FEEDING
WELLINGTON'S ARMY FROM BURGOS TO WATERLOO

FEEDING
WELLINGTON'S ARMY FROM BURGOS TO WATERLOO

THE LIVELY JOURNAL OF ASSISTANT
COMMISSARY GENERAL TUPPER CAREY
VOLUME II

Edited by Gareth Glover

Pen & Sword
MILITARY
AN IMPRINT OF PEN & SWORD BOOKS LTD.
YORKSHIRE – PHILADELPHIA

First published in Great Britain in 2024 by
PEN AND SWORD MILITARY
An imprint of
Pen & Sword Books Limited
Yorkshire – Philadelphia

Copyright © Gareth Glover, 2024

ISBN 978 1 39904 146 1

The right of Gareth Glover to be identified as Author of this work has been asserted by him in accordance with the Copyright, Designs and Patents Act 1988.

A CIP catalogue record for this book is available from the British Library.

All rights reserved. No part of this book may be reproduced or transmitted in any form or by any means, electronic or mechanical including photocopying, recording or by any information storage and retrieval system, without permission from the Publisher in writing.

Typeset in Times New Roman 12/16 by
SJmagic DESIGN SERVICES, India.
Printed and bound in the UK by CPI Group (UK) Ltd.

Pen & Sword Books Limited incorporates the imprints of Atlas, Archaeology, Aviation, Discovery, Family History, Fiction, History, Maritime, Military, Military Classics, Politics, Select, Transport, True Crime, Air World, Frontline Publishing, Leo Cooper, Remember When, Seaforth Publishing, The Praetorian Press, Wharncliffe Local History, Wharncliffe Transport, Wharncliffe True Crime and White Owl.

For a complete list of Pen & Sword titles please contact
PEN & SWORD BOOKS LIMITED
George House, Units 12 & 13, Beevor Street, Off Pontefract Road,
Barnsley, South Yorkshire, S71 1HN, England
E-mail: enquiries@pen-and-sword.co.uk
Website: www.pen-and-sword.co.uk

or
PEN AND SWORD BOOKS
1950 Lawrence Rd, Havertown, PA 19083, USA
E-mail: uspen-and-sword@casematepublishers.com
Website: www.penandswordbooks.com

Contents

List of Plates	vi
Foreword	vii

The Further Recollections of Commissary Tupper Carey

Spring 1813	xii
5th Campaign: Advance into Spain, Battles of Vitoria and Pamplona, Siege of San Sebastian	1
6th Campaign: Entrance into France. Battles of Nive, Nivelle, Orthes, Toulouse. Peace, Return of Portuguese Army to Portugal. Go on a cruise and then return to England.	43
7th Campaign: Battle of Waterloo, Capture of Paris and occupation of its environs. Peace, British Army of Occupation in France and withdrawal in 1818	115

Appendices

A: Commissary Tupper Carey's Correspondence	250
B: The Court Martials of Deputy Commissary General Charles Pratt and William Moore	256
Index	259

List of Plates

1. Osma church and village.
2. The Battle of Vitoria by J.P. Beadle.
3. Allied camp near Urugne by Robert Batty.
4. A mule train near Enderlache by Robert Batty.
5. Pasaia Harbour (commonly known to the British as Passage).
6. A view of San Sebastian from Sao Bartolomeo Monastery.
7. The Battle of Nivelle by William Heath.
8. The Battle of Toulouse by William Heath.
9. General Sir Thomas Picton.
10. General Sir Lowry Cole.
11. General Sir Henry Clinton.
12. Arthur Wellesley, Duke of Wellington.
13. The Battle of Waterloo by George Jones.
14. A drawing of Summerland found in Tupper's papers.
15. Tupper Carey in later life.
16. Anne (Tupper) Carey.
17. Their son the Reverend Tupper Carey.
18. The Order of Chevalier of the Legion d'Honneur of Louis XVIII, which Tupper was not allowed to accept.
19. The Carey family mausoleum in Candie Cemetery, St Peter Port.
20. Memorial window and brass plaque commemorating Commissary General Tupper Carey in St Stephen's Church, St Peter Port, Guernsey.

Foreword

Volume 1 covered the early life of Commissary Tupper Carey up until the spring of 1813 and the rest of his career will be covered in this second volume. It spans the period from the launch of Wellington's great advance into Spain in 1813 until the end of the war in 1814, the Waterloo campaign of 1815 and the Army of Occupation in France from 1815 to 1818, when Tupper became arguably the most important Commissary working for the Duke of Wellington. To explain the sinuosities of the numerous roles performed by Tupper Carey during this period it would be best to refer to the second half of his own report of his services, written in the early 1840s:

> Services of Commissary General Tupper Carey officially called for by the Lords Commissioners of Her Majesty's Treasury while at the head of the Commissariat Department in the Island of Malta and dependencies
>
> In November 1812 he joined the [4th] Division of infantry under Lieutenant General Sir Lowry Cole, as Senior Superintending Commissariat Officer, with which he continued during the many arduous campaigns of the years 1813 and 1814. [He was present at the] celebrated actions of Vitoria and [siege of] Pamplona, entrance into France, battles of Nivelle, Nive, Orthes and Toulouse, until the dismemberment of the allied army in June near Bordeaux. When he [then] proceeded as Senior Commissary Officer with the whole Portuguese contingent, consisting of

vii

26,000 men, on its return through Spain and Portugal. [He] remained in Lisbon some time making up his accounts, then went to Gibraltar for the recovery of his health and returned to England early in 1815 and was put on Half Pay.

[He] joined the army under the command of the Duke of Wellington and [on] the 9th of May of the same year [joined] 2nd Division of infantry [Henry Clinton] in the Netherlands as Senior Commissariat officer, with which he served during the whole of the operations of the Battle of Waterloo, [and advance to] Paris, [remaining in France] until June 1816 when he was ordered to England to answer queries as [to] his accounts. [He] went out again in September and rejoined the Army of Occupation at Cambrai and relieved Deputy Commissary General Dumaresq and served during the three following years in the north of France, as senior of the two British Commissaries in a Mixed Commission, with the same number of French 'Intendants Militaires', the duty of which consisted in the general superintendence of the supply of the British, Hanoverian, Danish and Saxon contingents of the Army of Occupation in that country. [He] remained alone at Cambrai some time [after the army left], settling accounts with the French administration. [He] returned to England on the conclusion of the service in November 1818 and was [again] put on Half Pay. In the discharge of his last duty (The British part having for the last year wholly devolved on him) and which became extremely complicated and delicate owing as the interests of the army and those of the French administration being often times at variance, he had the satisfaction of meeting with the approbation of his superior officer Commissary General Sir John Bissett and his Majesty the King of France Louis the 18th, who was pleased to confer on him the Order of Knight of the Legion of Honour.

FOREWORD

In August 1819 [he] received orders to proceed and take charge of the Commissariat duties at the [Island of] Mauritius and sailed for that destination on the 11 March 1820 where he served upwards of three years until his promotion to the rank of Deputy Commissary General in July 1821, which led to his removal in the beginning of 1824 and was [again] put on Half Pay owing to the indifferent state of [his] health occasioned by campaigning. As otherwise then, Secretary Hill wished him on his arrival in England to have gone to Barbados and subsequently to New South Wales (at the particular request of Major General Darling the intended governor) and in 1826 to Canada, which he was under the necessity of declining from continued indisposition.

In March 1837 his health having recovered sufficiently, he was appointed to the charge of the Commissariat duties at Malta and served there until his promotion to the rank of Commissary General in 1845 and then retired [permanently] on Half Pay, the services of officers of his rank not being required for years afterwards, one only being employed.

Within less than a year of his return to England from duty with the Army of Occupation in late 1818, he married Anne Le Mesurier at St Clement Danes Church in Westminster on 11 October 1819. It is clear that Anne travelled with him to his appointments in Mauritius and Malta. During the long years of half pay, Tupper and Anne also regularly travelled throughout Europe. Their marriage was happy and produced four children:

No.	Name	Birth/Death	Marriages
1	Augusta	1821–94	Born in Mauritius Died unmarried
2	Tupper	1823–97	m. Helen Sandeman
3	Francis	1825–8	
4	Charles	1827–1905	m. Amelia Tupper

When on half pay Tupper and Anne routinely resided at the family Hauteville property until his own house was built, known as Sumerlands at Mount Durand, St Peter Port,[1] construction of which began in 1828 and it was probably designed by the locally-acclaimed architect John Wilson, Tupper's family moving in in 1831.

His father Isaac had suffered a severe paralytic stroke and was confined to one room of his house for upwards of 20 years, eventually dying in 1828. His wife Marguerite had a mausoleum built at Candie Cemetery for Isaac and her and to contain the next three generations of Careys. She died in 1837.

Tupper was awarded a Military General Service Medal when it was inaugurated by Queen Victoria in 1848, with seven bars for Talavera, Salamanca, Vitoria, Pyrenees, Nivelle, Orthes and Toulouse. He clearly played an important role in the Waterloo campaign but along with the rest of the Commissary Department, he was not awarded a Waterloo Medal. The current location of his MGSM is unfortunately not known.

As he himself states, he was never granted permission to accept the Knight of the Legion of Honour which was offered to him and Deputy Commissary General Bowles, who worked with him.

Tupper's later promotions were:

Deputy Commissary General 19 July 1821
Commissary General 24 December 1844

Tupper Carey died aged 79 at No. 13 Upper Wimpole Street, London on 26 May 1867. His body was transported to Guernsey and interred in the family mausoleum in Candie Cemetery. He has a stained-glass window and brass plaque dedicated to him in St Stephen's Church in St Peter Port. His wife Anne died at Sumerlands on 3 September 1875 and was interred with him on the 7th of the same month.

---

1 The house later became the Sumerland House Hotel and is now a luxury nursing home.

FOREWORD

His son Tupper got a BA at Oxford in 1845 and an MA in 1852. He was ordained in 1847 and became the curate of Longbridge Deverill until 1859 and later rector of Fifield-Bavant. The current owners of Tupper's recollections come through the marriage of his son Tupper to Helen Sandeman, who had two children, Albert (1866–1943) and George (1867–1948). Albert married Helen Chapman and had five children, the youngest of which was Peter Charles Sandeman Tupper (1902–76), the grandfather of the current generation, their father being Peter Charles Tupper Carey (1929–2006).

Tupper senior's youngest son Charles became a Brevet Major in the 63rd Foot and served in the Crimean War, fighting at the Alma, Balaklava, Inkerman and Sebastopol.

The Further Recollections of Commissary Tupper Carey

Spring 1813

The memorable events which had succeeded the destruction of the French army in Russia in the latter end of the past year forced the Emperor Napoleon to order drafts of his best soldiers to join him in the north of Germany, from Spain, Italy & wherever they could be obtained to assist in the organisation of another army to oppose the advance of the Russians & the rising defection of the Prussians, Austrians &c which step in addition to existing circumstances could not but produce a disheartening effect on the French army in Spain. And as every day added strength both to ourselves & the Spanish Corps in cooperation & about to take the field, the Marquis of Wellington did not stir apparently until every arrangement was complete to ensure his striking an important blow with every chance of success. Of his dispositions no one of us had the slightest conception for they were clothed in impenetrable secrecy & not one of his generals or other officers were presumed to be in his confidence, unless it was his Quarter Master General, Colonel Murray (afterwards Sir George)[1] through whom all the movements of the army were unavoidably communicated & arranged, and such was the precaution taken to prevent the enemy from ascertaining them in time to counteract them, that the business of his office was exclusively conducted by commissioned officers in whom of course every reliance could be placed. Even Sir Lowry Cole who commanded our division was invariably (I was fully satisfied) quite in the dark as to what was

---

1 Major General Sir George Murray was the Quartermaster General.

in contemplation, for I seldom went to headquarters without his enquiring from me for any information I might have picked up in the several offices in which I had transacted business.

Just before the commencement of the campaign the French armies opposed to us occupied various positions in connexion with each other, extending in our front from Madrid to Valladolid, Toro, Zamora & to the Esla more northward, with advanced posts in front of Salamanca &c. Whether we should make a dash at Madrid to our right, or in the centre towards Salamanca & Valladolid, or to our left towards the Esla & Zamora, was the question which no one could answer, as our troops were so disposed as easily to take either & it completely puzzled the French generals until they were unexpectedly undeceived by the sudden eruption we made in adopting the latter of the three moves by which we endangered their communications with France.

5th Campaign

Advance into Spain, Battles of Vitoria and Pamplona, Siege of San Sebastian

The long wished for orders came at last on the 16 May for us to commence our march & never was an army in higher spirits and more confident in their chief. Our force consisted of at least 75,000 Anglo Portuguese with swarms of Spanish guerrillas & regular troops on our flanks & his Lordship having been made Generalissimo of the Spanish armies they were directed to the best possible advantage, although they could not be reckoned upon as we did on the Portuguese now become experienced soldiers. Our column consisting of upwards 35,000 men was destined to turn the enemy's right, our movement was therefore to our left & was understood to be a delicate & difficult one by its separating us from the rest of the army, a large river dividing us, the banks of which were in many places inaccessible for crossing. We accordingly proceeded to the Duero on the 18th, crossing partly by a flying bridge at Pocinho and partly a little higher up Barca d'Alva [de Alva], the crossing was picturesque, the river being reached by a steep descent on the banks of which the troops were drawn up to take their turn, some by the bridge & ferry & other conveyances, and the cattle &c by the fords which being deep, the latter could hardly be got to cross, giving great trouble, the difficulty being to get one to lead.

I reached the high grounds overlooking the scene at the moment of the greatest bustle and as I knew I could not cross immediately, I remained a spectator for a while. The other bank was equally steep and those that had already crossed were perceived winding up the mountains as far as the eye could reach & that was at a long distance, for they had entered in[to] the province of Tras-os-Montes, the most mountainous & rugged in Portugal. Our *corps d'armée* consisted of five infantry divisions with a proportion of cavalry & artillery under the command of Sir Thomas Graham (afterwards Lord Lynedock [*sic*]).[1] The appearance of this rugged country was most romantic & from its inaccessibility, not having suffered by the presence of troops so much as other parts we fared better, but found the towns & villages old and antiquated as if centuries had passed without producing any change.

We reached Torre [de] Moncorvo (tower of crow mount) an old frontier fortress, looking as old as the hill on which it was situated, and continued our march on the 22nd by Fornos, 23rd Laguaca [Lagoaca], along the frontier and skirting the river Douro encamping near Especiosa, and finally entering Spain for the last time, encamping at Muga [de Alba] near Carvajales [Carbajales de Alba] on the 29th.

It is said that when Lord Wellington crossed the frontier with the centre column marching towards Salamanca, he looked back towards Portugal & called out 'Farewell Portugal' & though he may have been sanguine at the moment, it does not appear consistent with his having ordered the construction of the hospitals before alluded to, two or three months back, unless indeed circumstances had so altered as to make him more confident of the future. Lord Wellington having come over from the column on our right to put us in motion again, we proceeded to the banks of the Esla, the cavalry fording and at once attacking small parties of the enemy who were guarding that part of the country. The fords however were hardly passable, some of the cavalry having been drowned in the attempt & as it was dangerous for the infantry to make the attempt, the pontoon train was

---

1 Lieutenant General Sir Thomas Graham became Lord Lynedoch of Balgowan in Perth, Scotland in May 1814.

5TH CAMPAIGN

at once had recourse to and in a few hours a bridge was constructed over which we passed and by so doing turned the position which the enemy had taken on the Douro. Unless indeed they had decided on attacking us, for as we were on the northern side of that river and the remainder of the army on the southern, we were so divided by that great stream that we might have been beaten separately, but the fact was the French forces were not sufficiently concentrated for the purpose and they abandoned that position leaving us to unite on the 4 June for ulterior operations, retiring slowly with occasional little rencontres in which our division did not participate.

Being now joined by a Spanish force it was necessary to make methodical arrangements for applying the resources of the country to the wants of the allied army by which the English, Spanish & Portuguese would be fairly attended to & as it might be amusing to know the dispositions made, annexed will be found the original instructions addressed to me. No great dependence was however put on what would be obtained through them although they were of some assistance; our great resource being in what we brought with us from Portugal & what was conveyed from the magazines in the rear on the transport attached permanently to the division consisting of 550 packsaddle mules which kept going and coming loaded with biscuit, forage, corn, rice & salt from those magazines. One peculiar mode of obtaining bread which had been resorted to be my predecessors[2] was again had recourse to on re-entering Spain and that was in employing from 15 to 20 Spanish women (peasants) in collecting it; they were strong sturdy bodies, between 20 & 30 years of age, natives of Castile, mounted on their own mules on which they perambulated the various villages out of the line of march and bringing it on [any] transport they could find, or if not we sent with them our mules and having got the article cheaper by far than we could do, with so many mouths to fill,

---

2 The commissaries previously attached to the 4th Division were William Wemyss, George Hodges-Newton, Alexander McNaughton and Thomas Dumaresq.

all scrambling to buy the little that could be obtained on the spot, they were fully repaid by getting the price we paid in the towns near which we happened to be encamped. Being women, no notice was taken by the French of what they were about and on many occasions they obtained bread in the villages they occupied (but generally beyond the line of operations), it being manufactured secretly & brought away when the enemy had left & this assistance we continued to receive during the remainder of the time we continued in Spain.

When once the army was concentrated, its maintenance was kept up with great difficulty, the country round about being swept of all it contained & having been already well stripped by the retiring enemy, whose adroitness at foraging was unrivalled. The exertions of the Commissariat were in consequence incessant, the generals meddled & grumbled when all human effort was of no avail, and Sir Thomas Picton,[3] noted for his violence & bad temper, once told the Commissariat officer attached to the 3rd Division under his command, with an oath, that he must make bread from stones if he could not procure it in any other way, and his interference at other times was most unjustifiable.

As the 3rd and 4th Divisions usually moved together, one division occasionally occupied the village or neighbourhood vacated by the other; in one of these instances it was for us to move & make place for the 3rd Division. The magistrates had been baking bread for us during the night & as soon as the troops had marched I was superintending its collection & removal, when Sir Thomas and Staff unexpectedly came into the village and on enquiring what I was about he immediately ordered me to desist and leave the supply for his own corps. I remonstrated as far as I dared, but got an abrupt reply to leave the place instanter and suiting the action to the word he directed his cavalry orderly who was riding behind him to escort me out of the village and some distance beyond. I knew the violence of his

---

3   Major General Sir Thomas Picton was given command of the 3rd Division in 1810.

5TH CAMPAIGN

temper and therefore took my departure without further delay, though boiling with anger at his having thus set the regulations of the service at defiance, for it was clearly understood that the supplies intended for one corps were on no account to be forcibly applied to the wants of another as it must have led to the greatest confusion. I galloped directly to report this circumstance to Sir Lowry Cole and being near headquarters at the moment, he rode at once to make it known to Lord Wellington, but as the churlish character of this morose though gallant soldier was well known, the matter dropt as likely to end in no satisfactory result.

The comforts of the soldiers in camp oftentimes depended on trifles and this was peculiarly exemplified in the occasional want of salt for cooking, which in a country like Spain, in the interior of which it could not always be obtained, in the requisite quantities from its being a government monopoly & brought from the sea coasts & mines only as it was wanted, became at times a great nuisance & prevented the men from enjoying their meals which without it afforded no relish & such was the dislike it created that many preferred mixing gunpowder in which there is saltpetre with their food rather than eat it without some saline ingredient. The inconvenience became at last so severely felt that arrangements became necessary to have it conveyed as other articles, and to form an essential part of the ration.

In the immense plains in that country, water was not always available although care was taken to encamp if possible the troops near rivers or springs, but as that could not always be attained, particularly when in presence of the enemy, the want was severely felt at a time when heat was overpowering & thirst excessive under a boiling sun without shade or shelter to mitigate its influence. And on this march, in more than once instance, great distress was experienced of this nature, and I perfectly recollect being encamped near a small spring, the only one from which a supply could be obtained for some thousands of men & animals, a scramble almost amounting to a fight soon took place for the least modicum, and the ground about it being soft became a perfect slough making the water a mere puddle of mud & at last the only way of getting any water from it was to put this compound into a vessel leaving it to subside, from which at length a proportion of discoloured liquid was obtained which absolute necessity alone could induce you to drink or make use of.

The troops being invariably encamped, the ground occupied for the purpose could not always be selected for its convenience particularly when our foes were in the neighbourhood, at times we might be in a wood in which the men soon obtained shelter by cutting down the boughs of trees & then it was delightful in the open air, but next day the probability was that we should have to put up with an open country with perhaps a tree here and there for the shade of which there was always great competition. And it must be ceded to the officer whose rank entitled him to it, many disputes occurring between the first possessors and those who afterwards laid claim from their superior grade, and the heat being almost insupportable the right was always insisted on; such were the vicissitudes of our lives which varied daily.

Being now in the plains of the province of Leon, the troops marched in masses which, or the dust they threw up, could be seen spreading over the country and as I usually remained behind if necessary for an hour or two to settle accounts with the peasantry, from whom supplies had been taken or obtained, I got on my horse & rode along the whole line until I joined my division, and it was amusing to observe the different characteristics of the two nations, English & Portuguese. The former marched grumbling at the heat of the weather, or some other inconvenience, they were exposed to, with but little jocoseness to enliven their progress, and if there had been an unavoidable short distribution of spirits particularly the day before, the taunts & threats addressed to the Commissariat officers as they rode along were anything but agreeable or subordinate to proper discipline & which obliged them to avoid the grumblers as much as possible by getting out of the way. On the Portuguese line of march

5TH CAMPAIGN

on the contrary, there was nothing but mirth and coarse sallies of wit, usually proceeding from some funny fellow one or two of whom existed in most companies of infantry, which made marching less tedious and occasioned usually a good deal of amusement by their buffoonery. There was a good deal of humour among these people in general & they had an odd custom of invariably giving a nice name especially to such individuals as had some personal defect or deformity under which designation they afterwards were constantly described & the real name omitted. Such was the case in respect to a General Sontag,[4] a Dutchman in our service whose nose was enormous & more resembled a large irregular potato thrown accidentally in his face, than the organ it was intended for & his sobriquet was *Nariz de Patata* (alias Potato-nose). I had two Commissaries under me, Cordeaux[5] and Charters,[6] one was lame & the other had lost an eye, and they both were invested with appropriate names, another whose name was House[7] was immediately dubbed *Signor Casa* (Portuguese name for house), and it was useless to enquire for either unless by using this baptismal denomination which is supposed to have originated from their Arab & Moorish descent, temper and character also influenced the appellation.

The expedients at times resorted to for fuel for cooking when the troops happened to be in a part of the country bare of it, or trees as a substitute was distressing for all parties, but as there was no alternative in those cases the magistrates were forced to give up a house or two to be pulled down. Of course, the uninhabited ones were usually selected & in the course of a very short time were demolished by fatigue parties from the camp, the owners receiving a pecuniary

---

4   Major General John Sontag was of Dutch heritage but left the Peninsula due to ill health in 1811.

5   Deputy Assistant Commissary General William Cordeaux.

6   Charters would appear to have been a clerk, as they did not appear in the Army Lists.

7   Another clerk.

consideration equivalent to the ration of fuel allowed to the troops; a poor remuneration for the injury done, which however very seldom occurred.

Having taken a little break after our extraordinary march thus far, by which we had succeeded in disturbing all the enemy's arrangements to check our advance and overcome the interruption which the River Douro might have occasioned. We commenced on the 5 June to make another dash at their right flank by moving on towards the Ebro and if possible, forcing them over that river, in succeeding in which Madrid & a great deal of Spain must be evacuated by them in concentrating their armies to oppose us. There were many positions between us & that river, on which the French might have fought, but they were passed one by one without any such attempt being made, even the celebrated Castle of Burgos was blown up and we were now racing with them to bring on an action. It was a most harassing effort without a moment given for rest, the duty being incessant without a moment's relaxation, for though the rides in accompanying the troops might give pleasure, the mind was so absorbed in the multiplicity of the arrangements in progress to obtain supplies even for the day's maintenance, that little or no relief could be enjoyed; we continued in pursuit but not in sight of the enemy, the duty of pressing them being performed by the cavalry in front.

We thus proceeded by Pina [de Campos] on the 9th, Villa Sondine [Villasandino] the 11th, entering the province of Old Castile on the 12th & reaching Villadiego the 13th & on to the Ebro, the approach to which presented the most bold & magnificent scenery. After a forced march on the 14th, our column crossed that river by the bridges of San Martin [de Elines] & Rocamundo & again thereby turned the enemy's right flank, while Lord Wellington with the centre & right column was pushing them over the same river by Ponte d'Arenas [Puente-Arenas]. By this time we were getting sadly in want of supplies having outstripped all our convoys coming up from the rear & the country affording but scanty resources, the rate at which

5TH CAMPAIGN

we were proceeding not even allowing time for corn to be ground & baked into bread. It therefore became necessary to issue flour to the soldiers leaving him to do the best he could with it & even that expedient began to fail, yet his Lordship would not relax in the pursuit, it being of the greatest importance to give the enemy as little time as possible to concentrate their troops (& give battle) which it was then said were all making for Vitoria.

The Commissaries of divisions of whom I was one, were in consequence summoned up to headquarters & there the Commissary General Sir Robert Kennedy[8] harangued us on the necessity of straining every nerve to prevent a halt taking place. He said it was not a common effort that was required, but one in which the welfare of the army & its success depended and that we must shew by our unremitting zeal & devotion to the service the interest we felt in the cause of our country. We promised of course to do our utmost and in doing so I knocked up two capital English horses which I had bought or I should say were bought for me in April in Lisbon and cost 50 guineas each,[9] one having broken down in its forelegs & the other run blind from incessant work.

No idea can be formed of the distressing situation in which the Commissariat were oftentimes placed in obtaining supplies when attached to troops (especially infantry) in the heart of Spain far removed from their provision depots, which were kept up from stores sent up the rivers, for though the country had abounded in wheat previous to the war, the constant throughfare of the armies had exhausted it & made the natives unwilling to give anything without coercion. A mode invariably followed by the French at the point of the bayonet when necessary, but forbidden to the British, where they did therefore get subsistence we starved. During this advance

---

8 Commissary General Robert Kennedy commanded the Commissary for most of the Peninsular War.

9 In excess of £2,500 each in today's terms.

the distress alluded to was severely felt, the march was continuous, the country was exhausted by the enemy retiring before us, we outstripped our convoys, and what could be collected in haste was a hand to mouth scramble which occasioned great anxiety to us all, not knowing oftentimes in the evening how the troops were to get bread the next day. Discontent spread among the generals & men & though no human effort but a half could bring a remedy, which the Duke would not listen to for a moment, it proved of little relief to the soldiers to be aware of it & this feeling was carried to such a pitch that none of us could ride along the line of march without being abused & insulted, the soldiers crying out at times 'shoot the fellow who is starving us' & such like expressions. Commissariat officers cannot of course boast of gallant deeds, but they could not but feel interested in the glorious exploits of the army & though unnoticed in the page of history, their meritorious & indefatigable efforts in the peninsula, in critical moments contributed in no slight degree to enable the troops to reach the enemy and bring on actions at the proper moment & with advantage.

Our march was through defiles, the mountains on each side of which were rugged & inaccessible, preventing the passage over them to procure supplies. There were numbers of vultures soaring about their tops eyeing & following us as if in anticipation of soon obtaining food of some sort or other, for singular enough they were usually harbingers of expected strife, though no doubt the constant loss of animals which our army experienced ensured to them more than a sufficiency of food.

In marching through one of these defiles on the 18 June, the head of our column unexpectedly (at last) encountered the enemy, who endeavoured to prevent our further advance and a skirmish followed round the village of Osma, the church[10] of which being the highest point of the valley, the enemy occupied the church yard from which

---

10 Santa Maria de Osma.

5TH CAMPAIGN

they were dislodged by a cannonade and on my going up to see the spot, there were among the dead, two men laying near each other, the tops of whose heads had been carried off as if cut with a knife apparently by the same shot both exactly above the mouth, their brains being bespattered on the walls of the church. The enemy retired and our division was not up in time to assist in the affair which was of trifling consequence. It was however, the forerunner of great events.

The 19th brought us still nearer to the great bodies of the enemy manoeuvring to gain time, but we would not be kept in check, though the difficulty of obtaining provisions increased more & more from the rugged nature of the country; and on this day a pound of raw wheat instead of bread was unavoidably obliged to be given to the soldiers as well as officers with their meat and spirits, the two latter of which had not failed us yet. Having halted on the 20th for (it was supposed) to reconnoitre & arrange the plan of attack, a good supply of biscuit & bread came up from the rear & fortunately the troops got a good meal with a sufficiency for the next day to keep up their stamina. The enemy was understood to be in position in front of Vitoria which was not visible from the mountainous nature of the country though the heads of the columns were just peeping into the basin in which that city was situated, so that we were quite concealed from their observation.

The French generals at the head of whom was King Joseph, had no idea it is believed, that the whole allied army was collected so near them, supposing the advance guard only to be at hand, and they were consequently taken by surprise. Their arrangements for sending to France the great convoys which accompanied them, consisting of all their plunder, stores, accounts &c not having but partially been carried into effect, they were therefore huddled immediately in the rear of their position waiting for an opportunity which never came.

By a change of arrangements on the 20th the 4th Division of which I was a member, became a part of the centre of the army, which army was divided in three columns of attack, as we were, of course, to be assailants. The left column under Sir Thomas Graham took a detour over the mountains to manoeuvre on the enemy's right & cut off if possible his communications with France by occupying the high road leading to that country, to occur at the same time that the centre column commanded by Lord Wellington in person would attack his position in front of Vitoria, while our right column under Lord Hill would press the enemy's left flank by an attack on a series of hills, or mountains which bordered on that side the basin in which I have said before, that city was situated, so that we formed three quarters of [a] circle round the French armies.

Every arrangement having been completed, the various troops in our neighbourhood moved to the respective points at which the attack was to commence early on the morning of the 21st and having myself put everything in order which concerned my professional duties, I rode forward with other non-combatants to an eminence from which we conceived there was a prospect of seeing distinctly much of what was doing.

As the troops got into action simultaneously, the cannonade on both sides produced a scene grand & animating, embracing as it did the chequered masses [of] red and blue of the infantry, with their bayonets flashing in the sun of our right & centre columns which, though apparently moving on a plain & sides of hills, found it intersected by ravines & rivers which had to be forced. By degrees we perceived that they gained ground & having come into close contact with their opponents the whole basin appeared a mass of confusion resembling a volcano, emitting columns of smoke, accompanied by the thundering noise of the cannonade & small arms which kept up the illusion. Thus the action continued before a decided impression was made on the enemy, who had to be dislodged from a series of positions, and as nothing further could be seen where we stood sufficiently near, we rode on again & I then followed my division as near as I could, or was necessary and got on the high road on the left of which & across it a hill had just been attacked & carried by

5TH CAMPAIGN

the 3rd Division with great loss. Our dead & such of the wounded as could not be moved, were laying in various directions from the bottom to the top & on crossing its summit there lay the enemy's dead & wounded & I perceived several of the French guns had been abandoned after an attempt had been made to drag them to the high road from the position in which they had been placed, by means of long ropes connecting the gun carriage with its limber (which limber containing the ammunition, is placed in the rear of the gun when about to be fired as far as the length of rope will admit, a mode adopted by foreign nations, but not by us) but the attack was too sudden & rapidly successful for it to succeed & after having dragged them some few yards and others a little further, the ropes had been cut or cast off & the gunner drivers had galloped off with the horses & limber leaving the guns in our possession.

As we advanced towards the city in the neighbourhood of which the action was still kept up, the great road became encumbered with more guns, caissons or ammunition waggons & other carriages, intermixed with the dead & wounded of the two armies in the utmost confusion & it soon became evident that the French army was in disorder & in retreat though the fighting still continued particularly on our left.

Sir Thomas Graham with his corps having succeeded in occupying a position which prevented the French army or its convoys, from retiring by the best & most direct road by Tolosa towards Bayonne in France; this successful manoeuvre was the ruin of the enemy & determined its fate, for after a violent effort made to reopen that communication which failed, the retreat could only be effected by cross roads impracticable to wheel[ed] conveyances, the whole material of the French army fell therefore into our possession & I lost no time in hurrying on to be a spectator of its capture.

Leaving Vitoria immediately to my left & passing by its suburb I at once found myself in the midst of the uproar; the cavalry had just dashed through the throng of carriages of all descriptions to prevent their escape, but the badness of the road had affected that object. It was near the gateway of the city leading to France that the convoys had been parked and I came up just as the Countess Gazan,[11] wife of the chief of the French Staff was made prisoner. She appeared in great fright (although an officer of the cavalry was endeavouring to assure her of safety) & sooth her despair (thinking herself I suppose in the midst of infuriated men likely to take her life). She was taken into town in her carriage as soon as possible & she was afterwards sent towards the French army by a flag of truce. King Joseph it was said at the time nearly met the same fate, he having but time to get out of his carriage & not a moment left to lay hold of his hat to get away in the scramble.

The convoys consisted of Spaniards in the French interest[12] fleeing from their country, numbers of officers wives, *filles de chamber* &c &c in their several carriages, waggons full of the plunder of many years from all parts of the country, others conveying the voluminous accounts of the French administration, a large military chest & considerable reserves of ammunition with a miscellaneous proportion of articles which an army encumbered with spoil could be supposed to have collected. The work of plundering had begun on our part, assisted by numbers of Spaniards, and many of ourselves whose situations & rank should have prevented them, joined in it and I saw in the bustle officers carrying off bags of gold on the pummels of their saddles,[13] other persons were ransacking carriages & tearing down the linings for what they could find, some were carrying off paintings, rich dresses of silk & such other articles as they met with, or suited their fancy, there being an ample choice of everything. In short it was a scene of endless disorder hardly to be described, and as

---

11 Marie Reiss (1777–1831), the wife of General Théodore Gazan de la Peyrière.

12 Known as *Afrancesados*.

13 The 18th Hussars were particularly implicated and searches revealed much that had been plundered, but by no means all.

5TH CAMPAIGN

attempts on the part of the unfortunate people owners of carriages had been made to get away by taking the first road or lane that presented itself in the confusion & had eagerly been followed by others, which endeavours had failed by the leading carriages getting into slows to prevent their proceeding which stopped those in the rear. These sort of roads & lanes were in all directions strewed with them and many having contained the papers & accounts alluded to considered of no value by the plunderers the contents were ransacked & thrown to the winds in all directions. For a time, money alone had been found in the military chest, waggons & private carriages, but an accident revealed a large supply concealed in other conveyances, for a tumbril containing ammunition having blown up by the carelessness of soldiers about it, it was found to have had a false bottom containing money which the explosion dispersed on the ground. The discovery spread like wildfire and gave a new impetus to exertion and large sums were discovered in almost every ammunition waggon & even in the gun limbers which also had false bottoms with the powder & shot above. Immediately after the battle an order from his Lordship was issued directing that the whole of the money found should be paid into our military chest, but it was but partially obeyed as only a very inferior amount was collected compared to that which it was calculated existed to the extent of above one million sterling if not more and I recollect that a long time after the action very many of the soldiers had still considerable sums in gold in their possession, a circumstance which could not be wondered at when the beaten armies were carrying off years of extortion & pillage from almost every part of Spain, from Cadiz to the spot on which they met their defeat.

The number of vehicles of every description including 150 guns amounted, it was said at the time, to 1,600 from which an idea may be formed of the property which existed and the extent of the scene of wreck which everywhere presented itself when the whole fell into our hands & the work of ransacking was at its height. I think it right to say I was only a spectator of what occurred, for though invited to join in the pickings I resisted it, not deeming it consistent for an officer holding the King's Commission to do so and afterwards I had no reason to regret it.

Other convoys had succeeded in escaping into France before we could come up, otherwise there would have been no end to the spoil which might have been too great a temptation to the troops & affected their discipline.

When tired of what was taking place outside the walls I went into the city to have a glimpse of what was passing there and endeavour to obtain supplies should any have existed within its walls. All however was confusion and dismay for as Vitoria had been the great thoroughfare of the French armies into Spain (& everyone connected with the intrusive king) backwards & forwards from which great pecuniary advantages had been derived, the inhabitants were evidently reconciled to French rule, and indeed well disposed towards that nation, they therefore received us not only with indifference but displeasure, astonished & stupified as they appeared to be at the sudden transition which threw them in our power, having expected that the united armies of France commanded by Buonaparte's brother, himself a king, would without doubt have driven us back. I quickly perceived also that in such a maze of confusion there was little to expect in obtaining any nourishment for the troops. I therefore went in search of them before night and fell in with them as they were encamping (after having driven the enemy away at a considerable distance) in the midst of another description of spoil, part of which was soon made available to keep up the system, consisting of large droves of cattle & sheep which were found abandoned. Every man helped himself as he pleased & an unnecessary and wasteful havoc was the consequence, but their exertions during that memorable day having been great and crowned with glory, they were left to do as they pleased.

Singular enough, very few prisoners were made on the occasion, attributable to the enemy having abandoned their guns early, when

5TH CAMPAIGN

they found themselves pressed on their flanks & having afterwards nothing cumbersome to impede them, their retreat became a flight which could be performed more rapidly than their pursuers could follow. It is a curious coincidence that this victory was achieved on the same spot as a former one by the Black Prince[14] in support of Peter the Cruel.

The 22nd, the day after the battle, saw us again on the move in pursuit and our road towards Pamplona was through a valley on each side of which were high mountains making a sort of defile and the traces of the enemy were perceptible in their endeavours to impede our progress by burning & destroying every house & shelter which could be serviceable to us and of which we soon felt the bad effects by heavy rain coming on in the evening and which lasted during the night, accompanied by little or no accommodation under which to get for protection, the un-comfort of which was greatly increased by none of the baggage or provisions being able to reach us owing to the line of march being encumbered by other troops, so that we had to rough it as disagreeably as could well be imagined.

In the midst of the gloom & misery of such a night & when everyone had sheltered themselves as they best could, I heard a cry of 'Turn out for bread', which was re-echoed throughout the bivouac and quickly men with hungry stomachs came rushing about enquiring where, where, but there was no response, and they had to return from whence they came disappointed and grumbling at the deceit practised on them. At the moment I was quite satisfied nothing had arrived and I ascertained afterwards that it was a mischievous hoax practised by some of the 7th Fusiliers old soldiers, on the 20th Regiment who had

---

14 Edward of Woodstock, more commonly known as the Black Prince, was the eldest son of King Edward III. He undertook a Spanish campaign in 1367 in support of King Peter of Castile, who had been forced to flee, relinquishing the throne to his bastard brother Henry of Trastamara. He defeated Henry's army at the Battle of Najera some 40km south of Vitoria.

not been long in the peninsula and had not had the experience of their more knowing comrades.

In the course of this march a good deal of straggling & loitering was perceived among the soldiers, some of whom had fallen out of the ranks and appeared to be fatigued more than usual, and there was at last a suspicion that an overweight of plunder was the cause. The knapsacks were therefore unexpectedly examined on parade previous to the march & in many of them bags of dollars of different sizes were found which fully accounted for the slow movements of those that carried them, who had tried no doubt, as many had done before, to exchange treble the value of their silver for the more portable article of gold, in which they had not succeeded from the rapidity of the pursuit & want of opportunity. All these dollars were handed over to me as the bearer of the public purse ad interim, until distributed equally among the soldiers, officers of course not sharing in this sort of prize money.

On the 23rd the weather continued wet and unfavourable with shocking roads cut up by the retreat of one body and the advance of the other, as well as by the hindrances put in our way by the enemy in destroying by fire or otherwise everything within reach, the night being hardly more tolerable than the preceding one. On the 24th however, the weather cleared up and our advance came up with the enemy's rear guard posted in a strong position. They were attacked without loss of time and there they lost one of the two guns which they had succeeded in carrying off from Vitoria, it having been disabled by a shot from our artillery, which injured some part of the carriage & being unable to remove it any further it was thrown over a cliff and found by us soon afterwards. The other (a howitzer) they succeeded in conveying to France. Next day the pursuit was resumed, but the enemy was too nimble for us unencumbered as they were and soon reached Pamplona in such disorder that the governor of that fortress would not allow them to enter, from not having a sufficiency of provisions to give them & to meet a siege, as well as from the

5TH CAMPAIGN

apprehension that his garrison might be alarmed & become tainted by the existing insubordination in the defeated army, and be prevailed to join them in the retreat to their country by the pass of Roncesvales.

On the 25th we reached the small village of Berrioplano from the heights of which Pamplona was visible & situated in an open plain completely fortified, including a citadel. There were no suburbs beyond the ramparts and it appeared in the distance like a large, long & high building with the tower of the cathedral overtopping it. We were obliged of course to keep at a respectable distance as the garrison fired at anyone who dared to come within the range of their shot or shells.

A French corps under General Clausel[15] which had arrived near Vitoria, too late to be of any assistance in the action, retired by another road to that of the defeated army on hearing of the result, but so slowly that Lord Wellington determined on cutting it off if possible.

Accordingly on the 26th he took with him four divisions of infantry with cavalry &c, of which the one I was attached was one & our march was directed on Tafalla in the province of Navarre towards the Ebro & then to Aibar & Sanguessa [Sanguesa] through a most beautiful & diversified country of dale & mountain. Our pursuit failed however through the treachery of the alcalde (chief magistrate) of Tudela, on the Ebro, over which there is a bridge, who informed Clausel of our movements and as that bridge enabled him to cross or recross & move on either bank of that stream, he was enabled to elude the trap laid for him, for otherwise there was a probability that his escape could not have been effected as he had others of our troops following him from Vitoria.

Our endeavours having thus been frustrated, we retraced our steps towards Pamplona & arrived in its neighbourhood on the 6 July. We then were ordered to form the blockade of the place & occupy to the north of it, Villalba [Villava] hardly more than a mile distance,

---

15 General Bertrand Clauzel.

consisting of an open village on the high road to France & at the foot of the first rise of hill forming a part of the spurs of the Pyrenees, and there we remained watching the garrison until the 18th of the same month without having erected a barricade or other defence against any sortie which might have been made. Our only safeguard being that of pushing our pickets and sentries at dark as near the ramparts as possible and withdrawing them just before the dawn of day, by which the enemy were never aware of this precaution. They could however, distinctly see our red coats in the village which being held in great respect, no attempt was made to molest us though we of course were on the *qui vive* and ready to turn out at a moment's notice. It was rather foolhardy, but success & experience had given us great confidence.

This halt was of great service to us, for our previous marches had been incessant for seven weeks traversing Spain from Portugal to the frontier of France, during which many flank & rapid movements over rivers & mountains, harassing to the soldiers & indeed to everyone, were of daily occurrence. And I may add that with my experience, I found it to have called for greater exertions on the part of the Commissariat than at any previous periods of the peninsula warfare. My responsibilities were greater & required incessant exertions day & night, for when the troops had got to the end of their march for the day, our duty commenced in seeking for supplies in the neighbouring country till night put an end to our exertions, and no conception can be formed of the strain such a service occasioned on the mind & body & which alone could have been borne by the young & healthy who could with light hearts submit to every annoyance & to the threatenings of the officers & soldiers at any existing deficiency of provisions, no good reason being admitted in exculpation, though impossibilities prevented their being procured.

Pamplona before which we were quietly reposing, is the capital of the province of Navarre and the key to the entrance into Spain from France, through the Pass of Roncesvalles & being most completely fortified, the holding of it by the French became of the greatest

5TH CAMPAIGN

importance in the event of their driving us back. Its situation was such, unfortunately in the interior of the country, far distant from the seacoast as prevented our bringing up a battering train to besiege it. We were therefore unavoidably forced to adopt the more tedious operation of starving the garrison into a surrender by a strict blockade and their stock of provisions being known to be scanty, hopes were entertained that it could not hold out long. Which was not realised, as it only capitulated on the 30 October after having consumed every particle applicable to human existence including cats & rats & been on short rations nearly the whole time of their being thus surrounded by enemies.

The events in the north of Europe so detrimental to the fortunes of Napoleon, combined with those passing round us, induced him to send Marshal Soult[16] to try and retrieve his affairs by making another trial of strength with our army. His arrival at Bayonne speedily spread among the peasantry with the additional intelligence that he was actively employed in reorganising the French troops preparatory to attacking us, and this intelligence had hardly got into circulation when orders arrived for us to transfer the blockade to a Spanish corps under the Conde de Abisbal[17] & subsequently Don Carlos de Hispania[18] and march the 19 July to the frontier and occupy the Pass of Roncesvalles. Villalba [Villava] our recent quarters was accordingly made over to our allies who had hardly taken possession when they began to fortify it in the best manner in their power. I had to remain near it for a day after the departure of our troops, in settling some accounts and I soon perceived their precautions had not been taken in vain for the French garrison on discovering that we were no longer on the spot, began to make sallies for the collection of supplies, which brought on repeated conflicts between them which generally ended

---

16 Marshal Jean-de-Dieu Soult.

17 General Henry Joseph O'Donnell, Conde de La Bispal, was of Irish descent.

18 General Charles d'Espagnac was wounded during the blockade of Pamplona.

in the Spaniards getting the worst of it. But as their numbers greatly exceeded those of the garrison the blockade was of course kept up though the latter succeeded in obtaining corn from the surrounding plain to delay their surrender; such was the contempt they had for those now opposed to them.

I lost no time in rejoining our people after a ride through a more magnificent country than I was ever in before, it being in the Pyrenees among a people different to those with whom we had hitherto lived. Their language, manners & customs being quite dissimilar to those in the plain. The Welsh & Scotch soldiers, particularly the former, understood many of their words, the men wore a flat bonnet very similar to the Scotch one, the leg below the knee being naked with a sandal tied to it and they were a fine athletic race & must have inspired respect from the Romans, who it was said journeyed through their passes but never held possession of them, which led to their continuing a primitive people among whom it became our lot to pass the next four months.[19]

After winding a considerable distance through defiles & over mountains, I arrived at the village of Biscarete [Biskarreta-Gerendiain] where I was to be stationed, though of course we knew not what an hour might produce in being ordered to go elsewhere. The place was situated in a narrow hollow without any view but the surrounding mountains. Wishing to get a peep into *La Belle France* I went as soon as I could to our advanced posts which occupied the high points overlooking that country & the pass [&] were picturesquely encamped in their bell tents on the reverse side of those heights to prevent their being perceived by the enemy. The view was beautiful and most extensive over the comparative flat country laying at the foot of the mountains with spurs or ridges intersecting it in various directions, the nearest & most distinct object being the town of St Jean de Pied de Port with a line or threads extending from it to near our

---

19 He talks of the Basque people.

5TH CAMPAIGN

feet, being the high road from that town to the pass which we were guarding, famous for the check experienced by Charlemagne[20] from the Saracens in his attempts to enter Spain.

From the height on which we were standing upwards of 4,000 feet above the plain, a feeling of the greatest exaltation could hardly be suppressed at the proud position we then occupied, having done more than could have been expected from us, in ejecting the French armies from the soil of the peninsula with comparatively a small force, but no doubt it was for a wise purpose, for there were too many visible signs that the Almighty [who] disposes of all things had wonderfully assisted us in the great & successful effort we had hitherto made to think differently. Our position was on the extreme right flank of our army facing France, which extended to our left over a continuation of the chain of the Western Pyrenees to the sea, a distance of 35 or 40 miles if I rightly recollect, by which we were enabled to cover the siege of St [San] Sebastian at one extremity & keep in check the garrison of Pamplona at the other immediately behind us, though it could only be done in a most disjointed manner from the inaccessibility of the country, with immense ridges of mountains intersecting the communications in every direction. While we were in the neighbourhood of Pamplona we had abundance of supplies, but soon felt a want in our present mountain fastness and being without money to tempt contractors to bring them up, I resolved to go to headquarters to represent the difficulties we were likely to experience if not immediately attended to. The Spaniard who had hitherto supplied us was a person of very respectable character, though he had been a smuggler in early life, but as it was a sort of profession & a lucrative one on the frontier & embraced by many whose situations were above it, it did not appear to injure

---

20 Charlemagne or Charles the Great (747–814) led an army into Spain in 778 AD, but despite taking Pamplona, the seat of Basque power, he did not trust the Basques and pulled out of Spain. During the retreat, the rearguard was overwhelmed at Roncesvalles Pass leading to the death of many, including Roland.

their reputation. Holding my bills for large sums already expended by him in our service, for which he wished to obtain payment, he volunteered to accompany and guide me by the shortest way & having confidence in him I willingly acceded to his proposal. Early on 23 July we started on mule back, with a sturdy Basque peasant on foot as a companion to take care of our animals on the road, he wore sandals & all he carried with him was a pole on which his jacket was tied. Knowing well our destination, my guide soon left the high road & took to bye paths and having every reliance on his knowledge of the country, all I impressed on him was not to go too near the enemies outposts. At times our way lead through wild ravines & forests, then ascended mountains & down them into the haunts as he told me, of smugglers, on tracks hardly broader than those made by sheep, on which our mules had to travel and as the smuggling trade had been discontinued for the moment from the presence of the hostile armies, not a soul was met with and wherever we passed it appeared a vast solitude. About noon he informed me that we should have to cross a small portion of French territory and enter a small village for refreshment, it was situated in a deep ravine and was not occupied at the moment by either army. The maire was a friend of my companion, old smuggling acquaintances I suppose, and after having partaken at a small public house of a good dinner, part of which consisted of a dish of well-dressed lampreys,[21] I was glad to get out of the risk of being made a prisoner by again mounting on our mules. I confess I had no apprehensions about it & if I had had they were removed by the good understanding, a sort of freemasonry, which I perceived to exist between my party & the villagers founded on a trade in which the principle of honour, though debased by its illicit nature, was most strictly adhered to.

We again commenced ascending a neighbouring ridge & passing over a bold country as before, we at length fell in on a commanding

---

21 Eels.

5TH CAMPAIGN

height with one of our advanced posts in front of the pass of Maya & immediately descended into the Val de Bastan [Valle de Baztan] situated in a valley in the midst of mountains, quite an oasis as it were in a desert, highly cultivated with Indian corn &c with good substantial houses. Passing through Elizondo, its principal town or village then occupied by a part of Lord Hill's corps, we continued our way and at dark arrived at Lezaca [Lesaka], Lord Wellington's headquarters, after a most exhilarating but at the same time, most fatiguing journey not less than thirty miles.

I at once had an interview with the Commissary General Sir Robert Kennedy & settled with him the business on which I came and was glad to go and lay down after a hurried meal, and though strong and equal to any exertion, I found the peasant, who had walked all the way, comparatively fresh after putting the animals in the stable & seeking in various directions for forage for them and food for us, which he dressed and of which we partook previous to taking our rest.

Next morning saw us on our return by the same road and I arrived just in time, for the grand attack meditated by Marshal Soult, which was about taking place on our various positions, extending the whole length of road or track I had been travelling on, his movements being directed on the passes of [Amaiur] Maya & Roncesvalles and had I delayed my trip for two days only, I would have been thrown in a state of great embarrassment in the midst of his advance, which would have appeared on each side of me without knowing which way to turn & I could not certainly have got back to my post until the affair was over. A division of our infantry got into this dilemma and wandered for some time in these mountains after losing their way by which, had the attack proved successful, their safety might have been compromised.

Having gone on the 25th [July] in the morning to speak to Sir Lowry Cole who was in the advance, I perceived from his manner that something was in agitation and on enquiring from one of the officers of his Staff with whom I was of course intimate, he pointed to the high road from St Jean de Pied de Port to the foot of the pass & said that usually it appeared like a white thread, but that then the colour was changed into a dark line and that it was occasioned, as it was supposed, by being covered by the French army moving to the attack. The force was estimated at upwards of 30,000 men while ours barely amounted to 10,000, too much for us to contend with, though our position was a strong one, liable however to be turned & which took place.

When their arrangements were completed their attack commenced and though we held our ground until night after an obstinate skirmish, our retreat became unavoidable as one of the regiments (the 20th) had been roughly handled & been obliged to leave their badly wounded to the mercy of their advancing foes, who we afterwards found had treated them kindly & praised them for their gallantry. When the pass was re-occupied by other troops of our army after the Battle of Pamplona. These men were collected round a good fire before they were abandoned, and a paper was pinned on each man's breast written in French by the major who tore out leaves from his pocket-book for the purpose, recommending them to the protection of the French officers.

To prevent obstructions in the retreat I was ordered by Sir Lowry Cole to order every description of supply on the road to go back immediately, and while in the execution of that duty, I fell in with Sir Thomas Picton and his Staff proceeding to the front, his division (the 3rd) being some distance in the rear and coming up in support. He enquired of me what had happened in the pass of Roncesvalles and [I] having described all I knew, he replied in his usual dry & sarcastic manner, that no wonder the affair had been unsuccessful, aware as he was of the incapacity of the officer who commanded, alluding to Sir Lowry; which opinion, in the manner it was conveyed & to so inferior an officer as I was, appeared to me most unwarrantable, in thus speaking of one equal in rank to him & who had hitherto greatly

5TH CAMPAIGN

distinguished himself. Such however was his manner and he spared no one, not even his Lordship if he thought they deserved it.

The retreat continued until the 27th [July] without molestation when a position was fixed on, on which to offer battle, by Sir Thomas [Picton] as senior officer in command on the last height of the Pyrenees between the advancing French army & Pamplona, about four miles from the latter, the high road passing through the valley of the Lantz on the left of the position & by which the enemy hoped to force us by turning that flank. From the disparity of numbers Sir Lowry [Cole] was not sanguine in succeeding to check him unless reinforcements arrived in time & he therefore directed me to send everything on the road further back not to encumber it, [until] clear of Pamplona in case of retreat, as the road by which it would have been effected skirting the foot of the mountain was barely out of gunshot of the fortress and having myself had to pass that way several times, the garrison amused themselves in shelling the Spanish troops employed in the blockade & in protecting the convoys of provisions &c passing to & from the army & during the battle which immediately followed, it was singular to find ourselves as it were between two fires, one from the town & the other from the French army pointing to[wards] each other.

Before Lord Wellington arrived great doubts were entertained of our success, but when he came just at the nick of time, his presence which was announced by loud cheers, animated the most desponding. He highly approved of the position taken, but on his way to it he at once perceived the weakness of the valley and while passing over the bridge that crossed it he got off his horse, tore a leaf from his pocket book on which he wrote an order for the 6th Division coming down as a reinforcement, to hurry its progress. It arrived without being perceived by the enemy, being on the reverse side of a ridge, just in time to cover our left flank & well it was so, for it was the general opinion that it might have otherwise been a serious affair which might have compromised our future stay on the French frontier & obliged us to fall back on the Ebro. But his Lordship was in the prime of life, indefatigable on horseback, invariably mounted on thoroughbred animals which enabled him to go from one place to the other in an incredible short time & by which in this instance as in many others, he was able to correct a difficulty & by it ensure success. Had he been an older man and less energetic, he could not have coped with such an able commander as Marshal Soult, with such an immense extent of difficult & intersected country by mountains & valleys to defend; while the Frenchman possessed a flat country, as a pivot on which to operate so that he could move to any point in half the time that his antagonist would take in meeting him with adequate numbers.

The action lasted partially the evening of the 27th and most decidedly the whole of next day and was most severe particularly for the division I was attached to, which on those days distinguished itself even more than it had ever done before. From the nature of the ground I could see little of the hottest part, it having been fought on the other side of the hill on which I happened to be & down a deep ravine situated between the two armies. From the wounded however, which were coming from the front, I learnt much of what was passing. The 40th Regiment of not more than 500 men in strength performed a most gallant feat, a dense column of the enemy amounting it was said from 8 to 10,000 men, crossed the ravine & ascended the hill on which this little band stood, without immediate support. Nothing daunted it, [they] allowed them to come on & when within fifty yards, gave them a volley & cheering rushed at them in so imposing a manner that the French went to the right about and the whole face of the hill downwards was in a few minutes strewed with their dead & wounded, such was the daring of these old soldiers. But several officers of the corps to whom I spoke afterwards represented the moment of the struggle as one of extreme anxiety, for the men well knew that there was no support immediately at hand and seeing at the same time the immense multitude coming up to attack them & which must have annihilated them could they have once taken possession of the ridge or crest of the hill, hardly any other troops in the world would have remained on the spot on such an occasion. The 23rd Fusiliers lost so many men in another part of the field that its regimental colours were necessarily withdrawn, there not being a sufficient number of men left to protect them according to regulations. Major Roverea, aide de camp to Sir Lowry Cole, was killed[22] while rallying the Spaniards who had given way on our right; he was brought to the rear slung like a sack across his horse and was immediately afterwards buried by a kinsman of his in sight of the enemy. He was a native of Corsica[23] & had been with the general since the campaign in Egypt,[24] and was a severe loss being a gallant & most intelligent officer. Colonel Le Mesurier, a first cousin of my wife, was also killed in this action at the head of a Portuguese regiment of the 6th Division;[25] he had been left as governor of Almeida in Portugal in our advance into Spain, but disdaining a life of inactivity he importuned Lord Wellington so perseveringly to be allowed to join the army that he was allowed to do so and fell gallantly leading on his corps in the valley through which the enemy hoped to relieve Pamplona.

The French army being repulsed on every point, night put an end to the contest, but in the morning of the 29th they still continued in position as the day before opposite to us, which left us in doubt whether or not they would again renew the attack or retire.

The hill which the 4th Division occupied & which was the key of our position, overlooked that of the enemy most completely & was so steep that no attempt had been made to get guns on it, but

---

22 Major Alexandre de Roverea, Sicilian Regiment, was Cole's aide de camp from 1809 until his death.

23 He was actually Swiss.

24 This is incorrect. Although Watteville's Regiment served in Egypt, Roverea was with two companies sent to occupy the island of Elba. He and Cole actually first met at Malta in July 1805.

25 Brevet Lieutenant Colonel Havilland Le Mesurier, 12th Portuguese Line Battalion, was severely wounded on 28 July and died of his wounds on 31 July 1813.

as they might be of use in case of the renewal of the fight, four of them were dragged up by fatigue parties of soldiers; the horses being taken out of the shafts as incapable of drawing them up the ascent which was too precipitous. Lord Wellington took his stand on this hill surrounded by his Staff with many other officers belonging to the troops on the spot. All were seated or on foot & he was watching with great intensity any movement which the enemy might make from which to discover what he was likely to do, and he desired everyone about him to point out what they could themselves perceive. I went up there for a short time to receive directions from Sir Lowry Cole (on some point of duty) who was in the crowd & while there I set my eyes (which were good, having a long sight) to work among the rest. Hardly a word was said, everyone being anxious to be the first to point out something new, but after all, his Lordship's eagle eye was the first to detect a movement which indicated a retrograde motion and orders were in consequence given for our turning aggressors & the next day the enemy were assailed in all directions & driven back on the road leading to their country leaving the garrison of Pamplona to its starving fate. Sir Thomas Picton turned their flank by a masterly move and succeeded in cutting off a part of their rear guard and a singular rencontre was then reported to have taken place between the French officer in command & the British officer who led our troops, the former being in the pass & the other descending a narrow ravine at the head of his men, each intersecting unexpectedly or crossing the path of the other, words passed between them, the Frenchman declaring that his antagonist was his prisoner, while the other pointing upwards to our troops on the heights & descending in imposing numbers & so situated as to command the line of retreat, ordered him to halt & surrender. The French officer saw at once there was no chance of escape and did as he was bid, from 1,200 to 1,500 men laying down their arms & becoming prisoners; they were afterwards formed on the right of the road in a small field waiting to be escorted to the rear & there I saw them very soon after. There were three battalions with

5TH CAMPAIGN

their officers & the sappeurs at their head, looking sulky & ferocious; the latter in the French army form a very distinguishing feature at the head of the regiments being large men armed with saws, swords & large burnished brass mounted hatchets, large fur caps, with immense bushy beards and large buff leather aprons. In this instance however they were not '*en grande tenue*' [in full dress], their beards being twisted into a tail hanging from their chin and the end of it tied to a buttonhole, giving it a singular appearance; they no doubt found this sort of rope a useless appendage in their captivity and got rid of it as an encumbrance; had they however foreseen that their detention was only to last about nine or ten months they would have retained it as a recommendation for future employment; its growth to the same size or perfection requiring years. These sappeurs were quite a contrast to the pioneers who similarly headed our own corps, being unfit for the ranks instead of chosen men, whose duty it was to assist the quartermaster in recovering and distributing the supplies & although when dressed a semblance of a show was kept up, being armed with pickaxes, spades &c.

The pursuit through the mountains by the pass of Dona Maria was continued with several sharp skirmishes from the 31 July to the 3rd of August & but for an unfortunate accident a considerable part of the French army might have been surrounded, their general having got information just in time by the capture of several marauders of our army of what was about befalling him by our proximity & he succeeded in making his escape with the loss however of many men and of a good deal of his baggage & supplies in a defile through which his troops had to pass & while moving on, on the 1st information arrived at the head of our column that the enemy were not far off & were endeavouring to save a convoy of provisions and ammunition they had with them. General Byng's[26] brigade was immediately ordered to take off their packs so as to make them more light of foot and start

---

26 Major General John Byng commanded a brigade in the 2nd Division.

in chase. They speedily came up with them & after a running fight a great number of the bullock carts were captured, besides prisoners, some drivers managed to get away with their cattle in the midst of the confusion but many others were taken and our division had as their part eleven yoke [pairs] with upwards of six thousand pounds of bread. The bullocks were the property of French peasantry and was the first actual French spoil we made; they were in high condition and each were covered with a linen cloth and had evidently been petted by their owners who had remained by them. It was curious to see them take their food, every mouthful of Indian corn straw being thrust by the man into the animals mouth as if feeding a child; a custom which we afterwards found to prevail in the part of France which we afterwards invaded. They valued these animals above any other moveable property & being reared for the plow [*sic*], the loss of them was greatly felt by the poor fellows who could hardly tear themselves from them, but having been taken with the army, their value & that of the bread became the prize of our soldiers who received from me £397 for them[27] & they were slaughtered as rations for the troops.

On the 3 August the French army was again ejected from the Spanish territory and our division halted on that day at Echalar [Etxalar]. We were again therefore with the main body of the army in the centre of our positions and did not return to the pass of Roncesvalles.

Our casualties in all the actions & by sickness since we left Portugal, from the end of May to the present time was considerable, amounting to a third of our numbers, the number of rations issued at our first starting being 9,000 & now hardly exceeded 6,000. Of course many of the sick and wounded were expected to rejoin their ranks on recovery.

By this change of situation we were enabled to get a peep at what was going on in the siege of St [San] Sebastian & more so on removing to Lezaca [Lesaka], Lord Wellington's headquarters, in the

---

27 This prize money would be split between the men.

5TH CAMPAIGN

immediate neighbourhood of which we remained for a considerable time.

Portugal had been abandoned as the pivot of operations from which stores of all descriptions had hitherto been forwarded by land for our use, but the left of the army being now established on the sea coast & surveying harbours & Bilbao was in the first instance, subsequently the neighbouring port of Passages [Pasaia] was fixed on for the same purpose by the ships discharging their cargoes there, consisting of everything required for its equipment, maintenance & every material necessary for the progressing siege. It therefore became an occasional point of duty for me to go to it & on my first ride there I ascended, on leaving our encampment, the heights above Lezaca [Lesaka] and on a ridge in my way a scene burst upon me of the most extensive and magnificent description, for on looking westward, there I saw the sea for the first time after an absence from it of three years, which made me the more enjoy it. Numbers of ships were seen on its bosom and in the centre of the view near the shore, was seen the besieged fortress in the shape of a conical hill, partly obscured by its fire and that of our batteries employed in breaching the walls. The hill from which I was enjoying the prospect was the last commanding height of the western Pyrenees bordering the flat country to the sea & from it the view was prolonged to my right by a continuation of the low land on which was situated the towns of Rentería [Errentaria], Pasages [Pasaia], Fuentearrabia [Hondarribia] & Irun the frontier one, with other smaller hamlets on the River Bidassoa which at that part divided the two kingdoms & beyond that was seen a slip of France. The Spanish army occupied the towns in this plain on the Spanish side, in support of our troops employed in the siege. In looking back from whence I had come inland nothing could be more picturesque and imposing than the position of the British troops for many a mile along the extended line occupied by their tents & huts spread on the faces of the heights, or studding the deep valleys, were seen like the Chinese wall [Great Wall of China] extending as far as the eye could

33

reach, and shewing the rude dwellings of the mighty mass of human beings collected in that alpine country, for there were the clusterings of the centre of our army.

It took some time to descend from the high ground & to cross the plain to my destination, which I at length reached through scenes of battle & animation attendant on the operations of the siege in progress & the crowded state of the country alive with men.

Pasages [Pasaia] is a singular place, being an inlet of the sea through a chasm in a range of high hills bordering it, which chasm is so narrow that its entrance can hardly be discovered by ships steering for it unless quite near to it and for a considerable distance the passage leading into the inlet inland hardly admits of more than two ships passing abreast, or I should say alongside. Looking down on it on one of my visits to the place from the hill overhanging, I perceived a corvette of ours of twenty guns snugly at anchor & so immediately was I over her, that I could easily have thrown a stone on her deck; she might have come higher up but it was not safe her doing so, for where she lay she could in case of emergency have slipped out to sea, whereas higher she might have been nabbed had the enemy suddenly broken through our positions and being for the protection of navigation she could not temporarily be better placed.

The town lays on both sides of the inlet as it debouches inland and to cross from one side to the other small boats are, or were used, the boatmen being all women, stout & powerful and who handled their oars with great dexterity; they had remarkably black long thick hair which hung down their backs to their knees and in some instances lower, in a braided tail & they appeared to do all the work of the port afloat. Having to come here occasionally during the autumn after St [San] Sebastian had fallen & Bilbao abandoned as a receiving port, I found numerous transports unloading all sorts of stores, among which were portable houses made of wood, which had been sent from England to serve as hospitals in the field and thus far there had been no difficulty in their conveyance, but to remove them in[to] the

34

interior, so many obstacles presented themselves that I believe no attempt was made & they remained when put together for the first time, as memorials of extravagant & ill digested arrangements.

Having in this my first ride, found myself in the neighbourhood of St [San] Sebastian, I got on horseback to get a nearer view of what was going on there; I soon reached the encampment of the besieging troops and from a height looked into the trenches & breaching batteries hard at work, but such was the smoke that I cannot say I got a very satisfactory view of what was passing and as the fortress returned the fire, it could only be perceived dimly towering like a peak rising out of the sea. I ventured no nearer being told that only officers on duty were permitted to do so; I therefore remained satisfied with what I had seen. There were intervals of repose in the breaching batteries, when the guns had got so heated that it became dangerous to load them for fear the powder might ignite before the balls could be put in. The firing was therefore discontinued and as there was a battery manned by seamen of the ships assisting at the siege, many strange stories were told of their proceedings when thus relieved from temporary exertion. They had a fiddler with them who played to their dancing and reckless of danger as these men proverbially are, to give more effect to his music, the fellow very coolly got on the parapet of the battery & there deliberately played for the amusement of his comrades exposed to the enemy's fire; but he did it once too often, a shot having struck the fiddle & smashed it to atoms & he was returned wounded by the splinters of the instrument, rather an unusual mode of being hurt.

This siege was a course of great vexation to Lord Wellington from the great loss of men in its progress & having been obliged to suspend it from the delays which occurred in sending from England an adequate battering train with a sufficient proportion of ammunition, which having at last arrived put our people in full activity to bring it to a termination and an eventful day it was when our efforts were crowned with success. The division I was with being in the mountains, did not in a body participate in the toils of that undertaking, but we daily heard of its progress and it having been understood that the troops in the trenches had got dispirited from the many difficulties they had encountered & repeated sorties of the garrison in which they had lost many prisoners, it was found necessary or advisable, to employ fresh men to assist in the storm. We were accordingly ordered to furnish 500 volunteers and the division was paraded for the purpose; when informed of the object such as chose to be of the number were ordered to step forward, but instead of the number required leaving the ranks, the whole simultaneously offered their services; such was the noble daring which animated the army & in consequence of which the men were told off in turn of duty. They were accordingly marched down on the 28 August two days previous to the assault which took place on the 31st.

That day was undesignedly fixed upon by Marshal Soult, Duke of Dalmatia, to make a dash at us for the purpose of raising the siege if possible, as his lines were not far from that fortress and owing to that circumstance the bustle among our troops from that place along the River Bidassoa & considerably to our right was general in the mountains. Our division was in motion early in the morning and marched & occupied heights gradually descending into the plain in which the Spanish troops were drawn up to prevent the enemy from crossing the river and again entering into their country. It was a post of honour for them and we were in reserve to assist them in case of need; from the ground we occupied, St [San] Sebastian was visible on our left as we faced the frontier & in our front the enemy's attack was expected. It was not long delayed and it was an imposing spectacle to see in one direction the place enveloped in a sheet of fire & smoke, rising up in a column in the air and in every other direction the development of the French attack pointed towards the heights of San Marcial & the opposition made to them on all sides in the plain & up the hills. The Spaniards behaved with great gallantry and on every occasion in which they repelled their adversaries which was anxiously watched & seen by us, we cheered them in great style. They no doubt heard these animating sounds in the midst of their exertions which without doubt encouraged them to persevere, for they well knew they would not be allowed to be overwhelmed without our coming to the rescue; such was their conduct however on that day, that we remained spectators of the fray, during which San Sebastian fell after a most obstinate defence, the garrison retreating to the castle on the summit of the hill, and the enemy was again ejected from the Spanish territory with considerable loss & mortification.

The day passed on in the turmoil of the fight until night, when a tremendous thunderstorm came on & found us on the ground we had occupied during the day high on a ridge & there we remained until next morning exposed to its fury with only such protection as could be collected in the shape of brushwood &c. Sir Lowry Cole had got up a bell tent under which he & his Staff lay snug enough, but towards midnight the pegs having got loose by the rain although frequently driven more deeply into the ground, a sudden violent gust upset it & notwithstanding every exertion made to re-pitch it, it could not be effected and there they were under the necessity of remaining until dawn exposed to the weather as the meanest of the men.

During the day of the action the place where the headquarters was to be for that night had been removed by Sir George Murray,[28] Quarter Master General, to a small village somewhere in our neighbourhood and Lord Wellington on his way to it at dusk passed through our position (for an encampment it could not be called) enquiring the road to it, as no one of his Staff knew its exact situation. None of us knew it either, except Major Bell our Assistant Quarter Master General[29] & that imperfectly; he was however ordered to accompany his Lordship. It was then pouring torrents of rain accompanied by awful lightning, in which they proceeded on their way & on returning

---

28 Major General Sir George Murray, Quartermaster General.

29 Brevet Major John Bell, 4th Foot, Assistant Quartermaster General.

to us next morning he told us that very soon after they had started they got bewildered from the excessive darkness and the road being hardly better than a path. Their only chance of getting on was by the continual flashes of lightning which set them right when going wrong. At last after going on for two hours, all trace of the path was lost in the darkness & they then proceeded quite at hazard looking with some anxiety for the slightest glimmering of light or indication to direct them, they wandered on for some time longer when his Lordship called out all at once, that he thought his horse trod upon something harder than usual. He alighted & while feeling the ground a flash of lightning shewed that they had got on a track, they followed it and one of the party perceived a light at a distance in the direction of which they proceeded & at last arrived at their destination. But the adventure was not yet over for all, for Lord Fitzroy Somerset[30] wishing to find his Lordship's quarters as soon as possible, spurred his horse on & in a moment after a splash was heard & a cry for assistance. The party came up and found Lord F[itzroy] had rode headlong, horse & all up to his chin into a mill pond, out of which he was immediately extricated and Sir John May,[31] commanding the artillery lost his way in finding his house & was all night exposed to the weather under an old wall which afforded him little or no shelter, such was a night's adventure in the Pyrenees.

All the enemy's efforts having been frustrated, we next morning returned to our quarters at Lesaca [Lesaka] & Lord Wellington was immediately after laid up with an attack of lumbago for three days & could not stir.[32] Fortunately all remained quiet & his momentary inactivity proved of no consequence.

---

30 Brevet Lieutenant Colonel Lord Fitzroy Somerset, Military Secretary to the Duke of Wellington.

31 Brevet Lieutenant Colonel John May, Assistant Adjutant General Royal Artillery.

32 This attack of lumbago can be dated accurately to a period around 10–13 August, therefore before the successful capture of San Sebastian mentioned already.

5TH CAMPAIGN

The castle on the peak of the hill at St [San] Sebastian persevered in holding out & the only way of subduing the obstinacy of the garrison was by giving it no rest, under a cannonade which rendered it aware that it was assailable though situated so high, but even that was not found to answer and in consequence a tremendous battery of mortars was prepared & I went to see the result of the effect it produced. And such was the precision of the fire that while looking on, the flagstaff on which the French tricolour was hoisted on the pinnacle of the hill was cut down by a shell and which was afterwards repeated several times, notwithstanding however this murderous exposure, against which they hardly had any protection, the governor doggedly held out until he could no longer endure it and finding no hopes of relief from Marshal Soult he at last yielded himself & garrison prisoners of war unconditionally on the 10th of September.[33]

On their surrender, curiosity was at its height to visit the place and so soon as I could find a moment's leisure, I rode there with several other officers. The trenches & approaches were still open & nothing done to level them & on approaching the walls of the fortress their battered state showed the effects of our balls, the ground being furrowed by them & objects destroyed in dreadful confusion, lay in all directions & although the killed had been removed out of sight, the effluvia which poisoned the air indicated that they were not buried deeply. The town itself was a heap of ruins and it was a work of difficulty, over fallen walls, broken beams, partial barricades & rubbish of every description, to make our way through the streets to the foot of the rock & ascend to the castle. Got in it at the reverse or sea side of it, to which the garrison had retreated as their last hold & in which they had evidently found but little shelter. The ground being a slope towards the sea, was cut up into large holes made by the explosion of the shells, to that extent as to make it an object of wonder that they were not all destroyed, for the only protection I could

---

33 The garrison formerly surrendered on 8 September.

perceive for most of them, were strong boards piled against the walls between which the men crept & being almost upright repelled the shells which in their rebound rolled elsewhere to burst.

The atrocities committed by our men on the inhabitants, when they broke in were most shameful, but when the obstinacy of the siege is considered & that the French evinced no feeling for the preservation of the town by protracting the defence beyond the rules of war, which occasioned a frightful loss of life on our part & infuriated our soldiery who were not all the best of characters, it is little to be wondered at that under such excitement, greatly increased by drunkenness under which the officers lost all control over their men, that less than was done could be expected. It has not however been satisfactorily ascertained whether it was us, or the French who first set fire to the town, but when it did commence to take measures to extinguish it was impossible, from being between the ramparts stormed by us & those of the citadel still occupied by the enemy, between whom fighting continued for ten [eight] days.

The destruction of the place created a great sensation throughout Spain fomented by the French party and it led to bad feeling against us, but there being no sufficient reasons for it, the importance of the capture for our future operations on behalf of that country was so great, that the excitement was allowed to take its course & it soon subsided by the superior interest arising from events which immediately followed.

In reoccupying our old ground near Lesaca [Lesaka] it was currently reported that we should soon make an eruption into France, but the rumour soon subsided and we quietly remained for a month without a move, attributable it was said to Pamplona still holding out & occupying many troops in blockading it. Nothing therefore occurred during that time of any moment and we were glad of the repose it gave us and our communications with the sea board being now on a safe footing, we obtained many good things from England (of which we had been deprived for a long while) by the reopening of

5TH CAMPAIGN

sutlers shops. And we were occasionally amused with an arrival of one description of luxury in the shape of fresh butter, which was brought into camp by a set of sturdy women from the mountains of Biscay, dressed in picturesque costume of their country, it being carried on their backs, as a soldier does his knapsack, in a wicker basket containing from 30 to 50 pounds, with which they travelled, thirty miles a day. These women ventured among us without protection and what they brought being excellent, to encourage them to come again, non-commissioned officers superintended the sale to prevent imposition & they were soon relieved it may be conceived of their burdens by numerous purchasers, so soon as their arrival was known.

Sir John Downie[34] to whom I have made allusion before[35] commanded a Spanish corps in advance of us and I saw him often, as I suppose he found it [in] his interest to keep well with his old brother officers who could occasionally assist him with something to eat, more especially as the Commissariat of that nation from inadequate resources, kept their troops in a state next to actual starvation. Even ourselves felt the same inconvenience & were obliged to issue occasionally Indian corn bread to our people, but it was so disliked that we could not often repeat it and yet outwardly the loaves looked most tempting, being baked in forms made of chestnut leaves ornamentally arranged, which left their mark stamped on the crust in very pretty designs, yet the prejudice could not be overcome. Our horses also fared badly at times from the difficulty of getting corn, and hay or straw became so scarce at last that they were unavoidably fed on leaves and tops of furze pounded, which latter they much liked.

---

34 Assistant Commissary General John Downie. He transferred to the Spanish Army, forming a private army of 3,000 men named the Legion of Extramadura to which he was appointed colonel, and he took to carrying Pizarro's sword. He was made a Brigadier General but was wounded (losing an eye) and was captured in an action near Seville in 1812, but the Duke of Wellington authorized a prisoner exchange for 150 French soldiers. He continued fighting on the East Coast of Spain for much of the war. He became a Major General and died in 1826.

35 In Volume I.

Sir John often requested me to accompany him to his camp and one day being tempted to do so, we had hardly reached it when a slight disturbance occurred between his advanced pickets & those of the enemy and having gone forward in his anxiety to know what was the matter, he requested me to follow him & which I did for a short distance. But the shot beginning to drop about us and perceiving that he was leading me into the thick of the skirmishing, I thought it as well to leave him, for not being on duty, had I been hurt I would have been laughed at for my pains. The affair was of no consequence, it having arisen from the bad feeling existing between the French & Spaniards, who on the slightest occasion disturbed the temporary state of quiescence between the armies. They were long shots which were exchanged, as the latter did not much fancy being in close contact with the former.

A winter residence in the Pyrenees was not much fancied from the sample we had experienced in summer, for the clouds attracted by the mountains produced constant wet which became most annoying under the inadequate covering of tents & bad huts, and the sublime & beautiful scenery by which we were surrounded was losing much of its interest. We were therefore looking for a change which might bring us into the plains of France, where we hoped winter quarters and a more civilised country would be met with. The army was nevertheless most healthy & in the highest spirits ready for any undertaking & it was not awaited for long, as the prevailing reports announced that we should be the aggressors in this mountain warfare & in general these precursors of events seldom failed to be correct.

6th Campaign

Entrance into France. Battles of Nive, Nivelle, Orthes, Toulouse. Peace, Return of Portuguese Army to Portugal. Go on a cruise and then return to England.

The Portuguese, having had much of this nature of service in their contests with the Spaniards in their own country, had organised batteries of mountain guns, three pounders carried on mules, the most powerful of the mules carried the gun slung on a pack saddle made on purpose across his back, another the wheels and the third the body of the carriage, the ammunition being carried by the rest. And there being many commanding points in action inaccessible to wheel carriages, these guns were conveyed to them and in five minutes could open their fire on the enemy when least expected & having brought some of them with us, they were found of essential service on many occasions. Arrangements were made for the attack but it was deferred from day to day by bad weather and [the] muddy state of the roads and it was only on the 7th of October that it took place.

It extended from the sea on our left to a great distance on our right, and the object was to pass the Bidassoa River, establish our footing in France and dispossess the enemy of a position of which the high peak mountain called La Rhune was the key and which they still held in the Pyrenees. Our division marched to the heights of St [Santa] Barbara where we remained some time as a reserve and in support of the right of the Light Division, whose attacks we witnessed and afterwards marched to occupy the ground as they won it from the enemy & advanced, in forcing them still further back. We only could see what occurred in our front but could distinctly hear the cannonade both right & left of us, a sure sign that the other corps of army were not idle.

Being on a commanding height & opposite to the one defended by the enemy the salient points of which had been fortified with a deep valley between them, our troops formed on it for the attack waiting for the signal to advance. It was shortly heard from the right and on they dashed with the skirmishers in front and the ascending heights of the mountain were soon in a sheet of smoke through which the troops were seen creeping up & progressively storming the redoubts & winning their way, though at times experiencing a check, then rallying for another effort. And our attention was more particularly drawn towards the 52nd Regiment which was creeping up to a strong redoubt, the possession of which the enemy was evidently inclined to dispute with determination. The skirmishers around it could we perceived, make no impression and in consequence the body of the regiment crept up unobserved into a little nook just under the work and when collected & had taken breath, a rush in mass was made at it. The enemy fired a volley but in an instant after, we saw the breastwork or parapet covered by a swarm of red coats and a stream of French soldiers flying & clambering up the higher ground still in their possession, in this manner the other corps fought their way and our division was ordered to descend, cross the valley and follow in support. We ascended the hills and halted for a time near a French encampment just captured called '*Le camp de la Bayonnette* [*Baionnette*]' which to us was the first specimen of our enemy's mode of creating a residence with better materials than were usually employed and certainly they beat us hollow in making themselves comfortable. For there was a species of order & neatness in laying out the huts & thatching them &c as might lead to suppose that they

6TH CAMPAIGN

were intended for a permanency & in imitation of a French town they had established restaurants, cabarets &c. The enemy having at last been driven from our front we halted for the night & slept for the first time on the French territory and though fighting was renewed to our right & left next day, our division came in for no share of it & as it ended in the attainment of Lord Wellington's object, we again went into camp near the town of Vera [Bera] to await as it was said the fall of Pamplona, now expected from day to day, but it dragged on all the month, without coming to pass.

Winter was perceptibly approaching and towards the end, set in with [a] severity which made our situation extremely disagreeable and injurious to the troops exposed as they were to its inclemency from inadequate shelter or cover, besides which the gales having set in made navigation dangerous & prevented the shipping from approaching the coast with supplies on which we principally relied for subsistence, added to which the cattle brought up from the interior of Spain for slaughter were dying along the road by hundreds and in the scanty pastures which the mountainous nature of the country afforded, to which they had not been accustomed. The cold also increased the victims and such as lived to be regularly killed for rations were so lean as to have the nickname given them of 'walking lanterns' by the soldiers for when slaughtered they appeared transparent when a candle at night was put into the carcass before being cut up; moreover all the forage within our reach was consumed and the officers' horses had actually to live on with, but an occasional feed of corn when it could be obtained and that only by sending for it themselves to the harbour of Passages [Pasaia] besides furze tops & leaves.

Under these circumstances everybody looked to a change with some anxiety and at last the gratifying intelligence arrived of the fall of Pamplona on the 31 October after the garrison had consumed every atom of provision & lived on rats & other vermin they could lay hands on. The rear of our army being thus freed from all obstacles to retard another forward movement, immediate preparations were made at once for commencing it and driving the enemy from a formidable chain of defences, consisting of field works extending on our left from the sea to the Nivelle River on our right, which had been erecting for a length of time and were considerably advanced to completion. The Val or Puerto de Vera [Bera] led to the heights of Sarre [Sare] and being in that pass our division was to attack those heights on which there were several field works and which led into France & into a comparatively flat country. As these works were to be escaladed, bags to fill the ditches were prepared, stuffed with fern & brushwood, which with scaling ladders were to be carried by parties accompanying those intended for the attack and as everything was quickly prepared, orders were given to hold ourselves in readiness for the advance, but owing to heavy rains & shocking roads three or four days intervened before it could be attempted.

On the 10 November however the weather having improved, the troops moved in great silence with the artillery carriages muffled to prevent the enemy hearing them and took their respective stations as near as possible to the French advanced posts and there awaited the signal to move forward. Lord Wellington was in our neighbourhood with all his Staff to direct the operation in which 20,000 men were concerned and just as the day dawned, the signal gun was heard and the rush was made by the artillery opening on the advanced redoubt. It was soon reached by the infantry, but in doing so the enemy after delivering their fire from their guns & musketry made no further stand, being perceived to leave it by jumping over the parapets the best way they could. The bags alluded to were at once thrown away and without further delay we found ourselves in possession of a very neat & well erected star work, constructed with sods [turf], with ditches &c and armed with several guns. On going to its rear by which the garrison had escaped, we found they had facilitated their descent in making of steps by sticking their bayonets between the sods of the parapet.

The next thing that fell in our power was their encampment which was quite a model in its way, consisting of a street on each side of

6TH CAMPAIGN

which two rows of huts were most tastefully erected with sods & very neatly thatched as if intended for a long residence. After some fighting the troops passed through the small town of Sarre [Sare], an open one without defences. The doors & windows of the houses were all shut with only a few frightened inhabitants peeping from behind their shutters, with evident apprehension as to their fate, if we should begin to plunder, or respect their property now that we were in France.

I remained some few minutes in the place & as they saw no violent measures resorted to, some crept out of their houses and as far as lay in my power I assured them that no ill treatment was intended if they conducted themselves peaceably. Afterwards however the Spanish troops did commit depredations which were immediately checked, but it was no wonder as they had great reason for retaliation. It was the first French town we had reached and though more of a village than a town we found it very superior to the places in the mountains which we had lately occupied.

As the battle was raging in all directions, as far as sounds indicated, the reverberations of the cannonade being conveyed from a great distance along the vallies [sic] and mountains, it became necessary for me not to lose sight of the division & therefore followed its movements as near as my duty required. I found it occupied in very close skirmishing with the enemy, closer than usual as there could not be, as far as I could judge, more than 30 or 40 yards between the advance parties, the French apparently being obstinately determined not to give way until their flank having been turned, they at last retired. The wounded were fast coming to the rear & a handsome young man, a volunteer who had joined the 20th Regiment in expectation of getting a commission was among them; he poor fellow received a most distressing wound, having been struck by a musket ball in the centre of his mouth which lacerated his lips and knocked in some of his front teeth but fortunately passed through his neck without touching the spine. I saw him afterwards as an officer rather disfigured but not the worse in health & when operated upon by a dentist his looks will not have been much the worst either.[1]

We continued to advance in support of other troops which were all on both sides of us and past [*sic*] various redouts & works which had been taken and at last got into the rear or a large star work still occupied by a French battalion, which had been left in it too long, for it was now hemmed in & [with] no means of escape, being surrounded by masses of our troops. It was situated on a commanding height and all we could see of it, keeping at a respectable distance was the parapet with a row of men's caps with guns presented, two attempts had been made to storm it by the 52nd Regiment which had failed with severe loss. The commandant perceiving at last that he was in an awkward position offered to treat for a surrender when summoned; a temporary truce was agreed upon to arrange the terms, during which many of us imprudently rode round the work to look at the garrison which was not a hundred yards distance. While doing so an officer galloped up & desired us instantly to withdraw as the truce might cease from one moment to the other; his advice was at once taken, but soon after the place surrendered. It however appeared that the commandant being a little the worst for liquor, insisted on written terms which had to be drawn up & there being no table, it was done on a drumhead which occasioned delay and an apprehension that in the midst of the negotiation he might have taken into his head to order his men to resume their fire. Perceiving that all was adjusted, we again drew near and immediately after the French regiment marched out with all the empty honours of war (the point which French vanity had most insisted on) and laid down their arms on the glacis. They were at once marched to the rear as prisoners, the men appearing rather more glad than gloomy, but not so the officers who evidently were much annoyed at this sudden change of fortune. In the fort there was a beautiful black poodle dog which was coveted by everybody

---

1 This Volunteer is not named in the regimental records.

and many were endeavouring to secure him; he had lost his master & seemed bewildered at what was taking place, but he soon found an owner in the person of one of Lord Wellington's aides-de-camp to whom it had been presented by the owner, the commandant after the signature of the capitulation, being no longer able to keep & feed him.

When this was all over, I went to the rear to hurry up the supplies for the division & make arrangements for the conveyance on mule back of the wounded to the rear & I joined it at night & found they had not had much to do in my absence.

In this action the enemy had been forced to give up a considerable portion of their country by which we were at last fairly established in the French territory and though it was a strip of exhausted land, still the invasion had commenced & the sacred soil of *La Belle France* was trampled upon by a host of foreigners. Headquarters of the Anglo Spanish & Portuguese army were established at St Jean de Luz, a considerable French town, from which all despatches were afterwards dated for several months

We remained some days in observation occupying a part of the conquered country and we and the Staff, were quartered in large farms from which the inhabitants had fled, but the property was respected. We were therefore most comfortably housed, but the troops were still under canvas & hutted. The roads to the seaside from which we drew our supplies had been so broken up by the transport, bad weather & troops moving to and fro on them, that in many parts they had become pools of mud, dangerous to travel on in the daytime & still more so at night. Many mules were drowned in them from exhaustion and heavy loads and were seen floating in these quagmires. One evening in returning to my farm lodgings from headquarters after dusk on a dark November night drizzling at the time, picking my way over which I had already gone several times and at about 100 yards from my temporary home the road being in a deep wooded hollow, I heard a person's voice evidently encouraging by high words his horse or mule to make an effort. I hearkened and it was repeated in accents of disappointment. I thought I knew the voice and therefore hallooed in return and on going to the spot, there I found a countryman of mine Captain William le Mesurier of the 24th Regiment, who was on his way to join his corps in the 6th Division to our right. He was seated on a bank overhanging the road, holding the bridle of his horse which was floundering in the mud and so imbedded in it that his own individual efforts or those of the animal could not extricate it. He had given over the attempt as hopeless & was making up his mind to pass the night in this forlorn situation when I came up to him & to his great content relieved him at once by inviting him to accompany me. He could hardly believe I was in earnest or that assistance was so nigh at hand, but I soon satisfied him that what I said was in my power. Having left him for a moment & gone to my farm, I returned with my servants & muleteers & immediately got the horse out of the slough in which he must have died in a few hours from cold; a blazing fire and a comfortable dinner awaited us with a bottle of good wine and having no bed to offer him, a large bundle of empty sacks were spread on the floor on which he slept most soundly wrapped up in a blanket & cloaks. He declared the transition was as great as he ever had experienced in his life and after as good a breakfast as I could give him, he resumed his journey on his horse which had been as comfortably treated as his master.

The weather having continued dismally bad & rainy, it was becoming seriously distressing to keep the troops any longer encamped; arrangements were in consequence made for putting them under cover and orders came for marching a few miles to our left to the village of Ascain, which we were directed to occupy until further orders and I believe no body of men ever began a march in greater spirits at the thoughts of having some sort of roof over their heads, for though an encampment is agreeable in summer, when the winter sets in accompanied by a succession of rains, there is nothing more miserable for all parties. The ground gets saturated with water and it

6TH CAMPAIGN

is impossible to leave the tent without being ankle deep in mud, and when the rain comes down heavy it makes its way through the canvas in a sort of mist, and if it does not perforate through the bed clothes or night cap, the moment you extend your hand on waking to get out of bed, whatever you lay hold of or feel, feels wet & clammy and what you put on, though covered as far as possible, is damp & chilly to the skin, an ordeal which young men only and men in the prime of life are able to withstand and keep their health.

On our movement taking place, the desertion of a Commissariat Storekeeper under my orders was reported to me, it was a very unusual occurrence, but when I knew who it was, I was only astonished at it not having taken place before, for he was a Frenchman (Pierre le Fevre by name) and was hired in the service a year before when we were still in Portugal and being a very smart fellow became most useful to the Commissary of the right brigade Mr Flanner.[2] How he came into that country we neither enquired or learnt, being satisfied with his conduct and exertions. Him and I often entered into conversation from my being within his reach who could speak French fluently and I became his protector whenever there was occasion for it. He used also to write to me occasionally and always addressed me as '*Mon General*' and though guarded in what he said regarding France, I could perceive he [h]ankered after his *chère Patrie*. The fact was he merely took service with us in hopes it might lead to his return, either by our embarking for England or as what occurred in our entering his country, being afraid to proceed then through Spain alone from the danger of being recognised and murdered. He started when all were asleep leaving a letter behind excusing himself in a most feeling manner for the step he had taken. The temptation he said, of again joining his family becoming daily so overwhelming that he could no longer resist it. He thanked Mr Flanner & myself for our kindness and hoped we would make every allowance for leaving so abruptly.

---

2 Deputy Assistant Commissary General John Flanner.

I fully sympathised with him and therefore no official notice was made to lead to his apprehension.

Ascain, allotted for our cantonment so long as Marshal Soult left us in quiet or we him, is situated on the River Nivelle which runs by St Jean de Luz into the sea. The place was poor without much accommodation & most of the inhabitants had left it. It was however in the low country and within easy distance of the seaport village of Socoa to which the transports were consigned and where they disembarked the provisions & stores, although the port of Passages [Pasaia] was still made use of for the same purpose. Our communications with England had become more & more frequent & regular, notwithstanding the difficulty of access during the winter from the coast affording no shelter or anchorage and in case of a gale coming in & blowing inwards, a vessel when once embayed was almost certain of being lost & which frequently occurred. Still the temptation of a good market & freights, overcame those obstacles and we were in consequence supplied with home luxuries of which we had been deprived while in the interior of Spain; potatoes, ale & porter, cheese &c became abundant and having been obliged to station one of my officers at the former port to receive supplies & send them to us we were occasionally regaled with fish & lobsters.

Straw & forage had progressively become extremely scarce, so much so that it was found necessary to get hay from England, which was however so sparingly sent that only the general officers, Staff and colonels of regiments could obtain it and that very inadequately for their horses. The subordinates were therefore obliged to depend as well as they could on the ingenuity of their batmen (grooms) in foraging with the occasional supply of corn (barley oats and Indian corn) which was fetched on the backs of their animals from the magazines of the two seaport towns alluded to when it existed there.

The enormous losses of cattle on the various roads from the interior of Spain coming up to feed the army, led to our government sending out a supply of bullocks from Ireland of which we occasionally

6TH CAMPAIGN

partook, but shipwreck and gales of wind on the voyage, occasioned losses almost equal in cost to the former modes of obtaining the animals, which led to its discontinuance.

Although St Jean de Luz was but a town of the 4th or 5th class & quiet in every sense of the word in ordinary times, the influx into it of the headquarters of the allied army and numerous persons connected with it, gave it an unusual animation. Most however of its principal inhabitants & magistrates had fled to Bayonne, but Lord Wellington's proclamations promising protection reassured them and many returned from time to time as they acquired confidence. It was a most gratifying spectacle to witness their arrival; they came of all ages, in convoys with their effects loaded on carts, having passed through the enemy's outposts to our own as if peace had taken place and to have induced them to such a hazardous step, satisfactory intelligence must have reached them of our honourable conduct, a confidence which was acted on throughout all the cantonments, thus to trust themselves in the midst of an invading army. His Lordship had however been most summary in repressing plunder & other disorders & had hung several Spaniards & Portuguese caught in the fact without trial or process, and in one instance which happened in our line of movement, a Portuguese & two Germans caught in the act drew lots as to whom would hang the other two, for there being no hangman on the spot & there they were hanging on the road when we passed by as a warning to others. One of the Germans having luckily escaped for the time the fate that awaited him, the execution took place under the superintendence of the Provost Marshal of the army who on such occasions had the power of summary punishment, his assistants having only the exercise of the cat & such had been the excesses of the Spanish troops on entering France, that the commander in chief was obliged to send them back into Spain, preferring to depend on fewer soldiers over whom he could exercise control, than have a set of exasperated men, anxious to avenge their country's wrongs added to his army, who by their bad conduct would have stirred up the mass of the population into insurrection against which it might not have been in our power to have contended successfully and yet when the dreadful enormities committed by the French in Spain & Portugal are considered the attempt at retaliation was not surprising and must have been expected.

As St Jean de Luz was within a morning's ride, I frequently went there on business; it soon acquired an appearance of bustle from the numbers of officers, functionaries & people congregating in it & making it in many instances a lounge from the neighbouring cantonments; some on duty & others from curiosity & to collect news, it being the source of all information and where everyone met to renew acquaintance. I occasionally visited there Captain Carey Le Marchant of the Foot Guards, son of the late Major General Le Marchant;[3] he had been wounded in the instep in one of the preceding actions and the wound would not heal, the surgeons were divided in opinion on cutting off the leg or not and while in this uncertainty a considerable discharge ensued which progressively reduced him to a skeleton and he at last died from exhaustion. He was a handsome tall young man, professionally clever and had he lived would have proved an ornament to the service, which by his death and that of his father lost two valuable officers. Shortly before his death I settled for him his father's pecuniary matters, which had remained unliquidated since the Battle of Salamanca in which he fell.

While the army was in a state of inactivity I was occupied in making up my accounts of the preceding months and it may be amusing to note the enormous prices paid by the Commissariat for various articles obtained from the country & contractors from which a slight conception may be formed of the ruinous sacrifices which England

---

3 Lieutenant and Captain Carey Le Marchant of the 1st Foot Guards had been severely wounded in the Action on the Nive on 13 December 1813. He died of his wounds on 12 March 1814. His father was Major General John Gaspard Le Marchant who had been killed in the Battle of Salamanca in July 1812.

6TH CAMPAIGN

had to make in the peninsula & elsewhere no doubt, in contending for political existence against Buonaparte.

Bread from 7 pence to 17 pence a pound: fresh meat in live cattle seldom less than from 2/6d to 3/- per pound: Rum a soldier's ration 1/3 of a pint from 1/1d to 1/5d, biscuit 17 pence per lb. Flour the same, rice 1/8d per pound. Wine per ration pint 1/8d to 2/4d; barley 6/8d for every ration of ten pounds, and 7d for every ration of straw of 12 pounds, equal to about £5 per ton and everything else required being in the same ratio[4] & which was partly caused by being paid in bills on which there was a heavy discount from the great scarcity of money in the Military Chest to meet those demands on it.

The mule transports attached to the army occasioned an enormous outlay and the tonnage in ship transports, for the conveyance of the provisions, stores, ammunition &c from one port to the other, was a still greater sink of expenditure and hard money or cash had become so scarce compared with the existing value of the bank note at home, that the Spanish dollar issued to the troops for pay & allowances at 4/6d cost the nation in procuring it by negotiation, nearly 6/- and those negotiations had to be effected all over the world and yet did not provide a sufficiency; our army at this time being *nine* months in arrear of pay and such was the financial distress at last, that to obviate it in part & [to] enable us to enter and advance into France and pay as we went on, an old hoard of guineas had to be sent from England as a last resource, by which and other means we were enabled to conciliate the inhabitants. For had we lived by extortion as the other

---

4   In modern equivalents:
    Bread £1.50 to £4.00 per pound (0.45kg)
    Beef £6.00 to £7.50 per pound (0.45kg)
    Rum £2.75 to £3.50 per ⅓ pint (0.188 litre)
    Biscuit £3.50 per pound (0.45kg)
    Flour £3.50 per pound (0.45kg)
    Rice £4.25 per pound (0.45kg)
    Wine £4.25 to £5.75 per pint (0.57 litre)
    Straw £1.50 per 12 pounds (5.44kg)

nations in the north of Europe, they would have risen in insurrection and most likely paralyzed our efforts, for as it was a partial rise did take place at the instigation of emissaries sent among them, but the people were too tired of war to join heartily in it, seeing as they did that we were doing all we could to protect their persons & property from the soldiery & it fell to the ground after having done some mischief to detachments coming up to join the army, as well as to the Spanish troops under Morillo[5] who contrary to orders, began making incursions into France from the country round Roncesvalles considerably to our right.

In the interval of repose from the 17 November to the 9 December & subsequently, Lord Wellington's pack of hounds went out twice a week, but I was too much occupied to think for a moment of going out with them. He had had them for two or three years & they were always to be seen on the line of march, the amateur huntsmen who turned out were numerous from the different corps, many in full fig[6] sporting dress which gave the assemblage an appearance of a field at home.

Our present quarters not being of the best description we began to hope for a change, few houses had fireplaces or glazed windows and it was only those who could contrive to erect the one, usually in the corner of the room & making a hole through the roof to let the smoke out, and using oil paper frames let into the windows as a substitute to the other, that could consider themselves comfortably accommodated. And we were the more desirous of a move from the certainty that we should fare better the more we got into the interior, but Marshal Soult was determined not only to prevent it, but soon renewed his former efforts to eject us out of France entirely. Accordingly on the 8th of December orders came to be in readiness to move at a moment's notice and soon after the division marched

---

5 General Pablo Morillo y Morillo, Count of Cartagena.

6 Showy full dress.

6TH CAMPAIGN

to the support of the other troops in our front & we were posted in the centre of the army & so placed that we could lend assistance either to Sir John Hope's[7] corps on our left, or to that of Lord Hill[8] on our right, both those flanks were in turn assailed for four days viz on the 10th, 11th, 12th & 13th during which days the attacks lasted most pertinaciously. From the ground we occupied we could distinctly see the enemy moving forward against the former corps then running back, advancing again and again repelled, reforming &c. We expected our turn to come next, occupying as we did a ridge near the village of Arcangues overlooking a similar height just opposite, on which the enemy were in force at about 5 or 6 hundred yards distance. A ravine or valley lay between us but we shewed no force, except a small advanced one, for the three divisions, consisting of not less than 17,000 men lay under the declivity of our hill on the reverse side of or from the enemy, the superior officers & Staff being only allowed to shew themselves on the ridge; all was quiet & a great stillness kept and sure enough, such was the arrangement, that had we been attacked the French would have indeed caught a tartar. Having had occasion on the 10th to speak to Sir Lowry Cole on duty, I happened to be with him on this eminence just as Lord Wellington & Staff came up to see (I suppose) what was passing in our front, of course I retired for the moment. They had a short conversation together & immediately after, his Lordship galloped away apparently to our left and just as I had re-joined Sir Lowry Cole bang came a cannon ball from a masked battery on the enemy's ridge which struck the ground under his horse's belly & covered me with earth & went bounding down in[to] the valley over the heads of the divisions, receiving a cheer from them as it sailed through the air. The noise made by the shot frightened my horse & I can't say I was over cool on the occasion, though there was no time for thinking of danger; he

---

7 Lieutenant General Sir John Hope commanded the 1st Division.

8 Lieutenant General Sir Rowland Hill commanded the 2nd Division.

sprang off the ridge instantly and when I looked up, I found everyone else had also disappeared from it. It was an affair of a moment & quite unexpected & was almost instantly succeeded by another shot which however came too late to do any harm, though it made a greater noise overhead from the supposition that there was a hole in it, as it whistled more like a shell than a shot; there was not the least doubt but that it was intended for his Lordship whose appearance no doubt tempted the French artillery officer to unmask his guns & take the chance of depriving us of our commander in chief, which had he succeeded in, would no doubt have been the signal for the retreat of our army out of France, for there was no general officer that had, it was conceived, capacity or talent to replace him in so important & responsible a situation.

The passing events in the north of Europe had led to the gradual breaking up of the Confederation of the Rhine and the various small German nations composing it had disengaged themselves from supporting Buonaparte and declared for freedom. This spirit quickly extended to their troops employed in the French army and having a portion of them consisting of Nassau levies opposed to us, intimation was secretly conveyed to Sir Lowry Cole that a brigade consisting of 1,500 men might most likely come over to us during the night (the 10th to 11th). The Fusilier Brigade commanded by General Ross[9] was therefore directed to receive them, the other troops being equally under arms to prevent a surprise if such had been intended and they came accordingly in the midst of pitch darkness, without ceremony, parade, or noise and as no preparations could be made for their accommodation they were unavoidably put in a churchyard until daylight when they were immediately marched to the sea coast to be embarked for England on their way to their own country. They were fine soldiery men dressed in French uniforms excepting their appointments, such as their belts & facings which were of buff or

---

9   Major General Robert Ross commanded the Fusilier Brigade.

6TH CAMPAIGN

orange coloured leather and cloth, the distinguishing one of their country when under the sway of Holland. A similar number with some cavalry intended to have done the same thing but being more in the rear mixed up with French troops they were prevented, disarmed & marched into the interior of France. By this defection the French army lost an effective force of near 4,000 men during the following two days, during which the corps to our right and left were engaged; the part we ourselves took was one of manoeuvring only, marching from one point to the other in support where it was wanted and on the 13th, the French having been defeated with severe loss in all their endeavours to force our lines & force us back out of France, withdrew reluctantly into their strong entrenched camp round Bayonne & other fortified points and we immediately after occupied the small village of Arrauntz, a little to the left of our former quarters in Ascain & nearer to Bayonne & the sea; we gained however little or no ground by these occurrences.

In these actions the Brigade of Guards was engaged & suffered considerably; a feeling of jealousy had arisen against them by the other troops, from having been for a long while back, kept in reserve and put in the best quarters & therefore much satisfaction was shewn when they came into action and it was said that many of their skirmishers were unnecessarily killed & wounded from standing upright in that desultory mode of fighting and not seeking, as more experienced men would have done, in laying down & otherwise covering themselves by trees, furrows, or other sinuosities of ground. Whether however this was said in derision or envy, I cannot exactly prove, but this I know that it was currently reported as a fact at the time.

The year ended without any other event of active exertion and a more eventful or glorious one could hardly have occurred both for Europe and our army, which latter had distinguished itself in a series of actions almost unparalleled in history and was rooted at last on its enemy's ground, though as yet in a small corner of it affording no great accommodation or comfort, for the weather was constantly wet, stormy and knee deep in mud and the roads hardly passable. Yet we had gained an important step which led to the attainment of the object which our country had in view.

We were miserably off for forage for the horses in the way of hay or straw which could only be procured in quantities hardly equal to a quarter of the usual ration, added to which our quarters were very cold & uncomfortable at such a bad season of the year; under such disagreeable circumstances therefore our Christmas & New Year's Days were passed with little gratification or enjoyment.

1814

Our stay in any place was of course uncertain depending either on the plans of the enemy, or our own & in consequence of some demonstration on their part, we marched towards Bayonne on the 3rd January 1814 in support of other troops, but it turned out of no moment & we returned back on the 6th & occupied the large village of Ustaritz on the River Nive to the right of Arrauntz from which we had marched and there we remained until the 16th of February following, with better accommodations and with greater intercourse with the inhabitants who became familiar with us and found that there was a great deal more money in our pockets than in those of the French troops. From a knowledge of the French language I got on capitally with them and thereby derived many advantages in obtaining supplies though the Basque language was still the prevailing one. The people were evidently tired of the war & conscription, especially the latter from its having swept away almost every young man capable of bearing arms. They were therefore tired of Buonaparte's reign and anxiously wished for a change.

In the middle of January the Duke of Angouleme[10] unexpectedly made his appearance at St Jean de Luz, much it was said to the

---

10 Louis Antoine Duke d'Angouleme was Louis XVIII's nephew.

6TH CAMPAIGN

annoyance of the Marquis of Wellington and though tolerated by his Lordship and allowed to remain at headquarters, no marked or outward distinction was paid him though of course treated with the greatest civility and he was not allowed to make any effort to induce the few French in the territory we occupied to declare in favour of his dynasty, as it might have proved injurious to our proceedings in endeavouring to support the Bourbons when the bulk of the nation might have been unwilling to re-admit them to reign over them. And it was only after the Battle of Orthes [Orthez] that he was permitted to take an active part in the restoration of his family & when the inhabitants themselves seemed in favour of it. I saw him often at St Jean de Luz; he was a middle-sized man without [a] distinguished appearance.

From the arrangements in course of progress in the latter end of January & beginning of February, there appeared every probability of our at last becoming the aggressors, by forcing Soult from his present positions and as I had occasion to go occasionally to Socoa our sea port on duty, I could perceive that some grand scheme was in agitation to pass the River Adour by unusual means, as large chasse-marées were engaging for the purpose and it was soon known that they were to serve as pontoons in the erection of a huge bridge to be thrown over that river below Bayonne, by which that fortress & the immense entrenched camp around it could be effectually blockaded on all sides and thereby oblige Soult either to leave it to its fate with of course a competent garrison, or risk a battle.

As a commencement to the operation & to attract the enemy's attention, our division with the others in the centre & right of our army, moved forward on the 16 February to attack the enemy's left; we belonged to the centre under Marshal Beresford[11] & Lord Hill commanded the right with which he manoeuvred & drove back the

---

11 Marshal (in the Portuguese Army) William Carr Beresford was a Lieutenant General in the British Army.

enemy's left and having succeeded in perplexing Soult as to what was the actual object which Lord Wellington had in view, we reached Bidache and halted there on the 17th & 18th then moved to Bardos for a day & returned to it until the 24th, watching the enemy & threatening his position across the river near Hastingues.

In the commune of Bidache, an extensive estate belonged to the Dukes of Gramont & Guiche before the revolution of 1792, and not having been sold but retained as national property, little or no change had taken place in it, the woods were still existing and the mansion which must have been noble from its extent, lay in ruins on a fine grassy knoll overlooking a very extensive prospect, it having been destroyed at the time & left apparently undisturbed to the period of our occupying that village.[12] It happened that in one of our cavalry regiments, which accompanied our column, the Count de Gramont's eldest son of that family, commanded a troop[13] having from a long residence in England as émigré been naturalized. He was quartered in the place and having had a good deal of business to transact with the maire I happened to be at the mairie when he came on some matter connected with his men. The Maire had got information of who he was and had determined on only knowing him as a foreigner or Englishman; he accordingly addressed him as Captain Gramont with such distant civility as almost bordered on rudeness, although no attempt was made by the latter to make himself known, or assume any pretensions connected with the rights of his family, although I dare say he had dropt [sic] some hints in the village on the subject. It was a curious scene as everybody present were aware of the circumstances & wished to see how the interview would terminate and it ended by the Maire coolly telling him that his application which related to a foraging party would be attended to. No idea existed at that time of a restoration and the Maire told me he could act in no other way,

---

12 The Château de Bidache or Gramont is still a ruin.

13 Captain Antoine de Gramont, 10th Hussars, later became the Comte de Guiche.

6TH CAMPAIGN

fearful of compromising himself with the existing government which might be retained and feeling as he did angry & disgusted at seeing a Frenchman in an enemy's ranks. Since that however, the property was recovered by the family, but I never heard of course how that functionary fared at his rude conduct.

My professional communications with the authorities of the several towns & villages for them to send supplies into our camp or quarters were hourly kept up and I frequently sent my letters or requisitions to places in the immediate neighbourhood of the enemy, taking the chance of getting something out of them and as an instance of shuffling out of a dilemma, I annexe a letter[14] of expostulation which I received from the principal inhabitants of a village in our front (the Maire having retired) requesting me to send transport for what they could spare, knowing that as they were between two fires I would not risk sending my mules which might be captured in the act, but whether or not they were sincere was not ascertained as in the bustle of the operations their plea was admitted & they were left undisturbed.

While thus employed in the centre of the army, the grand operation of throwing the colossal pontoon bridge over the Adour below Bayonne, before alluded to, was successfully carried into execution between the 22nd & 24th by which that fortress was completely invested & left by Marshal Soult with a large garrison to its own resources and he moved with the bulk of the French army to his left to put another hindrance if possible, to our further progress into France. The construction of this bridge, bringing the materials on the spot and laying it down in its proper place was an extraordinary proof of the experience every branch of the service had acquired in these campaigns and the design was so much beyond the usual course, that great doubt existed of its being successfully carried into effect, considering the difficulties to be surmounted in passing the bar at

---

14 Not extant.

the mouth of the river which at that season of the year was highly dangerous. But the energy of our Navy was not to be baffled and they performed as usual their part in it in gallant style; situated as we were, our corps of the army had no participation in that operation, being employed to keep up the enemy's attention and prevent his detaching troops opposed to us from going there to hinder its taking place. In allusion to the experience which the various departments & indeed every individual of the army had acquired through a service which had now lasted six years, Lord Wellington was said to have asserted that with such troops as he had, he could have gone anywhere and done anything & certainly as far as the Commissariat department was concerned & I may say the same of all the others, the organization had become so perfect that his Lordship made his movements at last without in many instances, ascertaining that they were feasible in respect to provisions &c merely giving his orders & not supposing that a doubt could exist of their being carried into execution.

Marshal Soult having separated himself from Bayonne his stronghold, to oppose us in the field, a grand series of operations commenced on the 22 February to bring him to action or oblige him to retire more inland by our forcing the passage of the rivers Gave d'Oleron and Gave de Pau &c.

The 4th Division accordingly marched with the other divisions, being as usual in the centre of the army under Marshal Beresford and after several days marching, during which we effected the passing over those streams without serious obstacle, but that of the fords being rather deep for those who had to go through them, others passing over pontoon bridges. We at last came up on the 26th with the main body of the French army in position near the town of Orthes [Orthez] where the action bearing that name was fought on the 27 February 1814.

Every arrangement having been made by the morning of that day (for it should be understood that many preliminaries are required to take place before all the columns of troops are in their right places & in readiness & on this occasion more so than usual) the divisions moved

6TH CAMPAIGN

forward to the attack & in this affair ours became jointly with the 7th [Division] the left wing of our army, destined to carry the village of St [Saint] Boes, on the heights above which & commanding it, the enemy's right was posted. After the action had commenced I rode up just as some men of our brigade of German artillery were in the act of burying their commander Lt Colonel Sympher,[15] who had just been killed by a cannon ball. He was an excellent man & much regretted and evidently the poor fellows were moved at their loss & at the work they were performing. As I ascended the heights leading to where our troops were in action, to my right lay in the low ground the town of Orthes [Orthez] with around it other attacking columns of ours of our centre & right wing and the features of the country being bold & hilly the scene was very imposing. I pushed on and quickly got quite near enough to the tragedy that was performing; the wounded were fast coming to the rear, the Portuguese bewailing themselves at their misfortune & the Englishmen growling at it, such being the characteristic of the two nations; among them was Lieutenant Colonel Donahue of our Portuguese Brigade (an Irishman).[16] He had been struck in the belly & though he still could ride, he sorrowfully told me that he was a dying man, for his bowels were seriously injured & his extremities were getting cold & he died shortly afterwards; I tried to comfort him but he said it was useless to give him any hopes, as he was sure it was all over with him. I offered him my services to accompany him to the rear but he declined, as his servant being with him could do all that he required; I had known him a long while having made his acquaintance in Guernsey some years before.

The struggle to obtain possession of the village and to debouche beyond it so as to make an impression on the enemy's position was most obstinate and being near enough to be more than a mere

---

15 Carey is mistaken here, Lieutenant Colonel Augustus Sympher was not killed as he was in Germany at this time, but Captain Frederick Sympher was killed at Orthez.

16 Lieutenant Colonel Daniel Donahoe, 11th Portuguese Line Battalion, was wounded at Orthez and died of his wounds.

spectator as the enemy's bullets occasionally reached the spot on which several of us non-combatants stood. The rattling of the shot on the roofs of the houses & the shouts of the soldiery, mixed up with the clatter of the musketry made the scene quite terrific and our troops had to give way for a time, our Portuguese brigade first and then the Fusiliers Brigade, it being found impossible for the columns to get through the street of the village & deploy into line immediately under the enemy's position on a height just opposite, studded as it was with artillery & infantry pouring down a deluge of shot & shell on anything that presented itself; and at that moment the anxiety was great as to [the] result of the battle. An impression however having been made by troops to our right on another part of the French position, the Fusilier Brigade (the [1/]7th, [1/]20th & [1/]23rd Regiments) after three hours fighting made another effort and at last succeeded in establishing themselves outside of St [Saint] Boes with immense loss to the 20th Regiment which was the leading one and had more than half of its officers & men killed and wounded; General Ross[17] who commanded having himself been wounded and it was awful afterwards in passing up the street & out of the village to witness the carnage which had occurred.

The action being thus restored in that part of the field and having been successful in other parts, the enemy began to give way in every direction, halting at times to give fight on various eminences, which intersected their line of retreat, but finding that they were getting outflanked on their left by Lord Hill's columns, the retreat became a run, the conscripts or young soldiers throwing down their arms and making their way individually out of our reach as well as they could and at the time it was asserted that they deserted in considerable numbers & returning to their homes under the impression that the war could not last much longer.

---

17 Major General Robert Ross.

6TH CAMPAIGN

In this action Lord March (now Duke of Richmond)[18] met with a very singular wound. He was struck in the chest and the shot passing out at his back was supposed to be mortally wounded through the body. His brother serving in another regiment, or on the Staff,[19] was in consequence sent for in great haste to be with him at his death, the premonitory symptoms of approaching dissolution did not however follow in their usual course, which astonished his medical attendants and after a little while & when a careful examination of his body had taken place, a blue mark was perceived immediately under the skin running round his side, from whence the ball entered to where it went out, by which it was discovered that the wound was superficial, the ball having been turned by striking one of the ribs & taking a slanting direction, the soldier firing at him not having been directly opposite to him. Being one of Lord Wellington's aides-de-camp and a very gallant young fellow and much esteemed by all who knew him, great sympathy was shewn for him when it was first made known that he had been shot through the body & likely to die & all felt great satisfaction finding that he was doing well. His gallantry was such that learning that his company in the 52nd Regiment was without a captain, he put himself at the head of it & there received his wound.

The French after the battle succeeded in getting away much better than was expected, attributable it was said, to a contusion received by Lord Wellington during the action the pain of which gave him sufficient annoyance to disturb his mind for the moment, but it did not last long as we soon saw him again on horseback. The results of this battle were however very great, for the whole of the magazines belonging to the enemy's army fell into our hands at Mont Marsan, Aire, Dax and many minor ones, with a considerable tract of country, which ensured to us the certainty of maintenance, for the more we

---

18 Captain Charles Lennox, 52nd Foot, Earl of March, was an extra aide de camp to the Duke of Wellington He became the 5th Duke of Richmond in 1819.

19 Lieutenant Lord George Lennox, 9th Light Dragoons, was an aide de camp to the Duke of Wellington.

advanced, the better the inhabitants appeared to be disposed towards us. Few fled at our approach and we paid in gold for what we took or was furnished to us, we therefore hardly felt that we were in an enemy's country. I met from them at all times the greatest courtesy which my knowledge of their language greatly increased, especially when I had to go about the country on duty without protection from troops, in which case the farmers entertained me, giving me the best of their larders and a *pate d'oie*, alias the leg of a goose pickled, a favourite morsel among them on which I often lunched. Had it not been for the ill conduct of the Spanish troops I am sure hardly a Frenchman would have been sorry to see us among them unless it was the veterans of the army who were of course all Napoleonists.

Soult having apparently retired to his left pointing towards Toulouse, left the high road to Bordeaux open to us which was at once taken advantage of by his Lordship, who ordered his left wing consisting of the 4th & 7th Divisions with their artillery & a brigade of cavalry under Marshal Beresford, to proceed to that city.

After the late action we had not pursued the enemy very far having halted at St [Saint-] Sever on the Adour River & remained there two days; we then marched to Grenade [-sur-l'Adour] on the 3 March and from thence to Mont [-de-] Marsan where immense supplies consisting of flour, forage, corn & brandy had been abandoned by the enemy.

This depot was in charge of a Lieutenant Ireland, Acting Commissary,[20] a young man, but whose head of hair was perfectly white and which he stated to have occurred in two days from a jet black, by the effect of abruptly hearing that his two brothers had both been killed in one of the late actions.[21]

---

20 Lieutenant Stanley Ireland, 87th Foot, acting Deputy Assistant Commissary General attached to the Royal Artillery.

21 Ensign De Courcey Ireland and Ensign William Ireland, both of the 87th Foot, died of illness on the retreat from Madrid respectively on 12 and 13 November 1812.

The towns we were now passing through were greatly superior to those on the frontier, the French language was become more general & the inhabitants more inclined to take the events as they happened, giving us the decided preference to their own troops who began to be unruly, plunder & treat them as if in a conquered country to which they had been so long accustomed.

On the 9th we advanced to Roquefort in the Pays des Landes, a country consisting of sandy plains & pine forests & inhabited by people constantly on stilts, on which they moved about as conveniently & nimbly apparently as other men would do on foot. Fogs were very prevalent and it was a strange sight to meet a party of these people carrying their produce to market thus suspended as it were in the air, some having sheep on their shoulders & others baskets &c & when seen at first through the haze they appeared gigantic & almost supernatural, being all dressed alike with slouched hats. The stilts appeared tightly strapped to the legs & knees & elevated the men to the height of ten or twelve feet and in passing through the villages they were seen speaking to people in the bedroom floor, lounging with their arms on the window sills. Their roads were also peculiar, many being boarded like a floor & others with rough beams or logs of wood laid across & closely fitted from the difficulty of finding a foundation for metal (small stones broken up in equal size) or other more substantial material. Our next day's march was to Captieux & to Bazas the day after the latter, a nicer town than we had yet come to. The church was said to have been built by the English when they occupied that country in the time of the Edwards.[22]

After the battle of Orthes [Orthez] a disposition favourable to the Bourbons having manifested itself, the Duke d'Angouleme was allowed to follow the army moving on Bordeaux and he was a day's march in our rear. My avocations obliged me to be frequently at the Mairie of Bazas to transact business with the Maire and while

---

22 Bazas Cathedral was built in the thirteenth century by Bishop Arnaud de Pii.

there it was intimated to him that one of the prince's retinue was arriving; it appeared to perplex him greatly for as yet there had been no open demonstration in favour of the family. He arrived immediately afterwards and announced the approach of the duke, the poor Maire retired soon after into an inner room, to consult with the other members of the municipality, on what was to be done and after some minutes they all came out evidently distressed in mind, for the dilemma was really of the most serious nature. For as the Maire was a man of large property, if he gave the prince a too welcome reception & that the dynasty did not again ascend the throne of its ancestors, he was a ruined man, and on the other hand in receiving him coolly and [if] the restoration followed, his conduct was sure to be visited with severity. When I saw him he appeared like a man under sentence of condemnation, but he had taken his determination & had decided on the reception being the best he could give.

Although we occupied the town, no honours were paid by us on the occasion, the duke alighted at the Mairie & was received at the foot of the steps by the Maire & other functionaries; the square contained some groups of individuals here & there, a faint cry of Vive les Bourbons & Vive l'Empereur, were heard without causing any disturbance, curiosity being apparently the principal object of those who were present. The duke soon afterwards went to church to Mass, accompanied by the Maire &c and then retired to the lodgings appropriated to him. His arrival however soon occasioned considerable excitement among the people, who were divided in their political views & opinions, it having been the first place in which an attempt at a public demonstration in favour of the Bourbons had taken place; those who had become rich by the purchase of national property, being the most violent against a change & in favour of the present regime.

My billet or lodging was in the house of an *ancient* noble, who had lost nearly the whole of his property at the Revolution, he was of course elated at occurring events and was incessant in his enquiries

6TH CAMPAIGN

on the state of affairs & on the hope he might entertain of having everything he had lost restored again to him. He thought apparently of nothing else, but I could give him no satisfactory information as to what might be [the] result of what was taking place, as it entirely depended on the proceedings of the allies in the neighbourhood of Paris of which we were entirely ignorant. Nothing however could throw a doubt or gloom on his expectations & happy he determined to be, on the thoughts that all must go right though in the end his bright visions of the recovery of his property were doomed to disappointment.

The next day's march brought us to Langon on the Garonne River where we remained for two days; the advance of our troops had departed for Bordeaux and we were to have followed them next day, but in the meantime counter orders came for the half of our division, which was a source of great disappointment as we all wished & expected to see that fine city. We were however gratified to hear that Marshal Beresford with our sister division had had quite a triumphal march on the 12 March, the inhabitants pouring in on the road from the various villages to see them pass by and the municipality of Bordeaux at the head of which was Count Lynch the mayor (of Irish extraction)[23] came out in state to welcome them to the city, in which they were most warmly received, and the Duke of Angouleme having accompanied them in their progress, the Bourbons were proclaimed & the white cockade worn, but we as yet remained neuter & sided with no party.

Our head commissary, Deputy Commissary General Ogilvie,[24] accompanied Lord Beresford and being a bold and meddling character thought he might do business in his way by endeavouring to make some prize money: he accordingly manned a boat, went down the river

---

23 Count Jean-Baptiste Lynch was Mayor of Bordeaux from 1808.

24 Deputy Commissary General James Ogilvie was with the 3rd Division. He captured single-handed the French sloop *Recquin* off Bordeaux.

and finding a panic among the shipping he took possession of several as prizes, among which a French corvette of 14 guns, which though with only a few hands might have repulsed him without difficulty, but putting on a determined appearance no opposition was offered; he thought that he had thus secured a pecuniary advantage & struggled hard afterwards in his claim for it; all the captured property however being considered to belong to the army in general, he gained nothing by his enterprise but the chance of being knocked on the head.

Opposite to Langon on the other side of the river the small village of St Macaire [Saint-Macaire] was situated & in it forage corn and hay belonging to the French army was ascertained to be secreted. I went over in a ferry to know the fact & cause them to be brought over for our use; the maire demurred delivering them, on the plea that we were not in possession as yet of that side of the river and that as the cavalry of his own country patrolled in the neighbourhood he would not be justified to give them up, for in so doing he might be severely punished. Besides which he told me that I was not in safety in remaining where I was; his object I perceived was to intimidate me if possible. I therefore sent for a detachment of soldiers & placed them on the captured property, seeing which he set about getting them conveyed across without delay and he afterwards told me that in being forcibly obliged to give them up his responsibility had ceased and he was exonerated from any appearance of disaffection to the existing government. Three or four days after a small detachment of ours was surprised in the same village & made prisoners.

On the 15 March we retraced our steps to Bazas, and from there to Captieux, making forced marches to rejoin Lord Wellington's part of the army operating in the neighbourhood of Toulouse, towards which Marshal Soult was retiring as his base of defence & to cooperate with Marshal Suchet who was in Catalonia. Nothing remarkable occurred in our march until we joined the army on the 25th by which time the enemy had been driven across the Garonne and was occupied in fortifying the heights round that city and the bridge approaches over that river.

6TH CAMPAIGN

While crossing some part of the Pays des Landes before alluded to, I had occasion to make a requisition for bread on a village in a retired part of the country, sending at the same time some mules to fetch it. When they returned I was much amused on going down to inspect what had been brought, to see the animals apparently loaded each with four large flat cylinders more like solid cart wheels than anything else, each weighing from forty to fifty pounds. The muleteers themselves seemed to enjoy the joke never having seen the like, and on enquiry it was found that the inhabitants of the village, not having had time to bake bread of more suitable dimensions, had sent what they usually prepared for themselves. The process of baking was as follows; a fire was kindled on a large flagstone appropriated to the purpose, until it was heated to the necessary extent and being cleared of the hot ashes, the dough was laid or spread on its surface to the required dimensions; afterwards the ashes were again heaped on these loaves until baked, two of them being more than a company of soldiers could consume.

As we progressed towards Toulouse we neared the Upper Pyrenees and on clear days it was a beautiful sight to see that range of mountains extending to the left as far as the eye could reach, covered with snow and the peaks diversified in a variety of shapes, burnished by the rays of the sun like so many rays of silver pointing upwards, in the most clear azure sky which could be imagined. We were however too busy and actively engaged to look on such sublime scenes with that calmness & pleasure which they would have created under any other circumstances.

Before we had joined the army a good deal of manoeuvring & partial affairs had taken place and we quickly got in the midst of the operations to force Marshal Soult to retire from Toulouse or at any rate to enable us to cross the Garonne, which must be effected by bridges of pontoons, as he held the only permanent one over that river, which bridge was the southern outlet of the city guarded by a fortification called a *tête de pont*. Attempts to cross were in the first instance made above the city by a part of our pontoon train being laid down, but it did not answer owing to the badness of the weather, the marshy nature of the banks on the opposite side and the appearance of the enemy in force to oppose it. That he might however be deceived and distracted, such pontoons as could be spared were left there with troops in support and the largest proportion of them were in the night of the 3 April silently & secretly conveyed to Grenade below the city & on to the banks of the river. Four divisions of infantry (one of which [was] the 4th, our own) with cavalry & artillery marched down to cover the operation, the place fixed on over which to throw the bridge on our side was at the foot of a bold eminence which was crowned by upwards of twenty of our pieces of artillery, the fire of which if necessary could have commanded the other side of the stream which was a dead flat for a considerable distance and the infantry were so disposed on the hill as to cover it like an immense swarm of bees of various colours & must have been an imposing sight to the enemy had he been there to witness it.

Every preliminary arrangement having been completed by dawn of day by the Royal Staff Corps,[25] the artificers of which composed the working party, they at once commenced when the light allowed [an] object to be discerned; a small boat was first pushed over with a small detachment & the first rope of communication having soon been fixed, the pontoons were taken down from their carriages & launched on the water. As the work progressed & in the incredible short time of five hours the bridge was completed without an enemy having been perceived to hinder the undertaking, although during the construction everyone was anxiously watching for the appearance of such a disturbance. The scene of bustle during these five hours was most animating and created much interest as on its success a door was (as it were) opened into a much more extensive, rich and new

---

25 The Royal Staff Corps was the army's engineers, controlled by Horse Guards rather than the Ordnance Department.

6TH CAMPAIGN

part of France, than we had as yet occupied. Everything connected with the security of the bridge being at last completed, the cavalry first descended to it, dismounted & led their horses over it, which being but a fragile affair after all could bear no great collected weight. The infantry followed, their respective bands playing the tune of the *British Grenadiers*.[26] and then the artillery, the guns of which were unlimbered & dragged over piecemeal.

Two divisions of infantry (the 3rd & 4th) thus crossed under most enthusiastic feelings, immediately advanced & took a position, but no one appeared to stop us. The cavalry then dashed forward, we the infantry following and we all shortly came on the high road from Toulouse & Bordeaux like an apparition to the dismay of the people, who had no immediate expectation of seeing us pouncing as we did unawares on them & finding their loaded waggons going up and down leisurely as if the passage of the river was an impossibility. As we were all Anglo Portuguese who had crossed, keeping up the strictest discipline, the inhabitants got over their fright quickly and as we only took possession of what actually belonged to the French government & army, the *routiers* or cartmen proceeding on the road with merchandise, or other goods connected with trade & belonging to individuals, were astonished and amazed when told that they might proceed on their journey and fear nothing. At first they had attempted to run away but being reassured, the best understanding was soon established between us & the peasantry; it was certainly making war most honourably and it was with proud feelings that we perceived the effect it produced on those who might otherwise have been considered our enemies; in fact we were only warring against the existing government.

The rest of the day passed quietly, the enemy leaving us unmolested. We occupied a small village into which the Staff officers

---

26 The *British Grenadiers* is a traditional marching song which originally dates to the seventeenth century and is still the regimental march of quite a number of regiments.

were quartered, the troops bivouacking outside. This isolated part of the army was commanded by Sir Thomas Picton, the surly old fellow before alluded to and Sir Lowry Cole our general was next to him & of equal rank. The former was not expected to take his quarters among us & the best house was accordingly selected for the latter & the baggage was put into it; unexpectedly however orders came to make room for Sir Thomas and his aide de camp having approved of Sir Lowry's house, most unceremoniously ordered the baggage to be removed and remonstrance being useless it was done at once, all parties concerned being aware of the overbearing character of the general and that had his aide de camp ceded the point it would have got him into such a scrape as would have produced a severe wigging. Such was the extent to which military discourtesy was carried on at times even with officers of high grade, only senior perhaps to each other by a few months. Sir Lowry was much offended, but there was no remedy and he was therefore obliged to take the affront quietly, go to another house which was little inferior to the other, but the cooking having thereby been delayed, he had to wait some time for dinner. There never was a good understanding between these two fiery chiefs, for Sir Lowry was not over quiet himself.

The next day rain came on & became so violent that the river rose & swelling to a great height endangered the pontoon bridge; it was in consequence obliged to be taken up & well it was done for the French sent down floats & other lumpy articles which would have destroyed it and thus we were completely cut off from the rest of the army and at the mercy of the whole French force, the greatest part of which could have been detached to attack us from one hour to the other and we had no point or position on which to retire. The weather continuing bad & Lord Wellington seeing the eminent danger we were in, ventured across in a small boat to see what could be done, for we were not above 14,000 men in all & there was no rallying point to occupy so as to oppose an attack, the country round about being flats. It must have been a moment of great anxiety for him and the astonishment was that his opponent did not take advantage of it, for never had he such an opportunity of striking a tremendous blow at us, but he overlooked it in the great efforts he was making to render the fortifications round Toulouse as complete as the shortness of the time would allow.

On the 7th the river began to subside and hopes were entertained that all danger was passing, which was felt to be a great relief and on the 8th the bridge being re-established additional troops came over and led to an immediate advance on Toulouse only from 14 to 15 miles distance, in the neighbourhood of which we encamped, the cavalry having had some skirmishing with the enemy.

On the 9th all the usual symptoms of an approaching fight were evident. Mount Rave on which the enemy's position was established was visible from our camp, but it hid the city from our view.

On the 10th of April the Battle of Toulouse was fought. The 4th & 6th Divisions on that day formed the left of our army, but in consequence of the rivers intersecting the line of advance, they were obliged to march towards the centre of the position, cross a bridge then make a long detour to their left, the whole time under the enemy's fire and through a bog through which the artillery could not follow. As I was not required to accompany them, I got up on the roof of a house from which I could observe all that was passing. I watched the two divisions as they went along, the enemy endeavouring to check their advance by a cannonade, and while looking at Mount Rave I perceived a body of cavalry issuing out of a hollow road in the centre of it, evidently intended to act against our people. They were descending down on[to] the plain when being perceived on our side, a Congreve rocket was fired at them, but instead of taking the proper direction it rose up in the air and did no injury, but the noise which the tail of it made seemed to me so unearthly & astounding in its progress (having never heard one before) that if well directed could not have failed to have caused astonishment to all who heard it. A second one followed quickly and passing immediately over the heads of the cavalry or through its ranks, an instantaneous panic was visible & in a moment the whole dispersed and were seen flying in all directions up the hill, men & horses having evidently been frightened at the unusual sounds which this new weapon had produced and such was the effect that they did not make their appearance again. While watching that part of the field & the enemy's position swarming with their battalions, my attention was attracted to a movement in my front by the Spanish troops about 10,000, marching up the hill to the attack. Their advance was imposing and they succeeded in nearly reaching the top in very good style, but then the enemy attacked them with their usual impetuosity, in a trice succeeded in driving the whole down the heights in irretrievable confusion, some taking shelter under an embankment & others finding their way in the plain and had it not been for our cavalry which was in support & which immediately checked runaways encircling them sword in hand, it is doubtful if they would ever have rallied. By this time the two divisions alluded to as having proceeded to the left, had reached their ground and then commenced the general attack all round the enemy's position from our left & extending to the river & across it on the *tête de pont* by which Toulouse was encircled in a belt of vivid cannonade & musketry which required to be heard to be conceived. The contest on Mount Rave was most obstinate, our troops were seen advancing & storming the field redoubts, then giving way, again advancing & then concealed by dense smoke until at last after a most severe and protracted struggle, the result of which was for some time doubtful, the French troops were at last driven from the whole of the fortifications on the plateau of Mount Rave and obliged to seek shelter behind the defences in front of the town. As the action was ceasing I rode up to ascertain where the division would remain for the night, to cause the necessary provisions to be brought up to it and on my way met with several prisoners coming to the rear, among whom was one who had lost part of his nose by a sabre cut and taking me for a doctor he imploringly begged of me to sew it up shewing me the part which had been cut off in a pocket handkerchief. I told him that I was not a professional man, but that he would meet with many further in the rear. How he succeeded I cannot of course tell, for I had no time to spare for enquiries before dark to get to my destination. I soon found our troops and passed over the field covered with numerous dead & some wounded and from the heights we were on (Mount Rave) & on which we were triumphantly established, there lay on the plain below the city of Toulouse within cannon shot with the French army in it, almost surrounded or at least so on three sides out of four. Major (now General) Auchmuty[27] who commanded the light companies in advance, reported that he had three oxen in an outhouse which might be slaughtered for rations if required, for there was no one with them, their owner having been unfortunately killed while standing by him by the last cannon shot which had been fired. The animals not having been wanted for the proposed purpose were left on the spot & I was subsequently called upon to know what had become of them, to which I could only answer what I have described.

At dusk I returned to the house from whence I had seen the action & slept there until dawn, when I returned to the troops. The day (the 11th) passed on quietly though all were on the tiptoe of expectation to ascertain what would follow next, but early next morning on returning to my post, I learnt from the officers that the French army had evacuated the city & been heard during the whole night filing off on the high road leading to Carcassonne, within our cannon range their road or means of flight, having it is supposed been left purposely undisturbed by Lord Wellington to avoid a bombardment & attack on the town which must have occurred had they persisted in remaining in it, the inhabitants being understood to be favourably disposed to the Bourbons or at least to peace.

This action & the immense loss of life it occasioned, might have been avoided, for it was suspected that Marshal Soult was aware

---

27 Major Samuel Auchmuty, 7th Foot.

of the overthrow of Buonaparte at Paris some days before, but not having received the intelligence officially, he would not give absolute credence to it & acted as if it had not occurred. We on our part gave him little time for consideration, our object being that of preventing his making his position invulnerable by the completion of his fortifications & he was therefore attacked without delay.

The news quickly spread of the evacuation of the town & in it were found the generals, other officers & soldiers who had been wounded of the enemy, numbering it was said 1,600, together with a large quantity of stores &c. The municipality (alias the corporation) put themselves in communication without loss of time with Lord Wellington and begged leave to escort him into the town & take possession. They accordingly met him at the gates in full costume & when he made his appearance with all his Staff & many other officers among whom I was, they presented the keys & drawing their swords surrounded him & in this manner accompanied him to the square in which the town hall was situated. The procession was triumphal, for the streets through which we passed and the balconies & windows of houses were crowded with spectators greeting us and making the reception to appear to be given more to an army of deliverers than to one of an enemy entering as conquerors. Two squadrons of cavalry accompanied his Lordship as his bodyguard & a still greater number of officers, for all who could manage it wished to have an early sight of the first large town we had as yet come to. We quickly reached the square alluded to & His Lordship having alighted from his horse at the door of the municipality, went upstairs in the midst of a concourse of people & was received by the authorities in the Great Hall, on the right hand of which there was a small inner room with a throne in it, erected for Napoleon when he visited that part of the Empire. His Lordship was led to it & invited to sit on it which he very properly refused, but putting a foot on the first step he made them a speech in French, the purport of which was that he was not warring against the French people but against Buonaparte, assured them of his protection and hoped the war was at an end,

6TH CAMPAIGN

with other matters which I could not precisely understand from his pronunciation being anglified. He spoke nevertheless with fluency & much to the satisfaction of his hearers, most of whom were heartily tired of a state of things which had deprived them of their children, carried off forcibly and unrelentingly as conscripts to serve 'as food to cannon', an expression said to have been used by their Emperor when he saw young soldiers arriving to join the army.

News having arrived during the day, by two officers (English & French) who had been detained on the road, of the restoration of the Bourbons, His Lordship appeared at the theatre in the evening with a large white cockade and great rejoicings occurred on the occasion and that emblem was forthwith adopted as the national one. The people were extremely cordial & a grand ball took place soon after in the hall of the municipality given to Lord Wellington and such of the officers of the army as could attend. I was taken there by the gentleman (one of the old noblesse) on whom I was quartered, in company with his wife and daughter. All round the room a stand had been erected consisting of three or four steps, on which the ladies were seated as they entered, appearing like a stand of flowers, the mothers & old people at the top and the young folks at the bottom ready to be handed to the dance when called upon by their partners & throughout the evening they kept to those places. The fashion then prevailing of dressing the ladies was *a la chinoise* [Chinese], the hair being all gathered on the top of the head & intermixed with flowers so as to appear like a bouquet; no curls were allowed below which made the neck & forehead to appear very naked & as there were very few beauties to set off so unbecoming a fashion, few if any of us ran the risk of losing our hearts on the occasion. Not knowing as yet how to dance quadrilles,[28] I remained a mere spectator of the scene,

---

28 The Quadrille dance was introduced in France around 1760 but was not introduced to England until 1816 by Lady Jersey, when it became a craze. It consisted of four pairs standing at each corner of a square, each section of the dance being repeated by the other couples.

which gave me full occupation, not having as yet joined in so gay an assembly in France.

I can give no description of the city as I saw nothing particular in it in the midst of the bustle and constant occupation which took up every moment of my time. While standing one day in the square a small gun went off unexpectedly a few feet over my head and on enquiry the only answer given at the moment was that it was twelve o'clock but I afterwards learnt that a magnifying glass was so placed over the touch hole of the gun in question fixed on the balustrade of the balcony of the town hall that when the sun shone it ignited the powder in the pan exactly at noon making it a species of clock or time piece which announced to the neighbourhood the hour of the day.[29]

Marshal Soult being still incredulous of passing events in the capital of France and unwilling to give his adhesion to the new government, we received orders to pursue him, and accordingly marched towards Castelnaudary & reached La Bastide [Labastide-Beauvoir] on the 14 April; on the road the French army left traces of disorganisation most disgraceful to it, for they had pillaged the houses & ill-used the inhabitants as if passing through an enemy's country, while we respected property scrupulously by keeping up strict discipline.

We reached St Felix [Saint-Felix-Lauragais] on the 18th and there halted under the expectation of an armistice taking place, but we kept on the alert for fear of a surprise, as no reliance could be placed on any assurances of our foes short of a formal written agreement. Our encampment was on a height overlooking an extensive plain occupied by the French army, removed however some distance from us. Our requisitions for provisions, forage &c were made on the villages lying between us and I frequently visited them when a delay occurred in their transmissal. On one occasion I rode into a small town, which I was told mostly contained Protestants and on going into the Maire's house, I found by the pictures on the walls that he was one himself.

---

29 The only functioning sundial cannon now resides at Atvidaberg in Sweden.

6TH CAMPAIGN

On asking him for the provisions required of him, he told me that he had received no letter from me and had he done so would not have attended it, as he considered he was within the French lines and the French patrols came occasionally into the town. He advised me to leave without delay, as I might become a prisoner from one moment to the other. I suspected it to be a subterfuge and therefore wrote a requisition for what I had first demanded and left it to him to execute with a threat that if it was not attended [to] he might have a regiment of cavalry quartered on the place & it had the desired effect on seeing my determination not to be put off. Finding me conversant in his own language, we entered into conversation & I then discovered the cause of his coolness and indifference to serve us. With much feeling he regretted the possible restoration of the Bourbons, as under the dynasty of the Empire, Protestants enjoyed equal rights with Roman Catholics and in the change, persecution and degradation were sure to follow, and pointing to the pictures, you can he said, form some notion of the sufferings endured by my ancestors & others of our faith formerly. They depicted many atrocities such as breaking on the wheel, burning of houses &c all which subjects I must take down & I will most probably be deprived of my official situation when that bigoted race get again established on the throne. You must not therefore he added, wonder at the coolness of our reception which would have been to you our co-religionists, most cordial if divested of the danger which accompanies your presence. I really pitied the poor man and left him in hopes that his fearful anticipation might not come to pass. So indulgent had been the Imperial government, that Protestants had been allowed to erect a college for the education of their youth and the building was visible from our encampment.

While awaiting events there, the inhabitants of the towns & villages occupied by the French army were so disgusted at its licentious and disorderly conduct, as to induce many of the magistrates to come over & request Lord Wellington to occupy the country with his own troops and several came to me with their complaints, knowing I spoke

French, to ascertain the steps they were to take to get them conveyed to His Lordship. I advised them to go to Toulouse the headquarters, but nothing resulted from it as we immediately retired when peace was announced.

The contrast was a curious one on our side, for in preserving order supplies were abundant and large *routiers* or waggons loaded with provisions & spirits came on speculation from Toulouse & other places for sale confiding on our integrity & good conduct as well as on the certainty of being paid for them.

Within a ride of our encampment the great reservoir of water was constructed which fed the Languedoc canal,[30] considered one of the wonders of the world (or of the times it was built I should say) it connecting, by that description of communication, the Atlantic and Mediterranean sea. This reservoir consists of an immense high dam[31] erected across a valley connecting two hills, which hills joined together at the top of the valley where there is a considerable stream flowing down, a lake is therefore formed of considerable depth and extent and in the masonry of the dam the water is let down through cylinder apertures, when required, by turning large screws with the help of crowbars. When a party of us reached the spot, I went for the person attached to the works & who usually attended visitors. On our way down he told me in confidence not to be frightened or astonished when he applied the cross bar & turned the screws & not mention it to my companions beforehand that their surprise might be the greater; we all alighted (six or seven of us) from our horses & went through a long vaulted passage apparently leading to the centre of the dam, to the room or cellar w[h]ere the water was precipitated to a great depth down below. The man asked us if we wished the waters to be

---

30 Originally known as the Canal Royal en Languedoc, it is now more often known as the Canal du Midi. Built in the seventeenth century it runs for 240km (150 miles) linking the Garonne to the Mediterranean.

31 The Bassin de Saint-Ferreol is still the main reservoir for the canal. The dam, consisting of three parallel walls, is 786m long and 149m wide.

left down & which being answered in the affirmative, he applied his crowbar accordingly & such an uproar succeeded in this subterranean hole of rushing waters, that even I could hardly stand it; it appeared as if the whole dam was giving way from the immense pressure of the lake above & crumbling over our heads, the noise being re-echoed along the passages & such was the effect on the spectators that when I looked round they had all disappeared, some had run far into the passage or gallery by which we came & others had upset each other in their rush for safety and it was only when the cylinders were closed again that they thought the danger to be over. The superintendent advised us not to mention the impression we experienced that others coming afterwards might be equally surprised as ourselves and I think the secret was kept much in the same way as by those who had been deluded in going to see a wonder of a horse who was declared to have his tail where his head usually is.[32]

Marshal Soult having at last thought it advisable to recognise the new order of things, hostilities ceased and the 4th Division with other troops returned to Toulouse where we remained on 20 & 21 April & were present at the ball before described. Our destination was the town of Condom where we were to be stationed in conformity to a convention entered into between the Marquis of Wellington and Marshal Soult which established the portion of territory which each army should occupy until the country was evacuated by the signature of the treaty of peace.

On our way to our destination we reached L'Isle en Jourdain [L'Isle-Jourdain] on the 22nd, Aubiet 23rd, Auch on the 24th a nice town & Condom on the 26th where & in the neighbouring villages the 4th Division took up its quarters until the end of the succeeding month. Nothing material occurred on this march except that I lost my best horse by a singular accident; I happened to be quartered on a house which had no stable and my servants put my horses in

---

32 From *Mother Goose.*

an adjacent unoccupied blacksmith's shop or forge. Unfortunately an iron anvil in a corner of the place had a pointed end and it was supposed that the horse rubbed himself against it during the night, for in the morning he was found lying on the ground near it & dead, with his belly ripped open & his bowels partly out; the loss was great and would have been greater still had we been actively employed against the enemy. As it was, he had cost me 50 guineas a short time before.[33]

Condom, the place of our sojourn for the time, is a quiet little town & the chief one of a Bishopric, about twenty leagues from Bordeaux with about 6,000 inhabitants situated in a retired part of the country in which a considerable number of the old noblesse then resided, the Maire the Marquis de Cugnac[34] being one of them. The inhabitants had not been accustomed to see troops especially foreign ones, but the fame of our good conduct having spread far and wide, they were particularly civil and attentive, the only bar to sociability being the want among most of the officers, of knowing their language. As it was however, we got on uncommonly well with them, the bourgeois even tried to outdo the higher classes in their attentions & entertainment, but the old nobles though they had lost a great part of their landed property, kept aloof from those individuals who had enriched themselves by the Revolution. Being in the number of the Staff and chief of my department, I visited the upper folks & from being fluent in their language I was rather a favourite among them, but then I could spare little or no time to encourage this good feeling.

The ladies & the women in general appeared to us very ordinary in their appearance, badly dressed and without taste which led to their making little or no impression on the hearts of any of us. Our chaplain[35] however, fancied at one time that one of our acquaintances was looking sweet on him & when he found or fancied that she constantly

---

33 Nearly £3,000 in today's terms.

34 Jules Emilien, Marquis de Cugnac, succeeded to the title in 1813.

35 Chaplain George Jenkins was attached to the 4th Division.

6TH CAMPAIGN

fastened her eyes on him, and stared him out of countenance, he mentioned it to Colonel Bell our Quarter Master General,[36] who thereupon watched proceedings & soon ascertained the cause, but being fond of a joke he allowed matters to go on a little longer for the fun of it, until he broke the spell by telling him he had discovered that she had a glass eye. The loss of it might have been accidental but it was evident from what constantly came under my notice, that the people of this part of the country were not gifted with sound health or personal beauty for deformities of all sorts, humpbacks, ulcerations &c abounded among them to an extraordinary degree, particularly among the women one of whom at least in fine was thus afflicted & for which no adequate cause could be assigned, badness of climate could not be pleaded for a more beautiful one I had not before seen & the country being well cultivated appeared like a garden, the air was mild and temperate with constant fine weather & not oppressive as in more southern climates.

Provisions were accordingly cheap & good and the troops were in consequence supplied on the spot & paid in money, so that although it gave trouble in making the arrangements, no anxiety was experienced in obtaining them comparatively, to what occurred when the army was together and marching. The Maires or magistrates of the different communes (villages) lent their assistance in this respect and I annex a letter from one of them taken from a number in my possession, addressed to me,[37] in which will be perceived the opinion entertained of our troops & also the copy of one, by which some idea may be formed of the adulation paid to Lord Wellington; for though every allowance must be made for exaggeration there is a great deal of truth in them, our discipline being great and all classes being heartily tired of the war.

---

36 John Bell had become a Lieutenant Colonel on 12 April 1814.

37 Not extant.

Though their personal defects extended to their minds which were not of the most upright description, our expenditure in the midst of abundance was very much reduced, even allowing for some degree of imposition. As examples, bread was obtained for 3 sous or 1½d per pound,[38] meat 12 sous or 6d per pound[39] & a pipe of good brandy for £12,[40] the same quantity of which latter of bad spirits was paid for in Spain & in the Pyrenees at the enormous rate of £52.[41] The army may be said therefore to have been in clover, in having everything of the best quality & comfortably lodged; yet the Portuguese troops were unhappy and sighing for home, where they knew a reduced ration of rye bread and salt fish awaited them. Yet there was a charm in returning to one's own country which appeared to overcome in them every other gratification or feeling; not so with our own soldiers who only looked to the enjoyment of the moment without troubling themselves after the future. The weekly market day was one of bustle in our quiet little town & an idle lounge for the officers quartered in it, among whom several had their quarters overlooking the scene in the square. One of them happened to be on his balcony while another was passing by, the latter took some eggs from the basket of a market woman & began throwing them at the former, who immediately sent his servant for a supply, that led to a pelting match which only ended in exhausting the market, for as they were paid for, the fun continued some time to the amazement of the country folk who could not comprehend its thoughtlessness & extravagance.

In return for the marked and really kind attentions which every officer received in Condom during our stay in it from all classes, we determined to give a ball in the best style in our power, to include every decent person and invitations were sent at considerable distances to

---

38 About the modern equivalent of 35p per pound (0.45kg).

39 About the modern equivalent of £1.30 per pound (0.45kg).

40 About the modern equivalent of £600 per pipe of 126 gallons (573 litres).

41 About the modern equivalent of £2,500.

6TH CAMPAIGN

such persons as were recommended by our town friends. The Mairie or municipality house was placed at our disposal by the authorities & the 7th Fusilier officers undertook to decorate the principal apartment which was converted into an armoury, with a grand military trophy at one end of it ornamented with various Colours & a field piece at each side including stars made with bayonets &c & the other regiments took the other rooms & ornamented them as bowers &c according to their fancy in which a great deal of taste & variety was displayed. The whole was a subject of astonishment to the natives, who had never seen the like before, for no expense was spared either in decorations or in the refreshments or supper, the latter of which was as splendid as the place could afford. The ladies appeared as usual in their unbecoming Chinese fashion head dress, which having become familiar with us did not seem to us so *outré* [outrageous] as when we first saw it. Everything was done to enliven the scene and as dancing was a favourite amusement among the French people, everyone seemed to enjoy themselves. At supper there was no lack of champagne as a stimulant, with toasts and speeches in honour of *Louis le desire*[42] and of peace & there being no desire of separating, the day dawned and obliged the party at last to disperse. Good feeling prevailed throughout the night and the expressions of thanks from the invited were most charmingly expressed, and I doubt not the event will have long been remembered. As far as I recollect the cost of the entertainment did not fall far short of £300.[43]

It was well timed, for it was hardly over before rumours for an immediate move reached us. Peace had been signed and on the 28 May orders were received for the march which was to disperse us all in various directions; two regiments of our division[44] besides many others from the army, were ordered to proceed on expeditions to the coast of

---

42 King Louis XVIII.

43 About the modern equivalent of £15,000.

44 Three battalions were actually sent to America and Canada, the 1/7th, 3/27th and 1/40th.

the United States of America with which power we were then at war, the Portuguese to return to their country, the cavalry & artillery horses to march through France to Calais there to embark for England and the remainder of the troops to proceed to Bordeaux for embarkation. My destination, greatly at first to my annoyance, was to accompany the Portuguese army through Spain to the frontier of Portugal and there leave it to go to Lisbon, for I dreaded another summer in the hot plains of Castile having suffered in my health during five already passed under its scorching sun. I became, however reconciled to my lot on finding that I might have been ordered to America which was then considered a worse alternative and turned out to be so in the sequel.

The dispersion was not however to take place until we reached Bazas on the way to Bordeaux, which we reached on the 3 June & there the final separation of the armies of the two nations took place, who had for several years been fighting together in great harmony. The moment of departure was much felt by both and was made as ceremonious and complimentary as could be thought of; the Portuguese battalions first started, the whole of them being first drawn up in the square in front of the generals and Staff, the British lining the streets and before marching presented arms, their bands playing, accompanied by the most animating cheers which were continued as the troops filed away through the town. For as they passed in front of each British regiment they were received with presented arms, loud shouts & the respective bands playing the *British Grenadiers*; the scene was most enthusiastic and gratifying & it evidently made a deep & it is supposed a lasting impression on our allies, who had gained the most unfading laurels which their country will ever have to boast in its annals.

From the 5th to the 15th during which I remained at Bazas in the exercise of my new duty my employment was incessant, for arrangements had to be made as the respective brigades of Portuguese passed through in succession daily, added to which all the Spanish & Portuguese followers & servants of the British Army had to be provided for, who were ordered to accompany them in detachments consisting, as it may well be imagined, of a motley and disorderly crew of men, women & children (mounted on all sorts of animals) the accumulation of years & who gave infinitely a deal more trouble than the troops & after all the arrangements made for them, it was found impossible to keep the whole in order, for many would proceed in their own way, submitting to no control and it was only when apprehensive of danger & being plundered on the road, that they clung to the soldiers for protection.

The last of the troops having taken their departure on the 15th, I started myself for the frontier of Spain, passing over the same ground as we had already traversed through the Pays des Landes on to Bayonne, which being now open, I took a hurried peep in it. I found nothing but a dirty town not worth a description & soon left it on finding the garrison badly disposed & officers ready to pick a quarrel, the inhabitants not being much better inclined & uncivil. Such indeed was & had been the general bad feeling in the place that everyone was recommended not to go in, many duels having taken place between our officers & those of the French troops, in which several lives had been lost.

I passed over the bridge on the river which divides France from Spain on the 17 June, having rode rapidly from Bazas & I remained three days at Rentaría [Errenteria] incessantly occupied in superintending the supply of more than half of the Portuguese army and making arrangements for the Commissariat to empty all the depots of provisions, cattle & forage which had been stored up in the several towns in Spain on the road all the way to the frontier of Portugal, the principal of which were in Tolosa, Vitoria Palencia, Salamanca & Ciudad Rodrigo, with various intervening minor ones.

I reached Tolosa on the 21st & wrote a report to the Commissary General herewith annexed,[45] to give an idea of the mode & character

---

45 Not extant.

of epistolary correspondence of those days, also march routes of the several brigades of troops, found among my papers and I pushed on to Vitoria where I remained two days and there met with an old Commissariat friend in charge there. I observed that many of our trophies of the battle fought there, such as caissons & carriages were still parked there instead of being removed, shewing an instance among many others of the usual apathy of the Spanish nation or government.

I had on my way down resisted many importunities to take under my protection the *cheres amies* [dear friends] of officers returning to England, but apprehensive of such incumbrances I civilly declined the offers until persuaded by my friend to do him that favour. We started all three together and at a certain distance from Vitoria their separation took place. They had lived together several years, but as she was of [a] very inferior degree, though handsome & no children, they had mutually agreed to dissolve [their] partnership. I shook hands with my friend who recommended her to me & then [I] left them together for a moment riding on a short distance. She soon joined me, dried up her tears and in a day or two, or hours I should say, her spirits returned and she appeared quite happy in my company until I left her several days after on the road near her home, to which she returned with means no doubt to tempt any individual of her class to become her husband. Many there were who had thus followed the army, but very few succeeded so well as to ensure marriage & accompany their husbands to England. One I knew & she is now the wife of General Sir Harry Smith & a most exemplary woman.[46]

To get on as quick as I could to reach the head of the columns when the rear had passed on, I occasionally took my way by cross & more direct roads, accompanied by my clerk and two or three

---

46 Captain Harry Smith, 95th Rifles, gave protection to the orphaned 14-year-old Juana de Leon after the siege of Badajoz in 1812. They married within days and remained happily married throughout his later distinguished career, giving her name to Ladysmith in South Africa.

6TH CAMPAIGN

muleteers. On one occasion we passed through a most solitary & wooded valley or defile well calculated for the haunts of banditti, and whilst in the midst of it and quite unconscious of danger, my Spanish companions appeared uneasy & left off humming tunes as was their custom, going on in silence and evidently apprehensive of something likely to happen from one moment to the other, but being unsuspicious myself I took no further notice of their looks. And in an hour we emerged into a more open country without accident, much to their apparent joy, their knowledge of localities being of course keener than mine and on reaching the next village the inhabitants expressed their astonishment at our having attempted that road which was notorious for the robbers that infested it, but who it was supposed had a wider field of action for the time being among the numberless followers of the army on their way home covering the main road in all directions & becoming an easy prey if they attempted to straggle, probably however we escaped from being English & to the respect paid to us during the war. There was however a disposition to plunder abroad which the nature of the times gave rise to at this moment, for it shewed itself more daring than could have been expected, in an attempt made by a guerrilla party to carry off on the march the Military Chest of the Portuguese army & it would have succeeded had the escort not been advised in time & put on their guard.

To shew the aversion in which the Portuguese were held in Spain & the pomposity of the Spanish character on the most trifling matters, I had occasion one day to communicate on business with the alcalde of a small village on the roadside & having gone to his house and enquired for him, he was pointed out to me seated on some timber at the end of his yard, in conversation with two others and three peasants in dress & appearance. I went up to him & told him I wished to speak to him, on which he rose up with all the dignity a Castilian can assume & informed me '*Somos in consejo*' ('We are in council') and cannot be disturbed & I had to wait a few minutes until their deliberations were over. He took me no doubt for a Portuguese officer seeing that my uniform was blue, for on finding his mistake he became as civil as I could wish; such is man in Castile, looking down in his state of ignorance on every other being as inferior to himself.

Passing on our progress through the great towns in Spain we found the various trades in a very primitive state and much as they are described to have existed centuries before in England. Silver & goldsmiths, blacksmiths & every other profession occupying each respective streets, guilds or wards, so that if a certain article of either was wanted it was only necessary to ascertain in what part of the town it was to be obtained to avoid a long walk in search of a shop as must be done elsewhere; no change had evidently taken place for hundreds of years (I may say) in anything in Spain or Portugal before the visit paid them by the French armies & our own in 1808 & we were not likely to give them very prepossessing examples of civilization or inducements to change by our proceedings.

Our march lay to the right of Villarcayo, leaving Burgos to our left & after passing through Valladolid & other towns in the midst of business and annoyance from the impossibility of acting up to my instructions, from the dilatoriness of the Portuguese Commissariat, I gladly reached Palencia[47] on the 14 July & having had a little rest I made a report of my proceeding to my chief at Bordeaux herewith annexed.[48]

The heat had become excessive and I was sighing for permanent repose but yet not half of my journey was over, though it was from there that the right column of the Portuguese troops were to take their final departure for Portugal and I was not sorry to see them depart by degrees, although it was required that I should accompany them to their own country which they were to enter in different directions. The column I was immediately with, being ordered to proceed by Toro & Zamora to Braganza [Braganca] in Tras os Montes & the

---

47 He would have passed through Palencia the day before he arrived at Valladolid.

48 Not extant.

6TH CAMPAIGN

left one by Salamanca, Ciudad Rodrigo & Almeida, from which they were to branch off in various directions to their several garrisons in the cities of the Kingdom.

Toro is a very ancient city on the River Douro from whence and neighbourhood many adventurers proceeded to Mexico & Peru &c after their conquest, causing thereby a depopulation of which that part of Spain has never recovered, for the sites of many abandoned villages were pointed out to me on our march. From Toro I proceeded to Zamora and then entered Portugal by the rugged mountainous country of Tras os Montes and in the beginning of August reached the city of Braganza [Braganca], the residence of the Royal family of Portugal previous to their coming to the throne. The place is small without attraction and as on reaching it my active duties were at an end, I lost no time in proceeding to Almeida which I reached on the 8th of the same month with the intention of making up a voluminous set of accounts in its neighbourhood in peace and quiet, undisturbed by any distraction to which me and my clerks would be liable to in going to a large town.

In Almeida however a superior officer of my department, Deputy Commissary General Pratt,[49] a cunning old fellow wearing a wig, had been stationed to pay off the Spanish mule transport which had been attached to the army, the arrears of the hire of which amounted to an enormous sum and I was ordered to report myself to him; in doing which I mentioned my intentions of remaining near him, with the sanction of the Commissary General, thinking that I should be in his way in the object he had in view. He feigned having received instructions, by which I was at once to proceed to Lisbon and he accordingly ordered me to go there without delay, which I of course obeyed as a matter of duty and the sequel turned as I expected, for he took advantage of the opportunity to which he did not wish me

---

49 Deputy Commissary General Charles Pratt.

to be a witness and with the assistance of a nephew[50] he acted most dishonourably towards the muleteers & government. After a while his dishonesty was found out and he was disgracefully dismissed the public service, as unfit to serve His Majesty in any capacity whatever.

My intention of a quiet residence having thus been frustrated, I lost no time in taking my departure for Lisbon, by the same road (through Castelo Branco which I reached on the 22 [August], Niza [Nisa], Abrantes, Santarem &c) as I had so often travelled over before, but with this great difference that the towns & villages in the way had assumed an appearance of profound quiet & stillness, to which they had not been accustomed for years and not having had as yet time to repair the damages of war, there was an air of melancholy about everybody & thing which gave rise to many unpleasant feelings and made us anxious to reach Lisbon which we did in the beginning of September.

A state of peace in that capital abolished the wages of war and therefore officers instead of being quartered in private houses had in lieu an allowance to provide for themselves private lodgings, but there being a difficulty to find them furnished, I was under the necessity of hiring two large empty rooms, one to serve for an office and the other for my own accommodation in which I put just enough furniture for a makeshift, not expecting to make a long residence there. They were therefore anything but comfortable and became more miserable from a severe illness which laid me up almost immediately after my arrival. The last march through parts of France, Spain & most of Portugal in the hottest season of the year & anxious duties, knocked me up and I was seized with a bilious gastric fever on the 12th of September which obliged me to take to my bed and a Portuguese acquaintance thinking to do me service sent me his own native doctor, by whom I was treated in their way by mere simples without apparent benefit. Which obliged me to call in one of

---

50 Quite possibly Deputy Purveyor George Pratt.

6TH CAMPAIGN

our medical officers, who disapproving of what the other had done, got annoyed and most shamefully discontinued his visits and I was left to be treated as before and condemned by a '*jalousie de métier*' [professional jealousy] to get on as I could. The carelessness of some officers of the medical staff now that war had ceased had become I am sorry to say a very bad feature of their conduct & from want of effective treatment by this desertion, I had long to struggle against the disease. It was dreary to an extreme to be laying in bed as I did in a large room without carpet, curtains &c and seeing no one but the doctor, my clerk for a moment & my servant the whole day; I felt the extreme loneliness of my situation in a land of strangers, without a soul who could sympathize with me and thus I continued for weeks.

In this situation, I received a letter from the senior Commissariat Officer of Accounts, dated the 25th, urgently calling for my accounts to which I made with some difficulty an official reply next day, from which the following is an extract.

'From the 12th instant I have and am still, laid up in bed with a severe bilious attack which deprives me of making any rapid advance towards their completion. I am at this moment so reduced by weakness & want of appetite, the effects of the complaint, that it is as much as I can do to keep up for a quarter of an hour.'

My recovery was tedious and so afflicted my stomach by creating indigestion, that the smallest meals appeared as if I had swallowed a cannon ball, it taking hours to dissipate it. This inconvenience I have not been able to shake off entirely, for it has ever since troubled me in occasioning nervousness, which has prevented my following up my profession with that perseverance & energy I before possessed. I rallied however by degrees from the worst of the complaint and though much emaciated, I contrived to walk about & recover strength thanks to a kind providence and a good constitution, which hitherto had enabled me to brave the trials & privations of seven years campaigning & which had been fatal to more than half of the Guernseymen who as officers had been employed in it.

Captain McCrea[51] & Lieutenant La Serre[52] of the 87th Regiment were killed at Talavera: Major General Le Marchant at Salamanca;[53] his son Captain Carey Le Marchant of the Guards, died of a wound in the instep,[54] Colonel Havilland Le Mesurier was killed at Pamplona,[55] Ensign Le Mesurier of the 9th Regiment near Bayonne,[56] and Ensign Henry Le Mesurier, brother of the above Havilland, lost his right arm at Salamanca;[57] those who survived were Colonel Saumarez Brock 43rd Regiment,[58] Captains Peter Le Mesurier[59] & William Le Mesurier[60] the former in the 68th Regiment & the latter in the 24th Regiment & Sir Octavius Carey commanding a foreign corps in our pay and employed on the Eastern coast of Spain;[61] in the Commissariat there were besides myself Mr Saumarez Dobree,[62] Mr Radford and Mr Hardy,[63] and I should add Captain McCulloch of

---

51 Captain Rawdon McCrea, 87th Foot, died of his wounds on 3 August 1809.

52 Ensign Nicholas La Serre, 87th Foot, was killed on 17 July 1809.

53 Major General John Gaspard Le Marchant was killed on 22 July 1812.

54 Lieutenant and Captain Carey Le Marchant, 1st Foot Guards, died on 12 March 1814.

55 Lieutenant Colonel Havilland Le Mesurier, 12th Portuguese Line Battalion, died of his wounds in August 1813.

56 Lieutenant Peter Le Mesurier, 9th Foot, was killed on 10 December 1813.

57 Ensign Henry Le Mesurier, 48th Foot, lost his arm at Salamanca while carrying the King's Colour.

58 Captain Saumarez Brock, 43rd Foot, fought throughout the wars with only a single wound at Vimiero. He died on 22 April 1854.

59 Captain Peter Le Mesurier, 68th Foot, survived the wars.

60 Captain William Le Mesurier, 24th Foot, survived the wars.

61 Brevet Lieutenant Colonel Octavius Carey, Calabrian Free Corps.

62 John Saumarez Dobree, Deputy Assistant Commissary General attached to the 5th Division.

63 Mr Radford and Hardy were Commissariat clerks. Radford later became a Deputy Assistant Commissary General.

6TH CAMPAIGN

the Royal Engineers[64] who at the siege of Badajoz lost his reason by the effect of the wind of a cannon shot passing immediately over his head in the trenches of which he died soon after.

I found Lisbon very much altered since I left it in 1811, no bustle in the streets but the grass growing in them, hardly an English uniform to be seen, most of the military having departed for England, leaving a few soldiers in the hospitals and such individuals as were required to send away the stores of the army or wind up the accounts of the various departments connected with it. The River Tagus was also denuded of shipping so that all around appeared as if the city had been visited by some sudden event which had deprived it of its vitality & robbed it of its trade and resources.

The arrival of a part of the Portuguese army from France afforded a moment of animation in the reception given to it, among the demonstrations to celebrate so gratifying an event to the national pride, a Grand Ball was given in the Opera house[65] (one of the largest in Europe) by the senate & camera of Lisbon on the 14 October to the officers & highest classes of the community. I received an invitation card the original of which I annex,[66] and although hardly capable of accepting it, I determined on going were it only for an hour as it was expected to be something very superlative. The pit had been risen to the same height as the stage, both of which made a magnificent saloon for dancing; I went there with several brother officers in good time and there we found an immense concourse already assembled consisting of the members of government, municipal body, nobility, gentry, generals, magistrates, army, navy & many other persons which a capital contains of the first respectability, care having been taken to exclude improper individuals by everyone shewing their

---

64 Second Captain William McCulloch was actually severely wounded at the siege of Ciudad Rodrigo on 16 January 1812. He died on 10 February 1814.

65 The Teatro Nacional de Sao Carlos.

66 Not extant.

cards of admission at the doors, and that the crowd assembled might not interfere with the space allotted to dancing, the old people and such as preferred a comfortable seat occupied the four or five tiers of boxes, from whence they could at their ease look on the gay & youthful throng below. The *tout ensemble* presented a most brilliant *coup d'oeil* [spectacle] for everyone was in their best finery, stars and decorations abounded in profusion & the old nobility as well as others were covered with diamonds & other precious stones, for which they were renowned and which had been obtained from Brazil, rich in these productions; being heirlooms in families & the accumulation of generations since the conquest or settlement of that country. The display was such as to create astonishment and an English gentleman who happened to be present & pretended to have some knowledge of the value of jewellery, estimated that there could not be less than one million and a half sterling[67] of that description of property on the persons of those present, among whom the old dowagers were most conspicuous. I could not venture to dance and finding myself weak & uncomfortable from the great heat of the place, I took an early departure after having seen all the company & what was likely to be the routine of the evening; from others I afterwards learned that a grand supper followed and that dancing was kept up with great spirit until late in the morning.

During the month of October and part of November, I was busily occupied in making up my accounts & which I completed & sent in by the 20th of the latter month, by which time I had hoped to be ordered to go to England, but to my great disappointment, I was told that I must wait until their cursory examination.

My acquaintance in Lisbon was indeed limited and I did not feel inclined to increase it unwell as I was. It was confined to the family of old Mrs Morrough, the Irish widow who had been most kind to me on former occasions, but as it only consisted of an only daughter and a

---

67 Approximately £80 million today.

6TH CAMPAIGN

relation to whom she was engaged, I could not expect from them much sociability. I also visited an old Portuguese acquaintance, the postmaster of Castelo Branco, then situated in the capital, but as he was married to a young & pretty wife to whom he never introduced me, my visits were mere formalities & being himself old and jealous like all Portuguese, he was afraid I suppose, of an acquaintance which might become too intimate. I was oftener with an old clerk, also a Portuguese, who had come down from Coimbra to settle some accounts, he having become a contractor with the army after leaving the Commissariat, finding it more lucrative; he was a free mason and induced me to become one also & which accordingly took place while I remained in Lisbon.[68] It was an affair of danger for I was told the Lodge was watched by the Inquisition and in consequence the greatest secrecy was kept of its locality and days of meeting, individuals of the craft were kept on the watch outside as well as inside to prevent a surprise, which without doubt would have led to the incarceration of the native members. I was initiated in the limited mysteries of an apprentice & saw others go through the same ordeal. I did not however, remain long enough in the country to rise in grade and since that time I have had no ambition to pursue the trade, so as to attain pre-eminence in that brotherly institution.

A few days after I had got relieved of my accounts & of any other duty, I accidentally met in the streets with a Guernsey school acquaintance, Captain Dobree of the Royal Navy,[69] who commanded the *Zenobia*, sloop of war of 18 guns, on the station. He seemed much struck with my bad state of health and at once offered to take me on a cruise for change of air. I accepted most willingly his offer and having on that plea obtained leave from Commissary General Pipon[70] then head of the Department, I soon got ready, went on board & took

---

68 The *Grande Oriente Lusitano* was established in 1802 at No. 25 Rua do Gremio Lusitano, where it remains to this day.

69 Commander Nicholas Dobree RN.

70 Deputy Commissary General James Pipon.

possession of a small though comfortable berth in his cabin. Next day we weighed anchor and left the beautiful River Tagus for a while, shaping our course to the southward to Gibraltar, passing along the Portuguese & Spanish coasts. We were at war with the United States of America and therefore gave chase to every sail we saw, in hopes of falling in with their privateers or recapturing their prizes; success however did not attend our endeavours and after peeping into Cadiz but not near enough to land, at which I was disappointed as its appearance was most inviting, we proceeded on and two days after entered the Strait of Gibraltar having the two bold headlands of Spain & Africa on both sides of us. Gibraltar was perceived before dark towards which we held our course, but the wind having failed us, the captain ordered out the sweeps which are large oars manned each of them by several men & worked on deck, as in a boat by which we got on at the rate of three miles an hour. It was a fine moonlight night such only as is met in those latitudes and as we approached the Rock (as it is called) the height and grandeur of it was considerably magnified & gave it a more imposing appearance than in the day; we were soon hailed from the shore & then allowed to take our berth.

On getting up in the morning I found we were warped within the Naval mole, but not allowed communication with the shore in consequence of the yellow fever having raged there and been scarcely over. With the Rock still in quarantine, all our communications were carried on at the Lazarch or Parlatorio [visiting room], a building with a double balustrade in the centre, six feet asunder, those in pratique being on one side & those in quarantine on the other, with a guardian (or watchman) in the centre watching that no personal contact took place between the parties.

The new Governor General Don[71] had just arrived to take the command & lay near us in the ship that brought him out, but had not

---

71 General Sir George Don was Acting Governor of Gibraltar from 3 April 1814 to 15 November 1821 and again from 7 June 1825 to 10 May 1831.

6TH CAMPAIGN

landed & having dined in his company, the conversation turned on the annual visitation of that fever for years past, which from what he had ascertained was to be attributed to want of attention to the sewers & to the crowded state of the lodging houses in the town; the Moors especially being allowed to huddle together in considerable numbers in small rooms, the air in which became tainted & nourished the disease. Knowing (as he conceived) the originating cause, to which he was determined to apply a remedy, he had great hopes of succeeding and the result proved that he was right, for since the commencement of his government the fortress has not again been visited by that pestilence.

Being thus deprived of an interior visit to it, I availed myself of the use of the captain's own boat which he placed at my disposal & occasionally accompanied me, to row in various directions, visiting the front of the town, neutral ground and sandy isthmus, then the batteries, all along to Europa point & afterwards to the back part of the Rock. On the town or western side, the ride is gradual to the summit on which O'Hara's Tower[72] is situated from 14 to 16,000 feet from the level of the sea, but at the back it is inaccessible and almost perpendicular and is the haunt of numbers of monkeys; & the land side being also nearly the same, its isolated situation becomes more imposing, unconnected as it appears from the mainland. As a fortress guarding the entrance into the Mediterranean its position in our hands gives it an importance of which the Spaniards are very jealous, not only on that account but because it is the haunt of smugglers who under our protection introduce British manufactures & tobacco in almost every part of the south of Spain to the prejudice of their revenue.

One day we crossed the bay, landed at the town of Algeciras and made a short excursion into the country, but as the town had more

---

72 O'Hara's Tower was constructed in 1791 as a watchtower on the peak of the Rock, but was struck by lightning soon after and abandoned. It was demolished in 1888.

attraction to my naval friends than green fields, we quickly returned to it. It was small in size & nothing to distinguish it from any other & it afforded no sights for the amusement of the traveller; we had for dinner fresh anchovies, which swarm in the bay & tasted much like sprats. We hoped to have been allowed to land at Gibraltar before our departure and were encouraged in that expectation from our linen being washed on shore which served as a strong preliminary, but before the indulgence could be officially permitted a signal from the Admiral ordered us to sea without a moment's delay, and mine host got I suspect a sort of philippic[73] for having delayed his departure, as he did not appear in the best of humours the rest of the day; our stay there was of a week's duration.

Our orders were to proceed to the westward of Cape Trafalgar & cruise there & in the vicinity, in company with the *Gramisus* frigate of 44 guns commanded by Captain Wyse,[74] out of sight of land of course. In our way we steered for Tangiers in the dominions of the Emperor of Morocco[75] in Africa where we arrived next morning & anchored as near the town as the depth of water would permit near the ruins of the English mole;[76] the place looked quite dissimilar to anything I had before seen. The houses had apparently no roofs, the tops consisting of flat terraces hid from view by low parapets, no chimneys and from the anchorage the place appeared like a pyramid the base being on the edge of the water & houses rising one above the other to a peak on the hillside. On going on shore we landed near the custom house and had an interview with the British Vice Consul, a few Moors were present, quite eastern in their appearance & dress, dark complexions & piercing eyes. We

---

73 A verbal roasting.

74 HMS *Granicus* of 36 guns was commanded by Captain William Furlong Wise RN.

75 The Emperor of Morocco from 1792 to 1822 was Sulayman bin Muhammad.

76 Tangiers had been occupied by British forces 1661–83, when they had constructed the mole.

6TH CAMPAIGN

were advised by no means to stroll in the country, as the population was extremely inimical to Europeans to that degree as rendered it unsafe to accompany them anywhere. The captain of the port was the first person to whom we were introduced, a huge & unwieldy Moor dressed in loose robes with a large turban and long beard; he walked evidently with much inconvenience to himself and the cause being enquired into, as a mark of sympathy, he unceremoniously took up his garments & shewed us his legs which at once explained his incapacity for exertion, as he was afflicted with elephantiasis to such a degree that his limbs appeared like tree trunks of two large trees most disgusting to look at.

On entering the custom house all that we saw in the way of forms of office were three or four Moors or Turks squatted on mats on the ground, in a circle, with beads in their hands apparently in conversation, with neither desks, inkstands or paper to denote the transaction of regular business. Gunpowder of good quality was known to be in great estimation among these people, the purser therefore took two pounds of it on shore to present to the captain of the port for his good offices in obtaining what we required. On giving him the canisters in which it was contained, it was observed to him through an interpreter, that they were given as a mark of friendship, to which he haughtily replied that there could be no friendship between a Mahomedan & a Christian though a good understanding might be kept up and as we perceived that every one of these savage & dirty looking people scowled at us as we passed them, we decided on merely looking up a street, the nearest to the landing place and confining ourselves to its neighbourhood. The Vice Consul told us there was nothing worth seeing and advised our not going into the town as should we pass by a mosque we must pull off our boots and be liable to insult. We did not therefore get any insight into the manners and customs of that savage race who, at that time were ignorantly bigoted, intolerant and haughty and still imposed tribute on several European nations as a security for their merchant ships not being molested.

One of their cruisers, or rovers (I should say) lay at anchor very near us and appeared of about our size; she had a very large crew, rough looking vagabonds, Moors of course, but from what we could perceive of her equipment &c we could have given a good account of her in a short time had they tried us, which we of course did not anticipate from being at peace with that power. They are now, however, much subdued & their piratical trade is over, which renders their being dreaded less than formerly.

Tangiers was made over to us as a part of the dowry of the Portuguese princess whom our Charles II married, but because it occasioned a trifling expense to keep it up, his extravagance & corrupt conduct led to its abandonment, the mole was blown up, though the remains are still extensive. Had the place been retained great advantages would have resulted both in a commercial as well as political point of view, for an intercourse would have been carried on with the interior and we would have commanded the entrance of the Mediterranean on both sides.

Our object for going there being for the purpose of obtaining cattle & other livestock, as well as fruit & vegetables, they were procured by our Vice Consul and brought down to the shore, and two boats having been ordered to be manned from our ship to fetch them, one of the crew happened to be a Portuguese and while I was standing by the captain, he came up and begged not to go on shore being in fear of being laid hold of by the Moors who were at war with his nation and made slaves of everyone on which they could lay hands & all the arguments made use of to convince him that being in an English vessel was a protection not proving of any avail he was allowed to remain on board; a circumstance which I mention to shew the dread & antipathy which every Portuguese & Spaniard then had to the Moors & Algerians & the Italians to the Tunisians & Tripolese higher up the Mediterranean.

The supplies we there obtained were remarkably cheap, for example the bullocks though small, cost only from 10 to 12 dollars

6TH CAMPAIGN

each, equivalent from two to three pounds sterling,[77] a dozen moderate sized fowls or ducks nine shillings,[78] 400 eggs 6s/9d,[79] 500 ripe oranges, five shillings,[80] and everything else in proportion.

Our stay being no longer required at that place, we weighed anchor, made sail and quickly passed entirely out of the Straits and in the course of two days fell in with our consort with which we kept company for some days, cruising in an open order, the two ships being hull down from each other, the topmasts being only perceptible on the horizon. The mode of communication was therefore by signal and it was remarkable with what celerity a question was put and answered apparently impossible to a landsman, for though my eyesight was excellent I could not but with difficulty, discern the signal flags through a spyglass, while the signalman with the same instrument could tell the number they indicated as they were going up to the masthead rolled up in balls, such was the force of habit. When the ships therefore were at that distance it often occurred that the signal was given to close for the commanders to dine together & then separate to take their usual station.

While thus sailing off and on we gave chase to a brig having all the appearance of a privateer, and she being a good sailor had a long run and we carried away several sails before we could bring her to and then only after firing a bow chaser at her which passed beyond her. She then hove to and having boarded her, we found her to be the *Zenobia* of Guernsey with codfish from Newfoundland bound to the Mediterranean, a strange coincidence that of two ships of the same name meeting each other commanded by Guernseymen. They were happy to find that we were not an American man of war or privateer; they had not had an observation for several days and when we came

---

77 Equivalent to £100–£150 today.

78 Equivalent to £25 today.

79 Equivalent to £18 today.

80 Equivalent to £14 today.

up to them, they were out of their course steering towards Lisbon instead of the Straits. We therefore put them right and in return they sent by the boat that conveyed them the latitude and longitude, a present of a small keg of cod sounds.[81]

I was not aware when I embarked of the chances I ran of being present at an action at sea and though I escaped the disagreeableness of it, the risk was of daily occurrence and I went through the preliminaries. One morning after breakfast a sail was discovered at a considerable distance bearing down upon us. At first we supposed it to be our consort, but found on a nearer approach that she was not so large though evidently a ship of war and much superior to us. We kept on our course, repeatedly making signals which were not answered; at last the captain went down to his cabin and brought up his private signal book & from it a signal was made and having been disregarded as the others, he immediately gave orders to clear for action, which of course was done without delay; the guns were cast loose, the men stripped themselves of part of their clothes, the powder magazine was opened and every other arrangement made to meet the emergency. My friend told me plainly there was no place down below for me to go to during the engagement & therefore recommended my taking a musket & buckling on a cartouche box, which I did and stood by him; the men being all at their posts & ready, a dead silence prevailed while the two ships were closing, and on me the suspense produced peculiar feelings hardly to be described, for at that moment life was in jeopardy & while intensely watching our supposed adversary she at once hoisted her English Ensign & gave her number, to the gratification of most of us. For though no doubt all would have done their duty, the difference of force had it been that of an enemy, would have been too great to expect that victory would have declared for us, for she carried 26 guns with covered decks &c, Captain Dobree was very angry at the *ruse de guerre* of his brother skipper, who gave

---

81 The swim bladder of a fish, then highly prized as a delicacy.

6TH CAMPAIGN

for excuse that he was determined we should not escape him had we proved to be an enemy & therefore got us well under his guns before making himself known and he did not answer the private signal from having heard that the American cruisers had got hold of them.

On a comparison of the respective strength and capabilities of the American ships, which were to be engaged by ours as of equal strength, the difference was most preposterous. For example our frigates measuring 1,200 tons, carrying 36, 40 or 44 guns, 18 pounders, with crews from 300 to 350 men and boys many of ordinary description & low stature, were expected and did fight American frigates of 1,600 tons, 50 to 60 guns, 24 pounders, with picked crews of 500 effective men; our Navy at that time being so numerous that they could not be ably manned; and the result was that owing to that disparity several of our ships were captured in a sinking state.

At that time the Americans had a noted corvette, called the *Wasp*, which from being an overmatch to those of the same denomination in our service, had taken two or three of them[82] and as she was in the same seas as ourselves, there was a probability of our falling in with her and when the vessel before alluded to bore down upon us with all the appearance of this redoubted enemy, a suspicion arose that it might be her and on comparing her strength & means with ours, the disparity was great indeed, her tonnage was 500 tons, with a covered or main deck, 24 long 24 pounders with a compliment of 150 superior men, while we measured under 400 tons with a flush deck by which the men were entirely exposed to the enemy's musketry & the falling of spars &c & 18 carronades of 32 lbs weight of shot the range of which was very short, and a compliment of 120 men & boys half of which were inferior description, there not being among them more than 30 prime seamen, so that had the two ships met, victory could only be a miracle have crowned our efforts, for she could with her

---

82 The USS *Wasp*, although denominated a sloop of war, carried two long 12-pounders and twenty-two 32-pounder carronades. She captured HMS *Reindeer* of 18 guns and HMS *Avon* of 18 guns but was then lost with all hands in the South Atlantic in a storm.

long guns & keeping beyond the range of ours, have cut us to pieces; fortunately for us however, the opportunity of such a rencontre did not occur and I must acknowledge that I preferred not being at, or present in it.

Although our cruise was in winter we experienced no bad weather and it was passed in tacking & retacking, exercising guns &c, the most disagreeable part being in the frequent punishments of flogging which occurred much too often & at that time was most cruelly & in many instances wantonly inflicted in the Navy in general on the slightest grounds, at the will of the captain without court martial, on the spur of the moment & without reflection as if brutes only had to be chastised.

The period of my leave of absence being near its expiration and our consort under the orders of whose captain we were cruising, being in company, Captain Dobree asked leave to run into Lisbon, ostensibly to get water &c, but really to put me on shore. We reached it in two days on the 22 December 1814 and had hardly got over the bar of the river, anchored securely & got on shore, when a tremendous gale came on, which we would have felt most seriously at sea.

Coming in as we did from Tangiers last, we ought to have been put in quarantine and it was only by quibbling in answering questions, put to the officer at the Parlatorio, who first went on shore, of our having come direct from Gibraltar, that we got pratique.[83] I knew nothing of it for some days afterwards, as I would have been very uneasy; fortunately the deception was not discovered and nothing further transpired about it, otherwise it might have been of serious consequence. In exculpation however I must add that Tangiers was then healthy, without plague; we had no sickness on board & our cruise might fairly have served as a substitute for a quarantine, yet we had no right to put that construction on our proceedings.

---

83 Permission to land.

6TH CAMPAIGN

Having on my landing reported myself to Commissary General Pipon and completed the business connected with my accounts, by taking the usual oaths, that I had not directly or indirectly derived any advantage in the discharge of my duty beyond my stipulated pay & allowances, to which I could most consciously subscribe, I received orders on the 2 January 1815 to hold myself in readiness to proceed to England by the first convoy of ships, but as that was not to take place soon, I was permitted to take my passage some days after in the *Lady Arabella* packet proceeding with the mails to Falmouth, a nice snug, fast sailing bark, properly armed and of course in capital sailing trim. On embarking I found I was the only passenger and as we had a very long voyage, the time passed on most heavily. It was in the depth of winter with adverse & stormy weather, which to me occasioned much sea sickness & obliged me to lay in my cabin for several days and when I ventured to dine for the first time with the captain & some of his officers, it was almost impossible to sit at table, the motion was so great and lurches of the ship so out of the horizontal line that a sharp look out was required to be kept to prevent the contents of the dishes and plates rolling into our lap & our chairs from being tilted over to sprawl us on the floor, to the amusement of the more agile & experienced. When I succeeded in making my appearance on deck, I found that a sharp look out was kept after every sail which appeared in sight, for the American cruisers & privateers were understood to be numerous in the tract we were pursuing and as I had no desire to be made a prisoner after an absence of more than six years from home to which I was returning with great anticipations of satisfaction and delight, I felt I must say the greatest anxiety to steer clear of such an untoward event. Our orders were to avoid every suspicious vessel and run for it if they gave us chase & being a good sailor, if we could hold out our distance until night, there was a chance of getting away during the darkness, by altering our course or performing some other manoeuvre. The great object therefore was to ascertain at break of day that we had nothing too near us & if we had to make all sail from any suspicious vessel; not but that we were prepared for a fight with 14 guns & a good crew to work them on one side at least. We were however spared a contingency of that sort & were left to contend with the elements alone, which we found troublesome enough without any other adversary.

We lay to for two days during a very severe gale of wind from the north west in the chops of the channel & it blew so hard at the beginning before the swell got up, that the sea was one sheet of spray forced up by the wind. Whilst in that position & making no way of course, at about nine o'clock at night, being seated in the cabin endeavouring to pass the time, I heard an unusual noise on deck, but supposing that they were putting the ship about or doing some other business, I took no further notice; immediately after however, the captain came down and looking up to him to ask what they had been doing, I perceived that his face was as white as a sheet and he told me at once that we had narrowly escaped being run down and lost, for while he was standing near the helm, all at once a large ship supposed to be of the line or a large East Indiaman, shot by with the speed of lightning, like a huge phantom with all sail set running before the wind, so near that one of his yards touched our spanker,[84] so that had she been a few yards to her right and to our left she would have taken us amidship and passed over us without most likely perceiving it in the noise of the wind & the disparity of size, for we did not exceed 300 tons while she must have been [some] 1,400. The captain returned on deck immediately after taking a stiff glass of grog to steady his nerves & he had lanterns alight hoisted up to the top of his masts to keep any other vessel from coming so near us. The gale having subsided we resumed our course and after passing the Scilly Islands & the Lizard happily cast anchor in the harbour of Falmouth on the 28th of January 1814 [1815] after a passage of twenty-two days.

I landed, of course, without loss of time and was much struck with the difference between the country I had left and that to which

---

84 A gaff-rigged, fore-and-aft sail aft of the after mast.

6TH CAMPAIGN

I had come, in the former the climate was beautiful, people indolent & slovenly with muddy complexions & dark eyes & with hardly any (what an Englishman calls) comforts in their houses; while in the latter the weather was cold and inclement, cleanliness & nicety prevailed, the people were ruddy and almost every woman looked rosy & beautiful with that comfort in tuns which were entirely wanting in the peninsula at that time.

I started by the mail as soon as I could, passing through Exeter, Bath, Marlborough &c and having reported myself at the Treasury in London & obtained leave to go home soon after, I proceeded to Weymouth & reached Guernsey in the beginning of February, in a very indifferent health, which I almost forgot in the greeting I received from every member of my family who were all rejoiced to see me after an absence of more than six years & from a campaign the glory of which had not been surpassed for a century, for it restored to the British arms the prestige it had acquired at Cressy [Crécy], Agincourt, Blenheim & that experience which led to the gaining of the ever memorable Battle of Waterloo. In the period of seven years or six campaigns it was calculated that 120,000 British soldiers landed in the peninsula never returned to their country, having died there in battle & hospital.[85]

Posterity will wonder that no distinction or badge was bestowed on the junior survivors of the peninsula campaigns to mark a nation's gratitude for so important a struggle, which aided so considerably in over throwing the power of Buonaparte & was certainly the originating cause of removing the opinion entertained in Europe of the invincibility of his arms by giving them so many defeats; the Duke of Wellington refused every application made to him for many years, until at last the Duke of Richmond (his old aide de camp) took it up in Parliament & so pleaded the justice of such a distinction,

---

85 The best calculations show that 10,726 officers and men died of wounds and 24,914 died of disease and sickness in the Peninsular War between 1808 and 1814, a total of 35,630 deaths. Quoted from Samuel Dumas, *Losses of Life caused by War* (Oxford, 1923).

that it was at last ordered by that assembly & was issued in February 1849. The Commissariat having participated in the distribution, but only those who actually served with the troops in the field. I received mine accordingly, bearing seven clasps on which are inscribed:

Talavera – 27 and 28 July 1809 being then a clerk attached to the reserve artillery in the field.

Salamanca – 22 July 1812, then attached to the 3rd Dragoons as Assistant Commissary General in the brigade of cavalry under the command of Major General Le Marchant.

Vitoria – 21 June [1813].

Pyrenees – Battle of Pamplona 28 July 1813.

Nivelle – 10 November 1813.

Orthes – 27 February 1814.

& Toulouse – 10 April 1814.

I joined the 4th Division of infantry with the same rank as Senior Commissariat Officer of it, in October 1812 & served with that division during the period in which these actions were fought and to the end of the war.

Though I was present at the siege of Badajoz (stormed 6 April 1812) that of Ciudad Rodrigo (stormed 19 January 1812) and that of San Sebastian in September 1813, the troops with which I served, not having been employed in the trenches or in storming, but only covering those operations, were not considered entitled to a clasp or bar for those services.

In February 1816 I received a letter herewith annexed[86] from the Commissariat agents in London acquainting me that my Prize Money for the foregoing services had been received by them amounting £40 3s 11d[87] comprising a period of six years from 1808 to 1814.

---

86 Not extant.

87 Equivalent to £2,000 today.

7th Campaign[1]

Battle of Waterloo, Capture of Paris and occupation of its environs. Peace, British Army of Occupation in France and withdrawal in 1818

February 1815

The Peace of Europe having existed for some months previous to my arrival at home in the beginning of February 1815, and Napoleon being safely established (as it was thought) at Elba with all the appearance of making it his permanent residence, arrangements were made by the authorities in England, as well as throughout Europe, to reduce their armies & military departments on the lowest footing. I accordingly received a letter dated the 8th of that month intimating that I was to consider myself on half pay at the expiration of one month from the period of my landing in England which occurred on the 28th of the previous month.

Having come home in an impaired state of health I was not sorry to have some repose after the preceding campaigns & was recommended to go through a course of medicine to which I submitted, but while under its operation, Europe was suddenly convulsed by the astounding information that Buonaparte had escaped from Elba

---

1 A heavily truncated and adulterated version of Carey's Waterloo Journal was published as 'Reminiscences of a Commissariat Officer' in Volume 79 of *The Cornhill Magazine* of June 1899.

and unperceived by the men of war cruising round that island,[2] had made a disembarkation in the South of France with some of his Old Guard & was proceeding in all haste towards Paris in (as it were) a triumphal procession, not only unmolested by the army, but joined by various corps to it which were either in garrison, in the line of march, or had been sent to crush his attempt. This of course put an end to the further progress of reducing the army, which on the contrary was immediately put on the war establishment and all the other allied nations took the same energetic measures to oppose the common enemy towards whom no understanding was ever to be attempted, but war in its most decided character was determined on, to put down the now called 'disturber of the world'.

While confined to my room I received orders to proceed instantly to join the army in the Netherlands, in answer to which I sent a medical certificate proving my inability to do so; but feeling anxious to do my duty as soon as possible, I declined going on with prescriptions & having received a further summons from the Treasury to go when capable, I was patched up by the doctor and left Guernsey on the 22 April for London, taking with me my younger brother Sausmarez on the chance of getting him some appointment with the army,[3] together with a groom.

We reached London without loss of time & were not long in making our arrangements for clothes, saddlery &c, I bought two good horses for 50 guineas each[4] & started at once for one of the ports of embarkation, my brother & the groom rode the two horses and I myself went down in a post chaise, the expense of which I was allowed to charge to government. In our way we passed through Canterbury, visited its interesting cathedral & without incident

---

2 The evidence strongly indicates that the three French naval ships on patrol here wilfully turned a blind eye to Napoleon's flotilla.

3 Sausmarez Carey was appointed a clerk in the Commissariat.

4 Approximately equal to £2,500 each today.

reached Ramsgate, then embarked ourselves & horses in a transport pointed out by the Transport Agent & after a favourable passage reached Ostend on the 3rd of May.

From the numerous arrivals from England of all arms, cavalry, artillery &c, the place was crowded & in a considerable state of bustle, for as some arrived others departed, all having one object, that of joining the army without delay. We accordingly started next day the 4th, for Bruges & halted there for the night not wishing to tire my horses, which gave us an opportunity of seeing that quaint old town, formerly famous for its manufacturing importance; it was like all the rest of the country crowded with troops.

The next day the 5th, saw us on the road to Ghent, I by canal, a novel & interesting mode of conveyance & the horses by the road & there we staid [sic] to sleep. It was the temporary residence of Louis the 18th, his bodyguard & adherents who had followed him out of France. I tried to get a peep at him but could not as I understood he lived in great retirement.[5]

Ghent was also once a famous Flemish city, in the time of Charles the 5th Emperor of Germany,[6] but its former splendour had long gone to decay and dullness was its prevailing feature when I passed through, though its churches & squares still looked grand & fine. I do not however enter into any description of it, as it can be found better done in most traveller's books.

On the 6th I arrived at Brussels, the headquarters of the Duke of Wellington and reported myself to my chief, Commissary General Dunmore,[7] in whose office I found an official letter from him dated so far back as the 16 April appointing me to the 2nd Division of infantry

---

5 Louis XVIII resided at the Hotel d'Hane Steenhuyse in Ghent: his apartments can be visited to this day.

6 Charles V, Holy Roman Emperor (1500–58).

7 Commissary General Thomas Dunmore.

at Ath,[8] at the very time that I was laid up in Guernsey. The town was full of our troops which gave great animation to it; I was not allowed to remain long idle, but yet found time to get my brother appointed a Clerk in the Commissariat at 7s/6d per diem with rations for himself & a horse,[9] and being well acquainted with French, got as good a situation as could have been selected for him, that of being attached to Deputy Commissary General Hames,[10] who was senior Commissariat officer with the British cavalry (under the command of the Marquis of Anglesey[11]), with whom he remained during the operations of Waterloo, march to & occupation of Paris and until the dismemberment of the army at the peace, when all supernumeraries were paid off.

On the 8th I started from Brussels travelling on my own horses & next day arrived at Ath & immediately reported myself to Lieutenant General Sir Henry Clinton commanding the 2nd Division of infantry; the place was fortified and enlivened by our troops quartered in it & neighbourhood; the inhabitants were I thought, indifferent towards us, and the general opinion entertained of them was that they preferred belonging to France than to the union which had been formed for them with Holland, attributed to their staple manufacture of linen being prohibited from entering France since its separation from it, which obliged them to seek a new channel for the sale of it; another cause was the difference of religion. The people of the town were not first class and we therefore had little social intercourse with them, indeed everyone had other things to think of in preparing for the campaign expected to take place shortly. Of our sojourn in that town I have

---

8 The 2nd Division was commanded by Lieutenant General Sir Henry Clinton whose headquarters were at the Château de Beloeil.

9 Equivalent to about £20 per day today.

10 Deputy Commissary General Gregory Haines.

11 Lieutenant General Henry Paget, Earl of Uxbridge, was not created Marquis of Anglesey until August 1815.

nothing worth relating and I may say I had not one moment's leisure for recreation, my occupation being incessant in the organisation of the Commissariat machinery, preparatory to our taking the field and which organisation ought to have been commenced a month before.

On my arrival I found a complimentary letter waiting for me from the Deputy Commissary General under whose orders I was placed, he being attached to the corps of which my division formed a part,[12] it was dated from Grammont, Lord Hill's headquarters & conveyed a pleasing incentive to exertion in the discharge of my duty; we had served together in the peninsula & there he knew me well. The division of infantry to which I had thus been attached consisted as follows:-

Lieutenant General Sir Henry Clinton commanding with his aides de camp & Adjutant General, Assistant Quarter Master General & Chief Medical Officer.

| 1st Brigade | 1st
2nd
3rd
4th | Line Battalions Kings German Legion commanded by Colonel du Plat[13] stationed in Ath & environs, consisting principally of old Peninsular soldiers. |
| 2nd Brigade | Bremervorde Battalion
2nd Duke of York Battalion
3rd Duke of York Battalion
Salzgitter Battalion | Hanoverian troops commanded by Colonel Halkett[14] stationed in Bouvignies, Rebaix &c young soldiers, had not seen a shot fired & were little better than militia. |

12 The 2nd Division formed part of General Rowland Hill's II Corps. Deputy Commissary General James Ogilvie was in charge of II Corps.

13 Brevet Colonel George du Plat.

14 Brevet Colonel Hugh Halkett.

3rd Brigade	1st Battalion 52nd Regiment 1st Battalion 71st Regiment 2nd & 3rd [2 companies of the latter only] Battalions Rifle Brigade	Commanded by Major General Sir Frederick Adam stationed at Leuze & adjacents. Peninsular corps recruited since their return, half & half.
One troop of horse artillery, Kings German Legion 5 guns (6 pounders) and one howitzer. [Commanded by Major Augustus Sympher]		
One brigade of British artillery (Captain Bolton) 5 guns (9 pounders) and one howitzer		

The whole consisting of about 8,000 officers & men with 1,200 horses, so that I had a large family to provide for, in which I was assisted by six subordinate officers besides clerks & other persons of inferior degree.[15]

Sir Henry Clinton was a very particular man, tall & handsome, wore his cocked hat different from the usual custom having the cock in front; he was a good linguist and quite familiar with French & German, an essential advantage from having so many Germans under his command & as he required information from me to an unusual extent on every point of service, I had much to do to please him.[16]

---

15 General Orders of 23 April 1815 appoints the following commissaries to positions in the 2nd Division.
The Staff of the 2nd Division – Commissary Clerk Dawbiney.
Major Sympher's Troop of KGL Horse Artillery – Deputy Assistant Commissary General David Maclaurin.
3rd British Brigade of General Adam – Deputy Assistant Commissary General David Bowman.
1st KGL Brigade of Colonel du Plat – Commissariat Clerk Dalby.
3rd Hanoverian Brigade of Colonel Halkett – Commissariat Clerk Greig.
Also Staff Surgeon John Maling and Reverend to the Forces Robert Tunney were appointed to the 2nd Division.

16 Sir Henry Clinton was certainly not an easy man to please.

7TH CAMPAIGN

The month of May passed without any movement & the news which transpired related to the preparations making by Napoleon to commence active operations, but his arrangements were then considered incomplete & not likely to lead to the opening of the campaign before the end of June. I had however occasional enquiries from my chiefs on the progress making for a possible move which were not answered satisfactorily, for we were not prepared with adequate transport &c & yet no urgent notice was taken of them. In the meantime the troops had field days to accustom the several brigades to each other & act in unison, in one of which we went near the fortified town of Conde on the French frontier but with no hostile intention, the demonstrations of both parties being as yet on the defensive. The troops continued in their cantonments, the army in general occupying a wide range of country for the purpose of being better fed & accommodated & as no concentration of corps took place, not even of cavalry to the front, during the first fortnight in June, no symptoms of an immediate movement were indicated for us to suspect what was suddenly to take place & put us in immediate contact with the enemy, not but that the troops were held in readiness to march from one day to the other.

In this state of affairs an order unexpectedly arrived, during the night of the 15th [June] for the division to move early next morning, first to Enghein, thence to Nivelles & there wait for orders, our destination pointing towards Quatre Bras. I did not leave Ath before the middle of the day, having to make various arrangements for sending supplies after the troops, paying for them & for those previously received &c, but as I rode fast and the march was a very long one, I overtook them on the road, halted & taking rest for an hour or two beyond Enghein & which they did at various intervals though without their baggage which was directed to go another way; they then proceeded on & it was only during the night that we reached Nivelles, and therefore too late to assist in the affair of Quatre Bras which of course was over.

The opinion entertained at the time of that action was that we were surprised in our extended & outspread cantonments by the great celerity of Napoleon put in his movements which allowed no time for the concentration of the troops at the point of attack, in proof of which during the greatest part of the period the fight lasted, there was neither cavalry or artillery of ours to support the infantry which before it had got under fire had made a march of upwards of twenty miles under a summer sun and when thus fatigued had to contend with cuirassiers, lancers, infantry of course and a powerful artillery, by which they suffered most severely, nearly crippling a whole division and had it not been for a great fault committed by Napoleon in withdrawing corps of his army in reserve to that which was attacking us & was intended to be brought to assist when required, it was to be apprehended that the results would have been serious to us had the whole French force under Marshal Ney come into action.[17]

It was occasionally a subject of enquiry to know how Napoleon had succeeded in bringing up his army & concentrating it so speedily as at once to overwhelm the Prussians on our left and immediately after falling upon us apparently unprepared, thereby eluding the channel of secret intelligence which the Duke of Wellington & Prince Blucher depended on for information of the enemy movements. The fact is that he was too quick for the spies employed, the presence of his army having anticipated their communications. The following was the mode adopted which was communicated to me by a French Commissary General (Regnault) who was with that army & with whom I afterwards served in a '*Commission Mixte*' with the Army of Occupation in the North of France; he said that the Transport Service in his country including every agricultural wheel [*sic*] conveyance, was completely organised by the civil administration & could at all times be applied to military purposes; when therefore the troops

---

17 Marshal Ney was allocated two corps, those of Reille and d'Erlon, but owing to useless marching between the two battlefields, d'Erlon's troops failed to engage at all.

7TH CAMPAIGN

had to go a considerable distance to reach the army in progress of concentration, they were on emergencies, forwarded on as follows.

After marching a regular day's march which was over by nine o'clock in the evening, all the waggons of the adjacent country (if required) had been collected on the spot which took them another day's march, they then cooked & rested for an hour or two and a similar collection of transport having taken place a third day's march was effected before night, which having been repeated the next day without much additional fatigue, masses of troops were thus brought together very much sooner than could have been expected & certainly with greater celerity than could have been done in any other country, quite sufficient to baffle the calculations of the enemy generals. So immediate an attack was not therefore expected by the Duke, for I know that one of his favourite Peninsular generals (Sir Lowry Cole) wrote to him about this time from England to be allowed to command the 4th Division,[18] the same number he had in Spain, which was promised to him[19] & that he would be in time for the opening of the campaign. No wonder therefore that Napoleon was sooner on us than was expected.

Resuming the narrative of our march, the division being mustered at Nivelles on the morning of the 17th, to go where required, orders were received to proceed on the road to Waterloo leading to Brussels. We reached Hougoumont and continued a short distance onwards and halted on ground on the left of the chaussée on which we had been marching & there the division remained as a support to that point in the rear of the right of our position.

From the length of march we had made & from the bad state of some of the cross roads we occasionally had recourse to the baggage, tents &

---

18 Lieutenant General Galbraith Lowry Cole was given leave to remain in England in order to marry Frances Harris on 15 June 1815, before setting off for Belgium, missing the campaign.

19 A number of officers agitated with Wellington to get their old divisional number again, but others like Sir Henry Clinton refused to comply and the matter was dropped.

provisions had not come up, so that we were without any of the little comforts they afforded & from the active operations which immediately followed they only made their appearance some days after very much diminished, for a large proportion was eventually lost from panics & alarms occasioned by the apprehension of the enemy's detachments of cavalry reported to be in the neighbourhood & laying in wait for them in the midst of bad and muddy roads; the batmen got alarmed & to get away more readily, they cut the ropes of the baggage loaded on horses & let it fall; others cut the traces of the waggon horses, galloping off with the animals in all directions where they thought they could find safety. My cart containing my baggage, public papers and money was among them & was supposed to be upset & lost in the confusion, my clerk who had charge of it having lost sight of it & returned to me reporting that he did not know what had become of it and it was only at the end of a week that it unexpectedly made its appearance.

On the ground which the troops occupied there were no houses or other shelter, in or under which they might find accommodation, they were therefore obliged to make cover for themselves by cutting down the standing corn.

7TH CAMPAIGN

During the 17th the troops were arriving from all directions to take their respective places in the position and it appeared to me, who had witnessed the movements of our army in the Peninsula previous to a battle, that the concentration of our troops in this instance was attended with confusion, but fortunately with no bad consequences owing to the enemy continuing to advance slowly without pressing our men, who were falling back from the neighbourhood of Quatre Bras, by which we were enabled to complete during the day all the necessary arrangements for the expected fight of the following morning without molestation.

When on the ground which was marked out for our division to occupy, the position was pointed out to me on which it was presumed we should await the enemy; it extended to another chaussée to our left coming from Charleroi and considerably beyond it, both chaussées meeting in our rear & leading to Brussels, the several troops being posted as they arrived on the heights which formed the advanced face of the triangle of the fork looking towards France, the handle of which consisted of the chaussée leading to Brussels through the forest of Soignes. We were therefore posted on the right of our position & it is to be observed that in the Netherlands the centre of the great roads are regularly paved, owing to the nature of the soil which were it not for that expedient would become impassable after a fall of rain to waggons & even diligences of the country as well as to armies in motion; we were therefore fortunately situated in having easy access to each of our flanks.

During all these movements we had thunderstorms & heavy rain, which drenched us all & finding my division was likely to be stationary, I left them to go into the village of Waterloo where the headquarters had been established, that I might if possible obtain supplies or at least ascertain what was to be done to get them. I found nothing but bustle & confusion in the village, it being encumbered with troops &c I therefore determined to ride on at once to Brussels as there only, I hoped to effect my object and at the same time get a fresh horse, expecting to find my groom who was on it and who had orders to look out for me. It was late in the afternoon and the road was thronged with waggons loaded with supplies of bread & forage corn, baggage animals & other conveyances belonging to the army and I had hardly proceeded on a mile when suddenly a panic seemed to have seized everyone at the cry of the enemy being at hand. To me it was ridiculous from having just arrived from the front where all was quiet, except the occasional booming of guns at a long distance, but when a cry of that sort occurs among a set of men without anyone to control them, the disorder which ensues is hardly to be conceived; it gathers strength & to stem it is possible. Never did I witness a scene of such confusion and folly & to add to its bad effects, it was raining hard & we were in the Forest of Soignes. The servants cut the straps of the animals on which the baggage was loaded & let it drop on the ground, then jumping on them galloped off to the rear, others dispersed in various directions in the wood. The peasantry carrying provisions in the country waggons, hired or pressed, cast the traces of the harness & ran away with the horses, abandoning the waggons and as the tumult progressed down the road with approaching darkness, the apprehension of danger became general with the followers of the army as well as officers & detachments of troops on the way to join their regiments & the whole went towards Brussels like a sudden rush of water increasing as it went along.

With other mounted officers, we endeavoured to get ahead of the current (seeing the impossibility of checking it) by galloping in the forest away from the road, but we were brought up so often by enclosures and other hindrances that it obliged us to return to it & follow the stream[20] and as the crowd accumulated, stoppages became frequent from the mass being blocked up. The rain was incessant,

---

20 This is an interesting comment, given that the Duke of Wellington is said to have stated that an army could easily march through this wood as it had no undergrowth. It is clear that a number of tracks led through the wood and it must have been these routes that he referred to.

7TH CAMPAIGN

[with] no cover to go to and thus we were obliged to creep on by degrees as the tide flowed until 2 o'clock in the morning when we at last got into Brussels. Fortunately for myself I had a cloak strapped on the pummel of my saddle which helped to keep me, when on, free from a good portion of wet, but yet the rain did soak through during the many hours it continued to fall. Many there were however round about me who had not that advantage, being in their uniforms and one poor man in particular (a brother officer) who was next to me was in full dress with his gold epaulettes and white duck pantaloons, which from their brightness appeared to have been put on for the first time, but help him I could not; in general however we who were considered on the Staff wore surtout coats [greatcoats].

The destruction of property was very serious in this unaccountable affair, particularly for the officers who could not for a length of time replace what they had thus lost, the cause of which originated it is supposed in the fears of a few cowardly individuals, who commenced it fancying the enemy to be at hand & which spreading like wild fire could not be controlled. After all it turned out that there was not the slightest foundation for the panic.

I went immediately to an inn, but it was so full that room to lay down could hardly be found. I therefore got into a quiet corner of the saloon & after resting two or three hours, rose up again & having seen my horse well fed, went to the office of the Commissary General and was there informed that all the supplies were on the road & these I certainly saw them overnight in a dismal plight, but where they were now was to be ascertained. Finding that I could do nothing and that I might be considered too long absent from duty if I stayed longer, I started again for Waterloo after having vain enquired for my groom & second horse & passed through the sad relics on the road of the preceding night's adventure.

I arrived about 8 o'clock on the ground occupied by the division on the 18th of June, hoping that the baggage & provisions expected by roads different from that from Brussels would have made their appearance & put us at ease in regard to provisions & other comforts, but there was no tidings of them. Some meat had been given to the men & they had had biscuit issued to them before they marched for three days viz 16th, 17th & 18th, but with their usual improvidence it is likely little remained for the last day's consumption. Spirits they had none and they therefore fought the battle without any artificial stimulant to their courage. While on the field an individual came up to me & enquired if I spoke French & having answered in the affirmative he told me he had in his charge [at] a little distance off several waggon loads of biscuit for the Dutch troops, but he could not find them & as the drivers were afraid of remaining any longer where they were, they threatened to throw their loads on the side of the road & save their horses & waggons. I wondered for a moment what I should do the temptation being great, but finding the man very urgent & that no one would derive any benefit from the biscuit if left on the ground, I desired him to bring it up to the division. It was done without delay and I never saw people more happy & active in taking their departure when they (the drivers) had once got rid of their burdens. The heads of the casks in which the article was contained were then knocked out in an instant & the contents soon found a vanishing point down the throats of those who needed it.

At a distance from where we [were] situated, the French army was perceived congregating in dark masses on the ground from whence they made their attack, but from the extreme bad weather & consequent muddiness of the roads of the day & night before, their artillery must have had a toilsome march to reach it & which must have impeded the intended hour of falling upon us.[21]

Our troops were permitted to cook while all remained quiet, but as the onset was momentarily expected on the troops in our front, or first line (we being in reserve) the chance of succeeding was very

---

21 Certainly Napoleon seized on the wet ground as a reason why the time the battle commenced was delayed, but it is clear from the evidence that half his army was yet to arrive on the battlefield, being strung out in the rear beyond Genappe.

7TH CAMPAIGN

precarious and it so happened that those whose meat was preparing for soup, had at last to throw the liquor away, for at about 11 o'clock the men were ordered to fall in and stand to their arms & very shortly afterwards we heard the commencement of the skirmishing which was soon followed by the first attack on Hougoumont a little before midday. The cannonade speedily became violent but the balls did not reach us.

The general[22] seeing me still with the division called me to him and told me that I was to longer required on the field, but requested me to endeavour to find them out when the action was over & if possible bring up supplies. I remained a little longer looking on, until the troops received orders to change ground & I then joined other Commissariat officers similarly situated as I was. We retired a short distance to the rear watching the progress of the action, but as it spread from right to left the whole position became enveloped in a dense smoke and nothing could be perceived. We thought it therefore advisable to ride to the fork where the two chaussées met leading to Brussels to enable us more readily to learn what was passing and in case either of success or disaster, to be prepared to do our duty, or to follow in the retreat. After remaining there some time I conceived it necessary to go into Waterloo with two of the officers under my orders to endeavour to secure if possible some provisions, but we had hardly entered it when another panic worse than the last seized on the followers of the army and renewed the scenes of the previous evening, which put an end to any transaction of business. In this instance however there was some reason for it, for the Belgian troops had commenced deserting their standards, spreading reports as they came along, that the enemy was at their heels & it became so alarming that it troubled even many who doubted the fact. I hesitated for a time what was best to be done & followed the stream but considering what my duty required of me I turned back, repassed the village & went a little way towards the field to judge for myself and never did I see a more extraordinary scene.

---

22 Sir Henry Clinton.

FEEDING WELLINGTON'S ARMY FROM BURGOS TO WATERLOO

The road was thronged with Belgian fugitives in whole companies both horse & foot, intermingled with numerous wounded officers & soldiers, giving sad & desponding accounts of the progress of the action and numerous prisoners of all ranks & sorts, forming together a melancholy exhibition of the usual occurrence in the rear of a general action, added to which shouts were heard at a distance and immediately after a group was seen approaching and producing a singular & exciting contrast to those surrounding us.

It consisted of a detachment of Scots Greys and Inniskilling Dragoons bringing in two eagles just captured from the enemy, every man was wounded or disabled. One eagle was still on the pole of the standard & was held up high in the air, the other had been broken off the pole in the scuffle and was in possession of two other men,[23] who equally did their best to shew their trophies to the best advantage. The appearance of the men was not less striking; some had lost their helmets in the fray and had handkerchiefs bound round the[ir] heads, from which the blood was still trickling, others had their arms in slings while others had their clothes tattered as if they had been in personal conflict hand to hand & had been dragged in the mire. The horses appeared to have equally suffered by sabre cuts & other wounds in various parts of the body, in particular I perceived one as it passed on, had had a large portion of flesh torn off his rump by the splinter of a shell. In short I never witnessed such a grim & motley scene, for though shewing demonstrations of the most enthusiastic expectation, the men's countenances had not lost that air of ferocity which the mortal combat in which they had just been engaged must have produced. The tricolour flags attached to the eagle poles appeared to be about a yard square [0.91m], fringed with gold & quite new; the scene would have been a fine subject for a painting & the group could not have consisted of less than from 20 to 25 individuals, who

---

23 This must refer to the eagles of the 45th and 105th captured during the British cavalry attacks that defeated d'Erlon's corps. It is not known which of the eagles had a broken staff, but both were attached to full shafts when they were taken to London a day later.

130

7TH CAMPAIGN

continued on their way towards Brussels as fast as the encumbered state of the road would enable them. These eagles had been captured between one & two o'clock in the successful charge made by our troops against the attack of the enemy on our centre [left].

In the midst of this confusion one of my brother Commissaries with whom I was in company, got quite savage at the desertion of the Belgian troops & rushed at one of their commanding officers, remonstrated with him & ordered him to return to the field with his men, but it was all in vain, the crowd carried him away & had he not speedily extricated himself from them his life would have been in danger, for they had determined on flight and would not be stopped.

Having nothing to do in all this turmoil but to watch events, I with several others returned to Waterloo & followed the crowd in hopes that the panic might be over or lessened at least. We got into the Forest of Soignes and no wonder that an alarm could at such a moment be easily propagated, for the reverberations or echo of the cannonade of the action (in which from 3 to 4 hundred guns were at work) was astounding & enough to frighten those not under military discipline. The fugitives were not in such considerable numbers as the evening before, but they looked as frightened and as the enemy was not far off, it was easy to apprehend that some detachments of theirs might have found their way in the rear of our army and as the road & forest swarmed with Belgian deserters, horse & foot & dressed much like Frenchmen, in espying some of these fellows emerging from different points, it was not difficult to conjure them in[to] the shape of enemies. This kept up the impetus of running away & as this time, the right & left of the road was encumbered by the debris of the former panic, the scene altogether was most disheartening.

On each side of the chaussée there was a ditch in which lay the country waggons upset with their loads of sacks of corn & biscuit burst out & soaked with wet, in other places remnants of baggage &

among them there lay the carriage of the Duke of Richmond[24] upset and set aside as everything else, to enable the ammunition waggons to come up from the rear. The paved part of the road had therefore been cleared of all incumbrances and one of the various incidents which took place & shewed the power of discipline, was that of a detachment of artillery with ammunition deliberately going up to the army, against the stream of fugitives pursuing their way in the opposite direction and both equally bent on their object. It was a lesson to those whose duty it was to be with or near the army and having seen quite enough I returned to Waterloo and there joined other Commissaries who like myself must wait the result of the battle to be of any use. These were most anxious moments for us all, especially as the reports brought in from the front by the wounded were most discouraging. In this state of things no one dared to get off their horses, much less leave them for a moment, for in the confusion they might have been unceremoniously laid hold of by those who had none & who were hurrying to the rear.

Tired beyond anything at this state of suspense, I rode about 5 o'clock towards the village of Mont St Jean with two or three other individuals, for information; wounded officers & men continued to come down & now & then a cannon shot was seen bounding along, but nothing could be perceived but clouds of smoke over the hills and an incessant clatter heard of great guns & musketry. Having passed the boundary line of disorder everything appeared to be well regulated in the rear of the position and no confusion as far as we could see. We were not able to see any part of the action and the cause of it was owing to its being fought on the other side of the hills on which our troops stood, in a valley between the two armies.

---

24 The Duke of Richmond is sometimes stated to have hoped for the command of a projected III Corps, but it is clear from the Duke of Wellington's correspondence that he was not considered for such a role as he was too senior. Richmond, with his son who had been badly wounded in a fall from his horse, did visit the battlefield during the battle, but no account mentions the loss of his carriage.

7TH CAMPAIGN

While thus in expectation, we heard much to our satisfaction that the heads of the Prussian columns were at last coming up to our left and had been announced by a detachment of cavalry, who for a moment were taken for French & nearly maltreated.

Evening was advancing and nothing decisive had taken place and thus we remained riding here and there in no pleasing state of mind for no one can conceive without having experienced it, what suspense was under the circumstances we found ourselves with the distressing thoughts of the immense sacrifice of life momentarily recurring; as to whether or not a disaster might have occurred from one moment to the other to occasion a retreat, which must have been accompanied by very serious consequences. For without doubt what remained of the Belgian troops would have disbanded so bad an example might have been followed by the Dutch portion of our army & their state of excitement was in no way improved but the contrary, by the wounded who reported on what was going on most despondingly, asserting that many of the regiments were almost annihilated, though when closely questioned they knew nothing more than what had occurred on the spot on which they had fought.

As the sun was setting the cannonade appeared to redouble, come nearer to us as if the enemy was advancing; this continued for some time & then the sounds seemed to recede. We of course remained on the tiptoe of expectation to know what had occurred, but it was only about nine o'clock that we began to learn that our troops had at last repulsed the final attack of the enemy and were in pursuit. The certainty became soon after known from officers coming down from the field and announcing the victory, a gratifying reality which gave us all a contentment hardly to be described. The extent of so glorious an event was however only ascertained next morning when it was found that the French had not rallied to oppose their conquerors, but had become a disordered mass of fugitives escaping as they could out of our reach & more especially of that of the Prussians who were foremost in the chase.

During the anxieties of such a day & of the disorders occurring all along the road, it was altogether impracticable to obtain supplies & as it was useless to go to the troops empty handed & equally impossible to find them in the dark, intermixed as they must have been after their advance beyond the French position in confusion, it was the unanimous opinion of my brother officers similarly situated as I was, that we would best perform our duty by proceeding at once to Brussels which was the grand depot of provisions &c for the army and there we accordingly proceeded about ten o'clock.

The road was not so encumbered as the day before, but there were many melancholy scenes of the wounded endeavouring to get away as they thought from the reach of the enemy & obtain shelter, the villages of Mont St Jean & Waterloo being already full of them. We hardly reached our destination before twelve o'clock at night & one of the morning & though reports had reached of our being victorious, many of the people we still met in the streets would not believe it, so that the excitement was kept up until it was found that at least our army was not in retreat, nor the enemy approaching; we were of course cross questioned about it & though speaking positively, there was as yet a great deal of credulity with many whose fears exceeded their reason.

We lost no time in going to the first inn that could receive us and our horses, and we were glad to get a sopha [*sic*] or carpet on which to lay down as such a thing as a bed was out of the question, besides which there would have been scarcely time to get in & out of it as we must be again stirring at the dawn of day. We therefore quietly took a short repose & a little after three o'clock in the morning got on our legs again to attend to our duty, by going to the office of the Commissary General for instructions and I soon after received orders to take with me a convoy of provision waggons, with which I started off before I could obtain any intelligence of my groom and second horse, the former of whom had no doubt been panic struck & with many others had started for Antwerp or Ostend, conceiving the

7TH CAMPAIGN

French to be at their heels for even officers & men followed so bad an example who had not had the experience of former campaigns.

Our route lay through the Forest of Soignes and the chaussée road from the recent heavy rains & immense thoroughfare which had occurred on it during the last three days was a mass of mud; my horse most unluckily cast a fore shoe in the midst of it and in a short time began to get lame from the wearing of the hoof on the stone & dirty pavement, and what to do I did not know, as to find such a thing as a resident farrier at that time was impossible. I could not lead my horse long & walk without doing him up as well as myself altogether, I was therefore in despair at the idea that in not reaching the troops I should be considered as having neglected my duty. In this frame of mind & disagreeable dilemma, I walked on a little longer without hope of relief when all at once I spied off the road in a small nook of brushwood a farrier forge of one of the cavalry regiments. I at once went up and requested to have my horse shod; the farrier refused, being strictly forbidden to do so to any horse not of the cavalry. For a time all my remonstrances were ineffectual until I thought of the only expedient which might probably overcome the difficulty; I pulled out of my pocket a Napoleon (16s/8d)[25] which I offered to him. For a time he hesitated what to do, but on my again telling him that the public service absolutely required it, he set at once about the work and relieved me from a great load of embarrassment.

Our march was very slow of course and we passed through Waterloo now a busy scene, the medical officers being busily occupied in collecting and attending to the wounded. From there we proceeded to Mont St Jean and arrived about 9 o'clock at the fork of the road, one prong leading to Charleroy [Charleroi] & the other to Nivelles. Here it was necessary to decide which to take & I unfortunately took the wrong one that leading to Charleroy [Charleroi]. It was a

---

25 About £50 in today's terms.

great oversight on some officer's part whose duty it was to do so, not to have stationed a person at that particular spot to point out to all going to the army the right path, in consequence of which the convoy instead of reaching its destination at about one o'clock only got there at night.

We journeyed on a short distance and reached our position of battle; it was dreadful to see the numbers of the killed both men & horses on each side of the road. Many bodies were already stripped of their clothes and as we descended down towards La Haye Sainte the scene of carnage was still more developed and with the exception of a few parties wandering in quest of wounded men as well as plunder, all was as quiet as a churchyard. All round La Haye Sainte and on the chaussée leading to the French position the dead were innumerable, French & English intermixed & those which had fallen in the road had been trampled upon by horses & wheels of artillery in a mass of blood, flesh & clothes, hardly to be distinguished one from the other & in the hollow between the two armies on each side of the road there lay piles of dead Frenchmen & horses, among which were many of the Imperial Guard, the survivors of whom when they found they could advance no further, had disencumbered themselves of their large bearskin caps which strewed the ground & put on their forage caps to enable them to get away more easily. To add to their numbers were many dead cuirassiers still with their cuirasses on, some of which I could have easily brought away had I had time or someone to assist in stripping the dead bodies.

In examining La Haye Sainte I perceived the mistake which had occasioned its capture by the enemy; the great gate of its entrance was on the road side & being exposed to their fire was barricaded and could not be opened; the enclosures all round were also loop-holed excepting the face looking towards our position, which being immediately under our fire required no such mode of defence. So long therefore as its little garrison had ammunition they succeeded in keeping the post, but as soon as it began to fail their defence became feeble and they were at last almost all of them bayoneted.[26] It was consequently a want of forethought in not making a small opening in the face of the wall alluded to, large enough to introduce a barrel of gunpowder which in being neglected led to so serious an impression as was made in the centre of our position.[27]

We followed the chaussée in the midst of this field of death, which in addition to men and animals, was strewed with arms of every description until we reached the foot of the French position and where it was said Napoleon took leave of his Guard moving on to the final attack. On ascending to the top of the eminence we came upon the French guns scattered in various directions evidently in the way of being dragged to the chaussée from different positions, but which had failed by the muddy state of the ploughed land & the rapidity of our advance, which obliged the drivers of the gun carriages to flee for their lives by cutting the horses traces. I perceived that some of the guns had engraved on them *Égalité, Fraternité* & others the letter N; the carriages were sunk in the ground almost to the axle trees & as many as 180 fell into our hands & those of our allies.

We proceeded on & fell in with the Prussian columns coming from our left marching to join their army. They began to plunder the biscuit, many most animatedly and I had great difficulty to prevent it. Perceiving some troops to our right, I rode up to them & found it was a part of our division the 52nd Regiment commanded by Sir John Colborne (now Lord Seaton) moving off across the country towards Nivelles. I applied to him for a guard to protect the convoy but he refused it with some excuse and [I] was therefore left to my resources to get out of the difficulty as well as I could; in another army I might have commanded any number of men for that purpose.

---

26 Stories of the massacre of the garrison of La Haye Sainte were hugely exaggerated. It has since been proved that over half of the defenders survived the battle.

27 The troops defending the farm did run out of ammunition, but the ammunition was not found in the chaos on the road to Brussels and therefore no attempt was made at introducing ammunition via the farmhouse on the northern quadrant of La Haye Sainte.

I was necessarily obliged to continue on the chaussée as the waggons could not go on the cross unpaved roads, until I reached Quatre Bras, when I could take another chaussée to the right leading to Nivelles which I found was the destination of our army, an immense roundabout [diversion], but which could not now be avoided. The Prussians kept moving by us occasionally and I would most certainly have been plundered by them of the best portion of the biscuit, had it not been for the opportune arrival of a detachment of our German cavalry (the King's German Legion), the officer commanding which seeing my dilemma, immediately ordered some of his men to draw their swords & accompany the convoy & thus we moved on to Quatre Bras through Genappe. I there beheld in addition to many other debris of the French army, Napoleon's carriage[28] on the spot where it had been overtaken & plundered, around it there were Prussian soldiers scraping & sifting the ground in consequence of a report that some diamonds had fallen from their settings in the night scramble.

When once past Quatre Bras we fortunately saw no more of the Prussians & therefore jogged on quietly until we reached Nivelles, not however before nightfall, but in time for a most acceptable distribution to the troops of what we had brought up. This day's journey was a most troublesome one & glad was I when it was over, but as yet no baggage had arrived or been heard of and I was necessarily obliged to continue in the same linen & clothes in which I had been wet several times, for no cloak could completely withstand the heavy & continuous rains which had fallen during much of the three past days. I began therefore to be anxious about it, for with it there was sixteen

---

28 Two of Napoleon's carriages were captured in the jam to the north of Genappe bridge, by Major von Keller and his men: reputedly they were full of treasure. One of the carriages was given to Blücher, whose family recently gave it back to the museum of Malmaison. The other was sent to England for the Prince Regent, which was then sold to Mr Bullock who owned the Egyptian Rooms in London. It eventually passed into the hands of Madame Tussaud's but was destroyed by fire in 1925.

7TH CAMPAIGN

hundred Napoleons (equal to £1,330 sterling[29]) of public money in charge of my personal servant; the Commissariat Clerk who had the care of it having in a moment of confusion lost it and could not find it again & had returned to me making as good an excuse as he could, but which being unsatisfactory became a cause of uneasiness from an apprehension that I might never see it again. One hope only remained however and that was owing to the following circumstances under which that servant was engaged.

While arranging my small household on joining the division at Ath in the month of May, a respectable farmer from the neighbourhood called on me and begged me to take his son into my service, frankly acknowledging that it was beneath what he might aspire to for him, but as he was likely to be drawn for a conscript, it was much better that he should follow any other temporary pursuit in which his life and morals might be preserved, than that of a soldier. I entered readily into his feelings and took him as the driver of the cart conveying my baggage, public papers and money, as well as to wait on me and as he was intelligent, zealous and trustworthy, I had every reason to be satisfied with his conduct & had it not been for a French cook who also was with the cart and knew that there was a good deal of money in it, my mind would have been quite at rest about its safety.

The Battle of Waterloo was fought on a Sunday, as was the case in several previous instances in the peninsula and such was the incorrect accounts published immediately after of its details, that the Duke of Wellington in a letter dated 28 April 1816 expressed great disgust at them.[30] It was a momentous event for the whole world and when the composition of our army is taken into consideration the wonder is that such a victory was achieved, but it shewed a combination of skilful

---

29 About £75,000 in today's terms.

30 In this letter to Sir John Sinclair, Wellington wrote 'the number of writings [on the Battle of Waterloo] would make the world think that the British army had never won a battle before'.

commanders & brave soldiers, the former being of incalculable value & not often found in the British army.

Lord Londonderry in the last pages of his account of the campaigns of 1813 & 1814 comments on that subject[31] & shews the inferiority of the allied troops and the want of unison existing among them, and in expressing my own humble observations as an eye witness, I can assert with confidence that the Duke never commanded, as a whole, a worst composed body of soldiers, consisting of a mixture of veterans (his old Spanish infantry as he called it), recruits, Dutch & Hanoverian troops & the ill afflicted Belgians, who in not understanding each other's language must have occasionally caused misunderstanding. The British regiments, many of which had served in Spain, were completed or recruited, on their return from that country in the proportion of about half equally with those of the King's German Legion, both of which were considered the flower of our army and amounted in round numbers of cavalry, infantry and artillery to 35,800 men who bore the brunt of the action, the Hanoverian & Dutch troops were next in point of excellence, though inexperienced in the field & likely did their duty with the exception of the Cumberland Hussars from the north of Hanover, consisting of a fine body of horse & men who when ordered up to the front to charge, deliberately faced about & fled out of the reach of fire and could not be induced to return, for which they were disgraced by being broke up in detachments & employed in various drudgery duties,[32] and as [to] the Belgian troops, I saw so many deserting their posts during the action that the few which remained could hardly have been trusted or made use of. Some conception may therefore be made of the description of material which the Duke had to oppose to Buonaparte's army, consisting of 70,000 men of one nation,

---

31 Charles Vane, 3rd Marquess of Londonderry, was Minister Plenipotentiary to the court of Berlin in 1813–14.

32 Colonel Hake, their commander, was court-martialled and disgraced.

7TH CAMPAIGN

principally veterans, the remains of his grand military organization, beautifully clothed & appointed & led by old experienced officers who ought to have annihilated us much before the Prussians came to our assistance, for they were elated with their recent victory at Ligny & full of enthusiasm in their Emperor's cause. The arm of the Almighty was therefore on our side & to him must be ascribed the wonderful results of that day, for had the Duke been disabled or rendered incapable of command even for the shortest time, there was no one on our side to replace him & from the way he was preserved though he exposed himself in the thickest of the fight, he must be considered as having been under the special protection of an all-wise providence which undoubtedly governs the affairs of this world.

As I confine my descriptions to what passed under my notice and do not borrow from the narrative of others, I shall add an extract from the narrative of a medical officer who was employed in attending to the wounded in the neighbourhood of Mont St Jean after the battle, exemplifying the spirit which actuated our soldiery.

He writes 'after we had been a day or two here, a short thickset stout English soldier came into the farm with a cudgel in his hand, but with scarcely the vestige of a countenance; he stumbled upon me (having enquired for a surgeon) and said he would be obliged to me if I would put up his face. He had been struck by a shell, and the whole of the integuments of his countenance had been torn off, excepting at one point and were hanging over his shoulder, these he had been resolute to preserve but had not met with professional assistance. The forehead, the skin round one eye, the soft parts of the nose, a portion of both cheeks, the lips and one ear (I forget which) were literally detached and lying where I described them. Seeing the extent of the yet remaining attachments and that the separated parts manifested no sign of putrefaction I deemed the undertaking of replacement far from hopeless. By the aid of diachylon plaister,[33]

---

33 An adhesive plaster made by boiling together lead oxide, olive oil and water.

I certainly did succeed in restoring this poor object to the possession of the 'human face divine'. No persuasion could induce him to remain where he was; no he was in good health thank God, had a good stick, the French were licked and now that he was a man again he would go on to Brussels'.[34]

The arrangements of the Commissariat were not complete when the army was called upon to act, for many of its members were inexperienced & not mounted as they should have been, had marches therefore and active movements been prolonged for some days before this decisive action, the troops would I am afraid have been seriously inconvenienced from want of food, but it is not the case as was asserted, that they were without it on the 18th, for as far as those to whom I was attached, the contrary will be found in the annexed reports. The Duke nevertheless got angry with us without reason and in consequence we were deprived of the [Waterloo] medal though it was given to a division of the army at Halle in observation & which never heard of the cannonade of the action, as well as to many officers & men who were not actually in the field but only on the effective returns of their corps; and had he made the least enquiry he would have found that there was a vast quantity of supplies in waggons near Waterloo equal to several days consumption for the whole of the army, which as I have described, became useless by the panics occasioned by the followers of that army & for which the Commissariat were in no way accountable; for had an investigation taken place, the fault I am confident would have been ascribed in great measure to the disorder in which the troops with their baggage &c arrived from their various cantonments; for whatever may be said to the contrary, the army was not concentrated as it should have been to meet so immediate an event as took place.

---

34 This refers to an incident recorded by Assistant Surgeon John Gordon Smith, 12th Light Dragoons, recently republished by the editor as *Blood, Guts and Gore: Assistant Surgeon John Gordon Smith in the Waterloo Campaign* (Barnsley: Pen & Sword Military, 2022).

7TH CAMPAIGN

In the Duke's character there is a defect which at times shewed much inconstancy in taking prejudices against individuals which when once established could never be removed by any explanation & by which several deserving officers & I may include my department suffered most unjustly.

Whilst on the subject of provisioning the army I must mention a circumstance connected with the field of Waterloo which was mentioned to me by a French Chief Commissary. It was that during the action casks of brandy were brought on the ground, the heads knocked out and the men about to attack were allowed to help themselves; this admission was accompanied by an observation that we no doubt did the same, but to which I can give a direct contradiction, for I can positively assert that during the time I was with the troops both in the Peninsula & Waterloo, no spirits were issued previous to the action, but only in the evening when all was over & in the latter case none had come up to be issued before or after the battle. It nevertheless was an idea entertained by the French military arising no doubt from the gallant & determined way they were repulsed and afterwards attacked by our troops.

On the 20th of June the army moved from Nivelles and passing through the city of Mons, encamped in the neighbourhood. Whilst standing in the market (the usual rendezvous of the followers of the army) hoping to meet or stumble upon my baggage among that passing by belonging to the army, I spied my brother Sausmarez and enquired if he had seen it. He answered in the negative but perceiving at once that my collar and shirt were worse for wear he relieved me of that part of my inconvenience by giving me one of each which were folded very nicely in one of his pistol holsters instead of its usual instrument of war and in the one on the other side there was a lunch snugly stowed away, both very useful appendages when likely to be sent away on duty to places not affording such necessaries.

Our march route for the 21st pointed towards France and we crossed the frontier during the day, encamping (singularly enough) near the village of Malplaquet famous for one of the victories obtained by the Duke of Marlborough. In passing through it, I am sorry to say the troops finding themselves for the first time in the enemy's territory and at liberty, as they thought to do as they pleased, began plundering the houses & cottages I should say in good earnest and in a very short time thoroughly emptied them, leaving not even a head of poultry for the inhabitants who had previously fled. It was therefore necessary to check the evil in the bud and accordingly the Duke issued a proclamation pointing out that we were not warring against the French people, but against Buonaparte and enjoining strict discipline to the army and protection to all property, which had the desired effect as far as the troops under his command were concerned.

We reached Bavay the next day and as it was headquarters as well as the thoroughfare for the troops encamped in the neighbourhood, there was no slight bustle in its streets occasioned by the baggage, stores &c arriving from the rear. My division being nigh at hand, I was permitted to get a lodging if I could in it, but while in search, an order was circulated peremptorily directing all officers not belonging to His Grace's Staff to vacate the place so as to make room for Louis the 18th & his followers who were hourly expected in the town. I took the hint of course & went to seek accommodation near the camp, which I found in a very humble way and as uncomfortable as it could be from want of my baggage. I then attended to the despatch of my duties & thinking to be in time, I rode to get a peep at his majesty. His progress was slow but at last the procession made its appearance; our troops lined both sides of the road for a considerable distance with their Colours & bands of music and presented arms as he passed. He was in an open carriage bowing as he went along, followed by his Guards de Corps very handsomely dressed & consisting of young men of the best families of France who had followed in his retirement to Ghent, as also other detachments of troops who had done the same in sharing his fortunes. These were followed by a more humble train

7TH CAMPAIGN

of persons who though they swelled the pageant added nothing, but the contrary, to the interest of it, the demonstrations of loyalty on the part of the inhabitants appeared but feebly expressed and the ceremony was not of itself particularly imposing. In fact the place was too small to afford getting up a show of this sort, but being the first town he had entered in his dominions, it was supposed to be necessary. It was also the first time he came in contact with the army which had opened to him the way to return to his capital & he could not pass without receiving their salute. His feelings must have been a strange mixture of joy & regret in seeing those men who in replacing him on his throne, had well beaten his countrymen.

Our next day's march was to Le Cateau [-Cambresis] where we halted a day and there I got into a decent quarter (alias lodging) for the first time since the 16th after leaving Ath, a period of a week. I was of course most uncomfortable both in mind and body in consequence of no tidings having as yet reached me of my baggage and feeling now almost convinced that it was lost, I had made up my mind to report the circumstance to the Commissary General in respect to the public money, knowing that it must lead to an immediate investigation; but as I was in the act of writing the letter, I heard an unusual bustle below & in looking out of the window most gladly saw my cart as well as my groom and saddle horse & my faithful Belgian servant, who ran upstairs at once & reported that all [was] safe. It was no less gratifying to my clerk as myself, for he would most assuredly have been dismissed from the service had it not turned up. My servant reported that as they were proceeding along the road on the 17th from Ath towards Nivelles with a long train of baggage & supplies on their way to join the division, whilst crossing a heavy part of it they were suddenly alarmed by a cry that a party of the enemy's cavalry was upon them. In the excitement no one considered for a moment if there was truth in it, but all endeavoured at once to save themselves as well as they could, which led to the same scene of confusion as had occurred at Waterloo.

Waggons were abandoned on sticking in the slough, the baggage was thrown off from the animals to accelerate the flight of those who conducted them and my man told me that had it not been for the superior power of my horse & lightness of the cart, it would have been impossible to have extricated the latter from the mud, which almost reached the axle tree & this was afterwards corroborated by others who had been equally successful as himself. The alarm turned out to be a false one after all, although the reports of the action that had taken place had filled the country with consternation and gave cause for much apprehension. As it was however, those who escaped with their baggage roamed about several days before they could learn with certainty where to proceed to join us. This arrival was a fortunate event for me for otherwise it would have led to prolonged delays in the process of being officially relieved from refunding the public money amounting to £1,330 for which I was accountable and in a private point of view I escaped from having to replace at my own expense my baggage which to me would have been for a time most inconvenient. To my great care therefore in purchasing a good horse & cart & to the exertions of an honest servant, I mainly attribute my having escaped so unpleasant a dilemma.

My groom had also to make known his own adventures; he had been by me directed to seek for me as soon as possible either at Brussels or on the road leading to the army, which he could easily learn from other grooms having led horses like himself. As it was not then known that it was to concentrate in front of Waterloo, he was accordingly proceeding from the former to the latter place in search of me in the afternoon of the 17th when the first panic I have related overtook him and being inexperienced in the incidents of a campaign he turned about & fell in[to] the stream of the fugitives and the alarm having become contagious among the temporary residents & such of the inhabitants of Brussels as could fly to places of greater safety, he was as he said enticed onwards by the existing panic as far as Ostend, where he remained until the result of the battle had been ascertained

1. *Osma church and village.*

2. *The Battle of Vitoria by J.P. Beadle.*

3. *Allied camp near Urugne by Robert Batty.*

4. *A mule train near Enderlache by Robert Batty.*

5. *Pasaia Harbour (commonly known to the British as Passage).*

6. *A view of San Sebastian from Sao Bartolomeo Monastery.*

7. *The Battle of Nivelle by William Heath.*

8. *The Battle of Toulouse by William Heath.*

Above left: **9.** *General Sir Thomas Picton.*

Above right: **10.** *General Sir Lowry Cole.*

 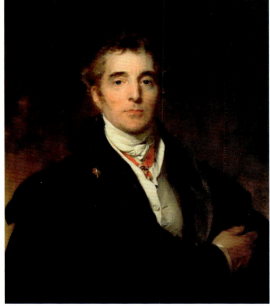

Above left: **11.** *General Sir Henry Clinton.*

Above right: **12.** *Arthur Wellesley, Duke of Wellington.*

13. *The Battle of Waterloo by George Jones.*

14. *A drawing of Summerland found in Tupper's papers.*

Above left: **15.** *Tupper Carey in later life.*

Above right: **16.** *Anne (Tupper) Carey.*

Above left: **17.** *Their son the Reverend Tupper Carey.*

Above right: **18.** *The Order of Chevalier of the Legion d'Honneur of Louis XVIII, which Tupper was not allowed to accept.*

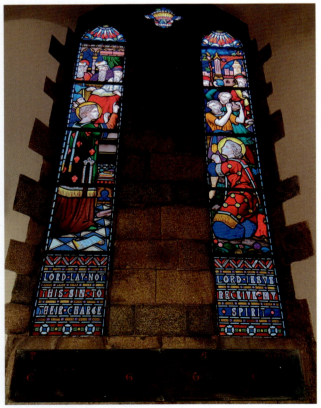

Above: **19.** *The Carey family mausoleum in Candie Cemetery, St Peter Port.*

Left: **20.** *Memorial window and brass plaque commemorating Commissary General Tupper Carey in St Stephen's Church, St Peter Port, Guernsey.*

7TH CAMPAIGN

& orders given for everyone connected with the army to proceed & join it, on the way he fell in with the baggage.

Having during the past week overtired the horse on which I rode and finding that even with two my duty could not be satisfactorily performed now that the army was in the field & moving forward, I enquired for another animal on which I could occasionally ride to relieve the others and was offered one by the neighbour of the person with whom I was lodging. He told me that it was a cossack (small & colour light chestnut & no beauty) which had come into his possession under the following circumstances. When a party of irregular cossack cavalry came into France the year before and passed through [Le] Cateau [-Cambresis], he had in his stable a valuable horse of his own & one of these fellows having been, with his horse billeted on him, both were near each other during the night. The conduct of these men was infamous, committing every excess with impunity and respecting the property of no one. Previous to their marching off next morning he took the precaution of going to the stable to look after his horse, when to his astonishment he perceived the cossack deliberately putting his saddle on his (the Frenchman's) horse. To remonstrate was his first impulse, but he was at once silenced by a blow of the whip which these people carry, called a *caucho*, resembling a small flail, the tongue being cut short & forming a stump which was most severe in its application. To attempt a rescue was an impossibility and therefore the robbery, or exchange at least, was allowed to take its course, not of course to his advantage for the poor beast was thoroughly done up, and it took some months to get him in condition when I became the purchaser for 14 Napoleons, a higher price by far than I would have given had I not been in want of such a conveyance.

The enormities committed by these barbarians, or banditti as they might be called, will never be forgotten or forgiven on coming into France in 1814; their saddle was a high peaked one, with a considerable space between the top of it & back of the horse, in which they could stuff many articles, beside which when plunder was abundant they

147

were seen with poultry &c hanging to various parts of this saddle; discipline or uniformity of dress not being thought of, and it was said that their formidable whip obtained for them when applied to the backs of terrified Frenchmen, or the threats of it, spirits & provisions when no other expedient could have prevailed.

The Duke of Wellington having as it was surmised, entered into arrangements with Prince Blucher for the march of the two armies towards Paris, the right of the two parallel lines of road was pointed out for us by Peronne, Roye, Montdidier, Clermont & Chantilly & the Prussians took the left by St Quentin, Compiegne &c & that we might not interfere with each other's supplies, we were to be fed by the country in our front & right & they by that in their front & left, which to us in particular was attended with great advantage as it prevented a great deal of clashing with allies who had no scruples to lay hands on anything that came in their way.

Orders were received to move forwards, and on the 26th we encamped in the neighbourhood of Lanchy & Beauvoir [Beauvois-en-Vermandois], without the occurrence of any particular incident, for the enemy had so far got ahead of us in retreating that no regular bodies were expected to be met with & therefore the probability was that we should reach the neighbourhood of Paris without obstacle. Part of the army had however been detached to our right to Cambrai which was holding out, but with which we had nothing to do.

Being now launched in the French territory & a uniformity of arrangement for the future supply of the troops which were to depend on the country having been determined on, with the approbation of the Lieutenant General Sir Henry Clinton, whose extreme particularity induced him to interfere in everything. A description of it will enable the reader to form an idea how armies are maintained when in an enemy's country; it was as follows.

When informed by the general in the course of the evening of the intended march for the next day, I went immediately to the Sous Prefect or Mayor of the town or village nearest our encampment, to consult

7TH CAMPAIGN

him on the means & capabilities of those through which we were to march as well as those near & in the neighbourhood of the intended encampment, shewing a statement of the rations of bread, meat, spirits, forage & fuel required, which he subdivided among the different places according to their resources. Letters or requisitions were then prepared for my signature & despatched by post messengers to the magistrates of the several local cities, so that the necessary preparations might be made in time; this done, I reported it to the general to satisfy him that he might be aware that no want would be experienced. Next morning after an early breakfast my duty was to ride in advance of the troops to several of the places from which the supplies were to be obtained to ascertain that they were getting ready, and I found almost invariably that the magistrates were punctually if not cheerfully doing what was required of them & that by the time the troops had reached their halting place, all the articles were arriving in camp for distribution and in some instances under the escort of the French gendarmerie. We paid for nothing, the expense falling on the inhabitants, but so admirable were the arrangements of the local authorities that the cost did not fall exclusively on the places who furnished the articles but on the whole department, which made it less onerous to all parties and therefore more willingly submitted to. This readiness was however mainly attributed to the strict discipline kept up and our only requiring what we were entitled to as rations In these excursions I was only accompanied by a Commissariat Conductor or my servant, and we rode at times out of the line of march & being as familiar with the French as the English language, I found the magistrates civil & communicative and learnt from them that those in whose neighbourhood we had encamped the day before, had written & recommended every attention being paid to our wants to ensure the same kind treatment which they themselves had met with, which proved a great stimulant to our getting everything done that could be wished.

The troops were regularly encamped, and the men only of good character with non-commissioned officers with passes were allowed to go in[to] towns for what might be required, but sutlers of course who accompanied the army were always at hand to meet in most cases the wants of the soldiery. The general good conduct of the men astonished the magistrates who could hardly believe it, until it practically came under their notice, not conceiving that an army of conquerors could thus behave themselves.

Such however, was not the case with our left-hand neighbours whose mode of proceeding was a perfect contrast, for on our line it was melancholy to see the inhabitants flying from the towns through which the Prussians were passing to avoid all manner of ill-usage & seeking protection in our part of the country, with what they could bring away with them. This treatment was no worse however, than what the French had done in their own country, a plea used to justify the retaliation.

Next day, the 27th, we crossed the River Somme at Hillercourt [Villecourt] and encamped in the neighbourhood of the town of Roye. No military obstacles were met with to impede our progress and under an impression that none would arise, I had no hesitation in riding unattended out of the line of march to ascertain that the provisioning was progressing in the several places ordered to prepare them. I met however occasionally a few stragglers of the French army, unarmed & quietly returning to their homes; we exchanged a few words together, but I thought it as well to move on quickly without appearing astonished at their presence and not to give them time to concoct among themselves any attempt on me should they be so disposed. They were generally young men evidently depressed by past events and conscious that the game was over.

The march of the 28th was directed towards Montdidier on to Crevecoeur [-le-Petit], looking towards St Just [Saint-Just-en-Chaussée] uninterrupted by events to the troops or incidents worth relating. Next day we moved on to Clermont and on the way rode some distance out of the line of march to a considerable town (the name of which I do not recollect), the head magistrate of which was

7TH CAMPAIGN

a Sous Prefect. In going into the square (market place) opposite the townhouse or municipality, I perceived a detachment of Prussian cavalry surrounding some loaded carts; having got off my horse I went upstairs to transact business with that magistrate. In the room I found the Prussian officer who commanded the cavalry below and on enquiring from the Sous Prefect if my requisition was in preparation, he at once declared that he could not attend to it owing to the Prussian demand. Perceiving at once that our ally had no right whatever to exact anything from the town, it being out of his limit agreed upon by our respective commanders, it became my duty to set the matter to rights, but to do so courteously was my object, for I perceived the Frenchmen present already began to chuckle at what would take place. I asked the officer if he spoke French and being answered in the affirmative I begged him to step aside and then represented to him how he was situated and the embarrassment he would occasion if he persisted in carrying off the supplies. He hesitated for some time but being determined that he should not gain his end, I civilly told him that if he did it, I would take his requisition with me and give it to the general of division who would forward it to the Duke of Wellington. This instantly decided the point, for he at once determined on withdrawing his demand and marching off with his men, leaving the loaded carts behind him, the contents of which I afterwards found to consist of cases of champagne, hams & other luxuries. The French authorities were delighted at my success & at being rid of those troublesome customers and I was requested to accept of them as a present for our officers in addition to the regular supplies which were soon in readiness. I refused them of course as it was inadmissible in our service, being only at liberty to accept from persons on whom we were quartered a dinner or other little attention they might feel inclined to offer.

While arranging these matters with the authorities and conversing with them on passing events, a French officer accompanied by two gendarmes entered the room & came up to us; it immediately struck me that his intention was of a hostile nature, conceiving that I had pushed on too far in advance of our column without escort. I put on however as bold a look as I could assume, but was at once undeceived on his observing that he was a Royalist and would thank me if I could give him any news of Louis the 18th for whose return he was most anxious. I told him that he was not far distant behind our army and might be expected in a day or two; on my telling this he took off his hat, waved it round his head & cried out most vociferously, 'Vive le Roi Louis dix-huit', which he kept repeating as he walked to the windows overlooking the square and having opened one, he stepped on the balcony, continued the cry which soon attracted a crowd below & to make it more impressive he wished me to shew myself, which I declined telling him that I could not appear to take part in what concerned Frenchmen alone. Having given full vent to his loyalty he retired as he came, but none of the authorities seconded him, which I suppose they did not consider advisable not knowing what turn affairs would take, or whether or not the Bourbons would be again restored. I was however treated with civility which indicated that they were not Buonapartists.

On the 30th our march was on to Chantilly and as usual took up our encampment in its neighbourhood; It was a famous hunting seat of the Royal family before the revolution, the palace had been destroyed but one could judge of the grand scale of the establishment by the extent & grandeur of the still existing stables.[35]

We were now approaching the capital without as yet meeting with enemies, but began to feel the proximity of our allies, their line of march & ours gradually approaching each other and though not intermingled, a short ride to our left would occasionally bring us in contact with their flank columns. Curiosity having led me that way, I fell in with a regiment of [Prussian] cavalry & in riding with them a short distance we came near a cherry orchard on the roadside, the trees of which were loaded with ripening fruit. A halt was made at so

---

35 Now the Living Museum of the Horse in the Great Stables of the Château of Chantilly.

7TH CAMPAIGN

great a temptation, the men dismounted, scrambled over the hedge, broke off large branches with which they again got on their horses and in an incredible short time the orchard appeared in movement along the road, the men eating the fruit at their leisure as they went along, exhibiting a specimen of the consequences of war as carried on by our allies & I regret to add that the same conduct was developing itself among the foreign troops attached to our army, for I perceived in passing through a town in the course of the day a commotion among the inhabitants occasioned by a detachment of dragoons of that force commencing to plunder and I saw several of the men deliberately enter the depot of tobacco and carrying off large rolls of the article, threatening to knock down anyone who opposed them. They would brook no interference and seeing that they were intoxicated I thought as well not to meddle with their designs as in their state they would not even respect an officer. Scenes of this sort became frequent and it was high time they should be put an end to either by a battle or peace.

Rumours of a cessation of hostilities were in circulation & yet our march continued without interruption, no doubt from our commanders being too knowing to be stopped by attempts at negotiations which might not succeed & give the enemy more time in preparing for the defence of the capital. At the end therefore of the day's march of the 30th of June, we suddenly beheld from the heights of the Pierrefitte [-sur-Seine], the dome of the Invalides shining in golden brightness in the distance, topping over the city of Paris with its numerous public buildings bounding the horizon and the town and plain of St Denis [Saint Denis] in the foreground, occupied by the French army barring our further advance. Under existing circumstances it was a proud & glorious sight which had not for centuries been witnessed by a British army.

A change in the movements of the two armies having been determined on, in consequence of the proximity of the enemy, we were ordered to halt & leave a high road clear which passed through Pierrefitte [-sur-Seine] to our right from the left, to enable the Prussian troops to pass us and proceed to operate a flank movement by crossing the Seine lower down and making an attack through Versailles, instead of in our front, which front we could perceive was strongly fortified by means of a canal & small river, the French posts occupying the great high road leading to St Denis [Saint Denis] & Paris.

Our troops had hardly withdrawn from the village which had been deserted by the inhabitants, when the Prussian columns began to file by. For a short time their march was orderly, but signs of disorder soon became apparent to several of us who were looking on. Doors were forced open by stragglers who began the pillage which found imitators. These fellows were perceived to enter the houses & return with what they could lay hands on, consisting of provisions, goods &c. Others threw similar things out of the windows for their comrades down below, with which they again joined their ranks; furniture was ransacked & the sacking of the beds were ripped up & strewed about, under the supposition that money was concealed in them, but as the plunderers dared not leave their ranks for long, they were succeeded by a stream of fresh hands who seemed to understand the business quite as well as their predecessors, so that in a very short time the work of destruction was completed and the village laid waste. In the midst of this disgusting scene Old Blucher made his appearance in an open landau evidently very angry, he got out & went into the house opposite to where he stopped; it was full of his soldiers & his appearance made them come out like a swarm of bees and he after them, but he was covered over with something white which he shook off as well as he could and we were informed that as he was going upstairs to empty the house, a soldier met him carrying a sack of flour holding the mouth of the sack in his hand, which in his fright he let go & strewed the contents over the Old Marshal who finding it apparently of no use to interfere personally, shrugged his shoulders as he came out, gave some orders & drove away & by this time the village had become a mere shell, each soldier having carried off what had come under his hands worth taking.

7TH CAMPAIGN

Extract from a Magazine

'The superiority of the British Infantry, officers & soldiers, was proved alike over both Allies & enemies at a combat near Paris after the Battle of Waterloo in 1815. A large number of Prussian troops had for several hours been endeavouring to drive the French from a suburb where they occupied one side of a street. Failing, they were relieved by a much smaller number of British troops under Sir Neil Campbell[36] with whom Lieutenant Colonel Napier (Sir Charles) went as a volunteer.[37] The British forced their entrance into a house on the French side, broke through the partition walls and stormed one house after another, till they completely cleared the district of the French.'

It was expected that as soon as the Prussian army had effected this movement a simultaneous attack would take place by us all opposite to our respective positions so as to enter Paris by force, a mode hoped for by many who looked forward for the plunder of so vast a city, but happily for humanity they were disappointed for it was announced on the 4 July to the army that an armistice had been entered into for the evacuation of that capital by the French army collected there for its defence & its peaceable surrender to the allied troops. From the 1st to the 5th of that month we therefore remained in a state of inaction, with our sentries & those of the enemy very near each other & watching any movement on either side but without disturbance, for so long as each kept their ground only without attempting to move

---

36 Colonel Sir Neil Campbell, 54th Foot. He had been sent to Elba in 1814 to keep an eye on Napoleon, but was never his gaoler and could not have prevented his return to France in 1815.

37 Lieutenant Colonel Charles Napier, 102nd Foot half pay, joined the army from the Royal Military Academy at Farnham after Waterloo as a Volunteer as he had no official capacity.

forward be they ever so near, nothing offensive was to take place & this was more cordially understood between the French & English than between the former & other nations.

Some part of our troops took possession of St Denis [Saint Denis] as soon as those of the French army had been withdrawn on the latter day & we ourselves (the 2nd Division) crossed the bridge in our front and took the road leading to our right with orders to proceed and occupy one of the barriers next to that of l'Étoile[38] under the understanding that as the French troops had evacuated the place we had only to appear at the point indicated & take peaceable possession; our troops therefore moved in column with Sir Henry Clinton & Staff in front without it being considered necessary for the light troops to be in front, as if advancing against an enemy. Under this feeling of security & when we had marched a considerable distance towards our destination, two or three officers besides myself, influenced by curiosity, rode ahead & having met a road to our left at a right angle to that we had come, proceeded on it for some distance presuming it to be the one the division would take & while in conversation & thinking of nothing but the pleasure of a peep into Paris, all at once several French dragoons unexpectedly rushed out at about two hundred yards distance on the road from behind trees which concealed them and made a dash at us at full gallop hollowing & bellowing in an evident state of intoxication. None of us being armed for an encounter with such fellows, we instantly wheeled about & returned to our troops and as we were well mounted we outran them, and turning the angle of the road alluded to came at once on the division, and while in the act of reporting the circumstance to the general, on they came little expecting to meet with a check. Before however they could bridle up, they had come so near that the general's orderly dragoon, in rushing forward to protect the general, without having had time to draw his sword or use his pistols, attempted to collar one of them, but in so doing missed his aim & laid

---

38 The Place de l'Étoile is where the Arc de Triomphe now stands.

7TH CAMPAIGN

hold of the man's pipe. The others, seeing the situation in which they were unexpectedly placed, fired their pistols & wheeled away leaping the ditch on the roadside & making their way across the fields as fast [as] they could. No one was hurt by the fire and the affair was so instantaneously over that nothing was done to capture them, having no cavalry with us to hunt them down, although had the general wished it volunteers from the mounted officers would have readily undertaken it.

The column was immediately halted and as it was now evident that the French army had not retired, the light infantry were ordered to the front & to load & thus we again moved forward ready to meet an enemy. We then learnt from the peasantry that the French troops being riotous and in a state of insubordination had not quitted the city. Seeing this & that detachments of French troops were visible in many directions, the general gave the order to halt & then sent his aide de camp with a flag of truce to the first outpost he could meet with, with a request to obtain an interview with any French general that might be near at hand. The officer quickly returned, and while looking up the road up which he had gone & returned leading to the city, we perceived a detachment of French cavalry advancing towards us at a furious pace and as they neared us a general was at their head preceded by a black trumpeter sounding his trumpet. It was a very amusing scene, the general took off his hat & enquired for Sir Henry who bowed in return; the Frenchman looked excited & commenced a speech by observing that it was not in the power of the officers to oblige the troops to leave Paris, indignant as they were at letting it fall into the hands of their enemies unfought for & he therefore could not answer for our not being attacked at any time although everything would be done by him to prevent it. He then declared that we were sullying the victory we had gained by bringing back the infamous family of the Bourbons which would be an eternal disgrace to us; and thus he harangued us in similar terms for some time, much to the annoyance of several of his hearers who I perceived were desirous of answering him & I must say I had the same feeling. But Sir Henry kept us in order & in a most cool & dignified manner told him that these were not subjects for which he had requested an interview, but simply to know if the barrier would be given up, which he had orders to occupy; in reply to which the French general said that under existing circumstances he could not at all make any promise and thus ended the interview, the party starting off the way they came & at the same violent rate. The language used was considered so offensive that the general's name was ascertained & made the subject of a report to headquarters, but probably no notice was taken of it in the then existing confusion of affairs.

Sir Henry Clinton not having received orders to force an entry, thought it advisable to proceed no further. He dispatched an officer to the Duke of Wellington's headquarters to report what had occurred & for instructions & as the evening was coming on we took possession of a large farm with outbuildings for the night, set to and barricaded all its entries with the waggons of the train, with every other precaution to repel an attack which had it taken place by a superior force might have proved of serious consequence, as we were completely isolated in the open plain without knowing of any other troops being at hand to render us assistance. After having placed sentries where necessary & sent mounted officers as sort of patrols (having no cavalry for the purpose) to feel for some other corps with which to open a communication, both officers & men laid down in their clothes or rested with their arms by them, wherever they could find room, no fires being allowed to be lighted for cooking to avoid drawing the attention of the enemy and thus we remained until the dawn of day without being molested & until information reached us from Neuilly that the French army had at last evacuated Paris during the night. Similar difficulties were experienced by other corps of our army in one of which an officer was severely wounded.

The division having fallen in early in the morning, we marched with much satisfaction to get into the high road leading from Neuilly to Paris and having followed it for some time we reached the famous Arche [*sic*] de Triomphe called the Barriere de l'Étoile & though

7TH CAMPAIGN

unfinished at the time, it appeared a most gigantic & splendid edifice. Passing it, we proceeded down the avenue leading to the Place de Louis Seize,[39] between rows of trees, the Palace of the Tuileries being seen at the end of them, forming a magnificent approach to the capital. We then entered the Champs-Elysees and received orders to encamp thereon without proceeding further.

My duty required that I should go on to see the Commissary General to receive instructions and I therefore rode in[to] the city which was already filled with Prussians; the inhabitants looked on with apparent indifference, some shops were open & others not, but as it was not the first time they had been thus visited, their surprise could not be so great as might otherwise have been expected. I was of course, delighted to find myself in Paris and I looked at everything with great avidity, but could not give my time at the moment to wander about for my gratification, as I had many official cares & arrangements to attend to, which fully occupied me for several days and as we were like a swarm of locusts wanting food (not to be denied), the French administration was put to a severe trial to provide the necessary supplies from the armies already arrived & others pouring in from different directions, which occasionally led to a scramble among the innumerable multitude. In the meantime the city was taken military possession of by the Prussians, some of them encamping in the gardens of the Palace of the Luxembourg; our troops were stationed in the suburbs only, extending from the river to the barriers on our left and my division had their right on the river occupying the ground on its banks from outside the gardens of the Tuileries and road leading towards the bridge of Jena & St Cloud, and there we remained some days.

All the streets of Paris were intersected by guns, loaded & matches lighted to fire down them at the instant in case of the rising of the inhabitants. Temporary stables were created of wood for the accommodation of the train horses & the officers and men occupied

---

39 Now the Place de la Concorde.

the adjacent houses so that it may be said the population was tied hand & foot; we ourselves had guns similarly placed to command the avenues leading to and from Paris.

So soon as Marshal Blucher had arranged his troops in their quarters, he at once (as it appeared) set about annoying the French people by an attempt to destroy the bridge of Jena. Passing that way two or three days after our arrival in Paris & while looking over the parapet which divided the road from the river, I perceived a number of workmen under the bridge boring holes in the piers just where the arches spring, for the purpose of blowing them up. It had attracted the attention of several Frenchmen who were looking on in a state of great excitement and being near them, they reproached me as an Englishman that such a work of vandalism should be permitted. I told them I had no power to interfere but that something would no doubt be done to prevent it and so it happened, for on the Duke of Wellington's remonstrances the next day an English sentry was seen on the bridge to prevent (as it was said) our men from wandering about into the Prussian cantonments, which included the Champ de Mars, just over the way & as the sentry could not be removed without some delay, the arrival of [the] Emperor of Russia in the meantime saved it from destruction. An idea was entertained at the time that Blucher had no serious intention of injuring it, for had it been the case he could have done it more expeditiously by excavating over each arch, loading the empty space with gunpowder & blowing it up; I understood that as a compromise, a change was to be made in the name of the bridge.[40]

Another of his annoyances was that of imposing a contribution of 100,000,000 francs equal to four million sterling[41] on the city of Paris, against which the municipality pleading want of funds the next day assembled the principal bankers of the city in one room & the former body in an adjoining one and having thrown open the

---

40 It was not renamed.

41 About £200 billion in today's terms.

7TH CAMPAIGN

folding door that divided them, he told them that as they combined the power and means they would not be allowed to separate until their arrangements were complete. The execution of this summary process was also interrupted by the arrival of the allied sovereigns & King of France, the latter of whom made his entry in state in[to] his capital some days after us, but I was not present, and it made little sensation as far as we were concerned.

The French army had retired behind the River Loire, and there appearing no intention of pursuing it, we received orders on the 14 July to move from the Champs-Elysees and go & encamp in the Bois de Boulogne with a large portion of our army. Plenty of straw was obtained and with plenty of underwood ready at hand, comfortable huts were erected under the impression that we should stay there some time while the future destiny of France was in the course of settlement by the crowned heads & their respective diplomatists assembled in the capital for the purpose, and peace signed. For we were still considered liable to a continuation of hostilities, the armistice being but temporary and we remained in that state for several months from an idea being entertained at one time of dividing the country between all the powers. The Prussian army however extended itself as far as Caen in Normandy with a view of covering more ground for obtaining provisions for the general supply of the allied army.

While the troops were thus encamped the general & Staff officers, including the Commissariat, were billeted in the village of Boulogne [-Billancourt], the camp being just outside, towards Paris and I went to occupy the house pointed out for my accommodation; it was locked up, the family having retired into Paris. After knocking some time a neighbour brought the keys and pointed out the rooms [that] were intended for me & my clerk, which finding comfortable we at once took possession. An old woman came soon after & made our beds and with our servants we were quite at home before evening.

Two days after, the eldest son of the family made his appearance & was introduced to me for the evident purpose of seeing what sort of folks we were; finding that I spoke French he seemed pleased at it, as well as I suppose at our appearance [as] from what followed, for on leaving he intimated that his mother would return home shortly & which she did sooner than was expected. Her name was Madame Briavoine, a portly dame, plain but amiable & of middle age, the widow of a merchant who had left her in easy circumstances. We quickly got intimate and conceiving that neither of her guests were dangerous folks, she gave us notice that her daughter & a niece and a second son would join her immediately. How she judged of our innocence I never learnt, unless she thought that the shrewdness of three women was more than a match for two men. They came immediately after & filled the house; the daughter was a pretty girl of sixteen & the niece a little older & tolerably well looking. The former was disposed to be agreeable, but the latter being engaged to an officer in the French army on the Loire was reserved & evidently concerned at our presence; the favourable impression made on our landlady led her to propose that we should dine together & indeed take all our meals with the family and seeing her bent upon it allowing of no refusal, I gladly acquiesced to it and the arrangement continued on the best of terms for nearly three months without one disagreeable moment occurring until we marched to Versailles.

I enter into these & the following particulars from being the only French family with whom I resided on familiar terms during my sojourn in France. As a proof of the lady's early confidence in me she requested me one day to go into the garden with her, where in my presence her gardener dug up a concealed cask which contained her plate & other valuables; on asking her why she did not take them with her in[to] Paris her reply was that she thought them safer at home, under the impression that the city might have been given up to plunder & such must have been the case had the French army persisted in remaining in it in spite of the authorities.

The immense number of troops now congregated in & in the neighbourhood of the capital occasioned much difficulty in

7TH CAMPAIGN

their maintenance, to attend to which gave full occupation to the Commissariat, especially in the article apparently of little consequence, that of firewood for cooking, which the French administration neglected to supply with regularity. We were therefore under the necessity of having recourse to an expedient which at once brought them to their senses from the extreme annoyance it occasioned among the Parisians, in seeing the ornamental parts of their public walks in the course of destruction & that was in cutting down several of the fine trees in the avenues leading into the Bois de Boulogne to convert them into fuel. No expostulation had as yet produced an effect but when it became known what we were doing & must be unavoidably repeated, our wants were at once attended to & the work or destruction ceased, such were the sad alternatives, or I should say realities, of war.

After our troops had had some rest after the last march, orders were issued to prepare for a review by the allied sovereigns who had expressed a wish to see the army which had so distinguished itself at Waterloo. The artillery & infantry were accordingly drawn up from the Place de Louis Seize & Champs Elysees on the left of the road leading to the Barriere de Neuilly (or l'Étoile) in close columns of battalions, the grenadiers in front with the officers at their head, the line being continued by the cavalry, pontoon train &c &c so that in riding down the road from the city, the great folks were enabled to see the masses quite near & receive a general salute as they passed, the bands playing, colours drooping to the ground (as is customary to crowned heads), officers saluting with their swords & soldiers presenting arms. It was a magnificent *coup d'oeil* from the concourse of emperors, kings, princes, generals & Staff officers of so many nations intermixed & dressed in a great variety of uniforms and mounted on the finest chargers. Though our ranks had been thinned by many losses, it was a moment of exultation to exhibit a body of men of whom our country had every reason to be proud. The men were not in general to be compared in stature with the corps d'elite of the allies, but they had stout hearts more than equal to huge bodies possessing less moral determination.

When once we were settled and duty more regular, Paris became the focus of attraction to everyone having either money, leisure, or curiosity, for by this time the inhabitants generally were getting reconciled to our presence and aware of the great pecuniary advantage which such an immense assembly of strangers was producing to them. Yet among them there were not a few who were discontented, including as it was suspected, retired French officers who scrupled not at times when they thought they could do so with impunity, to insult the allied sentries at their posts in various parts of the city, which after having been born with patience for a time, led to a proclamation from the Prussian Baron Muffling, Allied Commandant of Paris, notifying to the public in plain terms that the sentries thus threatened had orders to shoot the first person who provoked them by improper language; and the officers were ordered by their respective commanders on no account to appear in the streets without their swords which latter order was issued in consequence of the constant rows which were daily occurring in the Palais Royal[42] which had become the great & attractive lounge of amusement & dissipation.

Being occasionally in the place, I witnessed several of these disturbances which were invariably commenced by Frenchmen, principally half pay officers anxious to foment duels as a means of revenge for their defeats. But it having been ascertained that among them there were fencing masters & others skilful with the sword & pistol, it was resolved to give none honourable satisfaction, but when found unruly to bundle them out without further ceremony and this was done very summarily by the allied officers present. For when the row commenced they rushed to the spot from different parts & the ejection was at once effected. These scenes having come to the knowledge of the French government, every French officer who had

---

42 The Palais Royal faces the Louvre.

7TH CAMPAIGN

no business in the capital was ordered to leave it & thus the nuisance was abated.

Parades on a large scale became matters of frequent occurrence; one day it would be of the Prussian Guard & then of those of Russia & Austria, all corps of picked men of the most imposing appearance; the former guard consisted of ten thousand cavalry (cuirassiers), artillery, grenadiers & jagers, which generally marched down the boulevards to the Place de Louis Seize to await the arrival of the allied sovereigns before whom & their immense Staffs they marched passed [*sic*] in all the pomp of war; such was the care taken in the selection of these men that when in line by companies, a straight line might have been drawn across the tip of each nose from one end to the other. They wore a shako, to ornament which when required, a long feather was inserted in a sheath annexed to the scabbard of their sword & when ordered, these feathers were at once displayed, forming unexpectedly a sea of plumes where a moment before nothing existed but the top of the shako & a very small tuft. These guardsmen were better dressed than their comrades of the line, the colour of the coat was blue with gold lace on the collar, white duck pantaloons and they were so made up by padding about the chest & shoulders that a pin three inches long could hardly have reached the skin from outside. Each man wore a pair of white buckskin gloves & a gold headed cane and the waist was tightened to the smallest possible size, a fashion also adhered to by the officers, much to our surprise as nothing of this sort of distortion was in use in our army, our coats being comfortably fitted & unstuffed, but yet so long waisted comparatively, with the continental nations, that both peculiarities led to many caricatures exhibited in Paris.

At the moment the Prussian Guard were marching on the boulevards I met a countryman & friend of mine (Mr Savary Brock[43]), a tall, stout, broad-shouldered man and my uniform being a passport to go

---

43 Almost certainly Mr John Savery Brock (1772–1844).

anywhere, we mixed among & examined them in their occasional halts. He felt as he expressed himself almost a pigmy among them & could hardly conceive how such a set of men could be collected together & their ranks recruited. No doubt however they were more for shew than rough work, for it was said they were seldom brought forward to bear the brunt of an action but to decide it when absolutely necessary, it being no doubt difficult to fill up casualties. What added much to their martial appearance was their mustachios, our men being clean shaved except the cavalry.

At the Austrian parades the same routine of passing by took place, but the colour and fashion of the dress was different; the Hungarian Foot Guards appeared the finest of the troops of that nation. Their dress consisted of a low sugar loaf sort of bearskin cap, white coat, tight sky blue pantaloons and black gaiters beautifully fitted and very martial in appearance, their jagers (the Tyrolese in particular) dressed in green were also very fine men. Of the cuirassiers of the several nations I do not enter into particulars; they were no doubt splendid in their appearance, but were not equal to our Life Guards in size of men or horses. Their numbers however were almost countless, while ours were a mere handful.

The Russian display was in some measure different; the cut & colour of dress being distinct as well as the race to which the men belonged, the mustache [*sic*] being spare and greased and yet the pageant was equally splendid. There was a strong contrast to any other troops in the dress & features of the disciplined lancer regiments of Cossacks of the Imperial Guard, which had something of the Asiatic in it; they wore a muff cap & feather, tight coatee & very loose bulging pantaloons of the same colour tightly gathered at the foot, black belts with silver ornaments on the breast & pouch which in effect produced a good contrast, as also from being mounted on their high saddles & spirited long tailed horses & carrying long lances with which they were very expert.

In addition to the presence of the sovereigns & their personal Staffs at these military displays innumerable mounted officers attended to

7TH CAMPAIGN

witness them; in many instances ten & twelve deep jammed in mass, the great folks alone being in the front rank & looking directly on the troops as they passed by. In compliment to each other the sovereigns had interchanged colonelcies in their respective guards; thus Russia and Austria were colonels of regiments in the Prussian Guards & vice versa & which the troops were in the act of marching past, it was perceived that the sovereign whose regiment was coming up, stole away for a moment from his own Staff & went & put himself at the head of it marching past and saluting the sovereign of the nation to which it belonged. On one of these occasions a sudden move of position having taken place and no room left to keep a respectable, I should say respectful distance from my superiors, I suddenly found myself jammed in between the Crown Prince of Prussia & a General officer & there I was obliged to remain for some minutes knee to knee. I apologised to the former for my nearness, but seeing there was no help for it, he was affable finding that I could speak French. He was young with a feminine cast of countenance.

French artists made their appearance occasionally in these assemblies to take the likeness of their Majesties & other illustrious persons present, which at times put them in danger of being trampled upon, but seeing their object assistance was usually afforded them in being allowed to rest their papers on which they were sketching, on the pommel of the saddle. On some of these occasions I rode my cossack and having to pass through the Champs-Elysees to shorten my distance I usually leapt the low horizontal rails separating them from the high road and as he did it cleverly the Parisians who were looking on were much amused.

The parades were subsequently followed by reviews of the several armies in Paris & neighbourhood, on which days the troops manoeuvred in the field for several hours in imitation at times, of operations which had occurred in actions in which they had been engaged. The spot usually chosen was the plain of St Denis [Saint Denis] & were the sovereigns assembled to witness them when present at one of them, the troops not having had time to occupy their respective positions as early as was intended, the great folks had to wait to beguile the time and accordingly an immense circle of officers was formed round them in the centre of which they placed themselves and there a sort of field court was held as I could perceive numerous introductions, which made it an amusing scene for the short time it lasted. When all was ready, this prelude broke up & the army reviewed being ours, the manoeuvres were a representation of the attack at Salamanca, during the progress of it the Duke moved the troops in masses, in very broken ground everyone wondering how he could extricate them without confusion, but he did so most skilfully to the astonishment of the foreigners. The columns then marched in open order, the generals & Staff at their respective heads taking off their cocked hats in saluting, which had a good effect, usual with us, but not practised by the other nations. In the midst of the spectacle a curious circumstance occurred which drew the notice of all present; it was occasioned by the appearance of a large poodle dog, on which the figure of a dragoon was mounted, marching by himself at the head of the 7th Fusiliers; the dog being well trained & a great pet of the regiment, kept his distance most cleverly by occasionally looking back & deliberately trotting forward if he found he had lost ground & stopping if he was too much in advance. All eyes were on him for the moment & the sovereigns themselves could not help laughing at the animal's endeavours to perform a part to which held their attention from the troops while he was in sight.

When these reviews were over their majesties left the field accompanied by the Duke of Wellington & their numerous Staff & when he had proceeded a certain distance towards Paris he made his bow & left them, whereas the Emperor of Austria as senior potentate was followed to his residence by the Emperor of Russia & King of Prussia, the latter going home as last in succession, the proceeding being it was supposed, a point of etiquette.

The dress worn on these ceremonies by the Emperor of Austria was singular & almost grotesque; it consisted of a huge cocked

7TH CAMPAIGN

hat quite disproportional to his person, a plain military white coat without epaulettes closely buttoned with only one order on his breast, red tight breeches & high jack boots, serving as a contrast to the Emperor of Russia & King of Prussia dressed as general officers, the former with a little sword embroidered on his breast being the great order of Sweden and always appearing with a handsome & cheerful countenance, while the latter had always a melancholy look, occasioned (it was said) by past misfortunes & the loss of a beloved queen.

Among this galaxy of the great, Platoff [Platov] chief of the Cossacks[44] was more than ordinarily conspicuous in his dress, a mixture of Asiatic & European, and from wearing all the orders which had been given him by the different powers, strung like pearls round his neck & hanging down on his breast. In point however of dress, which attracted most attention from all classes both foreigners & Frenchmen was that of the Scotch regiments wearing the kilt, for the latter (the Frenchmen), in the Republican phraseology though familiar with the term *sans culotte*, had not before seen a dress answering that description & none believed that it existed until they had seen it. While the novelty lasted these troops were stared at in Paris by the curious whenever they appeared in the streets.

Having seen the elite of the Russian, Prussian & Austrian armies I did not attend their reviews, the grandest of which was that of the former power on the plain of Vertus[45] some leagues from Paris consisting of 160,000 men of which 40,000 were cavalry; it was described as a magnificent sight by those who were present & I had great curiosity to go there but could not obtain leave having business to transact during a considerable part of every day; moreover all the military pageants were becoming uninteresting from their uniform sameness.

---

44 General Count Matvei Platov commanded the Don Cossacks.

45 The Plain of Vertus was then famous as a vegetable-growing area: it was near Aubervilliers.

Objects of curiosity in Paris & environs were of course innumerable and the then celebrated gallery of the Louvre[46] (then intact) became the lounge of those desirous of seeing & examining its contents, consisting of the rarest works of art, the spoil of all Europe, England excepted. We had free access, as the custody of it was by alternate guards of the four great nations.

The Hotel des Invalides was also open to us and as conquerors we were enabled to see the grand plans of all the fortified places in the kingdom which were in the attics of the building, arranged on large tables shewing each city with all its fortifications, guns, ditches, sinuosities of ground, woods, roads, trees and houses, with a minute detail of the surrounding country so delineated as to produce the same effect as if seen from a height commanding the actual prospect; this sight was not usually allowed to anyone, especially foreigners.

The Palais du Luxembourg was also considered worthy of a visit as containing the grand paintings representing the victories of the French armies from the Revolution, which filled the walls of the principal saloons, but which were then covered with green baize, the reason for which I was told as an Englishman was that they were thus concealed not to outrage the feelings of the allies, for had it been known to the Prussian soldiers who were encamped in the gardens of the palace, their destruction might have taken place from one moment to the other. I was therefore deprived of the anticipated pleasure of looking at them.

Of course, I visited the Tuileries, Notre Dame, the Royal Library, Garden des Plantes, bridges &c, but as they are well known and better described than any attempt of mine to enter into details, I shall abstain from it.

While the negotiations were pending relative to what was to become of France and the terms or conditions on which peace was

---

46 The Louvre was renamed the Napoleon Museum in 1803. Some 5,000 artefacts taken from all over Europe were repatriated in 1815.

7TH CAMPAIGN

to be granted to it, (an idea having been entertained to dismember it) a violent letter of some unknown but influential Frenchman was put in circulation threatening a rise of the entire population to get us from the country, which had it been attempted would have occasioned incalculable mischief to the inhabitants, who never could have successfully combated without their greater leader, against a million of the best soldiers of Europe then in & about Paris & within a few days march of it, for we were at least that number of Austrians, Russians, Prussians, English including Dutch & Belgians and of the minor states of Germany, such as Bavaria, Hanover, Wurtemberg, Nassau, Baden &c & though an idea was entertained that this bold project was only intended to influence the negotiations with a view to obtain better terms & not to be carried into effect, yet it led to greater vigilance on our part to be prepared for it.

At this time other circumstances led to raise the anger of all classes while the capital was held under military subjection, for the museums were by degrees stript [*sic*] of the plunder they contained, every nation claiming what had been wrested from them during the war and when the operation commenced, it was a sad sight to visit the Louvre, for the floors of the rooms were strewed with the paintings &c already taken down & the cases into which they were to be packed; the frames being left on the walls as a dismal & blank memorial of that once glorious collection. The statuary of course experienced the same fate, the Venus de Medici,[47] the Apollo,[48] the Lacoon[49] &c being packed up to be forwarded to their respective destinations & in so doing the mode adopted was a singular one, a case being prepared & filled with liquid plaster of Paris the statue was lowered into it, the whole becoming in a few minutes a consolidated mass which could be conveyed any distance without danger of injury. We of course did not

---

47 The Venus de Medici was returned to the Uffizi Gallery at Florence.

48 The Apollo Belvedere was returned to the Vatican.

49 The Laocoon and his Sons was returned to the Vatican.

share by the dispersion of these treasures of art, although the French gave us credit for it in consequence of those belonging to Rome & some other of the Italian states being sent down to Havre for shipment to the Mediterranean (but as rumour would have it) to go to England.

It was contemplated at first to pull down the column in the Place Vendome commemorating the victories over the Austrians, in imitation of Trajan's pillar at Rome illustrating the conquest of Dacia, but it was limited to the taking down the statue of Napoleon from its top & erasing the Austrian eagles which ornamented its base.

A difficult operation was also undertaken in taking down the Venetian bronze horses which were on the Arc de Triomphe in the Place du Carrousel. They were claimed by Austria on behalf of Venice which then formed a part of the possessions of that power in Italy: when decided on, it was ascertained that there were not in that or any other of the continental armies, mechanics equal to the undertaking, in consequence of which our assistance was solicited, and Captain Todd of the Royal Staff Corps[50] with his men successfully performed it, no Frenchman being willing of course to disgrace himself by being concerned in it.

When the erection of the scaffolding was commenced on, the captain & his party met with opposition from the National Guard stationed at the Tuileries, being put by them in temporary confinement & as it evidently created considerable sensation in Paris it was found necessary to provide against a disturbance. I heard of the day on which the operation was to be accomplished & determined on being there if possible, the preliminary arrangements being of course completed. I went accordingly to the Place du Carrousel, and found it covered with Austrian Grenadiers; four open waggons containing each a considerable quantity of straw were at the foot of the arch and on a signal given, one of the horses was slowly detached from its base & bar on which it stood & was attached and gradually lowered

---

50 Captain Alexander Todd, Royal Staff Corps.

7TH CAMPAIGN

into one of the carts; the same was safely done to the other three in succession without the slightest accident or injury. Many Frenchmen were present & loudly expressed their rage & indignation, but it was all they dared do, for the allied force present was too great to be resisted. The horses thus snugly placed on their straw beds in their respective waggons were escorted out of Paris by the troops which assisted in the operation. Immediately after a report was circulated among the Parisians that the horses had all been injured while in the act of being taken down, for which there was not the least foundation, it being done to gratify their vanity & to disparage the mechanical powers of the allied troops.

The protracted presence of the armies was also a source of national vexation, though much money was made by the shopkeepers, yet they could not forget that the country had suffered & was still suffering many depredations especially in the country seats & homes in the neighbourhood of the capital particularly during the first days of our presence.

In one instance among numerous others, I recollect on going into one of these chateaux of large size, I found it stripped of a good deal of its furniture; fires had been lighted [*sic*] on its fine ornamental oak floors and from the want of other fuel the soldiers had used rich chairs & tables to cook their victuals with, the remnants of them being still visible among the ashes & the French being fond of decorating their rooms with looking glasses, they were all broken & we were told they had been smashed by the soldiers with the butt end of their muskets. A wag of a Frenchman had repaired one of the least damaged by pasting strips of paper over the cracks in imitation of boughs & having coloured them & added leaves he had written under it '*Manufacture de glasse à la Prussien*'.

The Prussian officers also in their conduct in Paris did not generally endeavour to conciliate the persons on whom they were quartered and no control being exercised over their proceedings in point of accommodation or provisions they were at times very oppressive, more perhaps to give a sample of what they themselves had suffered, when the French armies were in their country than from a malicious feeling. As an instance, it was currently mentioned at the time that a superior officer obtained from the municipality a quarter on the house occupied by the wife of a French general who had himself been quartered in his father's house in Prussia & had by his exactions grossly insulted the family; on presenting it personally to the lady he requested to see the lodging intended for him and appearing to be displeased at it, he demanded to see her own apartments which was done with great reluctance. While in it he sat on a rich satin sofa with one leg up and while telling her that it was his determination to occupy it himself and leave her the rooms intended for him, he amused himself in sticking the booted spur of the leg alluded to into the satin & tearing it; she became most indignant at such conduct but he calmly insisted on what he had decided & moreover that she would have to provide daily dinner for himself & several friends. Remonstrances were of no avail & with tears & vexation she perceived that resignation was the only remedy & she accordingly surrendered her apartments and the officer having occupied them for three or four days requested to see her and the interview having taken place he explained to her the reasons for his conduct, that she and her friends might have some conception of the shameful conduct of the French troops in their course of conquest in Europe. His object having been attained he apologised for what had occurred and would occupy the lodging at first intended for him.

Notwithstanding all these proceedings which were most galling to many Frenchmen, Paris continued to be the centre of attraction & the vortex of dissipation to all the lovers of pleasure, not only to the officers of the allied armies but to the numerous strangers (English in particular) who began flocking there & as many came from all parts of Europe, from the interior of the Russian empire to John o' Groats house in Scotland & Italy, the grouping at times in the streets of this gay capital had more the appearance of a masquerade than a scene in common life, for there might be seen the cossack of the

7TH CAMPAIGN

Don and the highlander intermixed with individuals of intermediate countries. A lounge on the boulevards to hear the magnificent band of the Emperor of Austria was the fashion, as it played every day, but the Palais Royal with its gay shops, covered bazaar and gambling establishments was much frequented.

Curiosity led me at times to the gambling table where I observed such scenes of distress by those losing their money that I only tried my luck once in putting down a Napoleon (16/8d). which having lost I did not repeat it; some of my companions were not so easily daunted, and I regret to say I was persuaded by them to lend them the contents of my purse, with which they did not I suspect enrich themselves, for they made no boast of it on repaying me.

No one can form an idea of the demoralisation going on in the accessories of those dens of infamy which are too shocking to describe and as I was tolerably prudent in visiting them, I cannot say I was the worst for it, but it was not the case with the young officers under my orders, for in paying them their pay once a month, I was obliged to retain with their concurrence in my possession a sum equal to meet their absolute wants for the period following and well I did so for the remainder of the money was dissipated in the course of a day or two. In one of these visits to these hells I perceived an unusual bustle at an adjoining table and having gone there, an individual attracted general notice by the boldness & extent of his playing. It drew the managers to watch him; he produced considerable sums in gold & bank notes to commence with, but the rise of luck in his favour was such that in the course of a very short time he carried off no less (it was said) than 60,000 francs which created [a] considerable sensation, for he continued to play only while fortune befriended him, but the moment he perceived it to be adverse he wisely discontinued playing.

It was amusing at times to join in the fancies of my brother officers, one of whom whose name was Strachan[51] took a desperate

---

51 Assistant Commissary General Alexander Strachan.

fancy to a very pretty Parisian girl of twenty while he was himself double her age & a great *savage* and she possessing all the lively gaiety of a Frenchwoman. Her parents imagined it to be a good match & therefore gave him every encouragement but the absurdity was that he understood very little French & spoke less, so that the main channel of communication for courting must have been made [more] by the eye than by the tongue. I was intimate with both and when in their company had often to interpret to them each other's thoughts and without vanity it would not have been difficult to have become the favoured swain had I fancied it, for I could easily perceive the intensity of love was principally on his side. In one of these conversations I was an accessory to his declaration to her of his affection; he was accepted and they were married soon after when it was soon found out he had nothing but his pay and his situation not so lucrative as was supposed; he afterwards made little progress in French and she as little in English so that their social intercourse did not much improve and not having seen them often when the army got more dispersed, I did not see how they got on but learnt that the marriage was not happy.

A curious circumstance which was prevailing topic of conversation with the army at the time occurred at the Elysee Bourbon,[52] the residence of the Emperor of Russia and it arose from the custom of the crowned heads having guards of honour attending on them from the four great nations in daily succession, each nation as I have before mentioned furnishing guards also in the same way over the museums &c. On the day the British Guards performed that duty in turn, the Emperor received as usual many of his officers & from some cause or other being angry with two colonels of his own guard he ordered them into the custody of the English colonel, with injunctions to hold them as prisoners & for them to be kept in the soldier's guard room. The officers, finding that they were his equals in rank took them

---

52 Now the Elysée Palace.

7TH CAMPAIGN

into his own room, without heeding the instructions he had received concerning them and there they remained until released. In the course however of the evening the Emperor heard of it & sent down an aide de camp to know why his orders had not been attended to, to which he received a most respectful but firm reply that it was contrary to the rule of the British service to degrade an officer until he was found guilty & that he could not treat officers of his rank otherwise than he had done and holding himself responsible for their security it must be left to him to act as he thought best to attain that object. No further notice was taken of his determination, although some said that it had been approved of by Emperor Alexander who was considered to be a very good man, yet it exemplified the extent of the despotism he exercised over his officers and subjects. Waterloo men dared much at the time.

While quartered in Boulogne [-Billancourt], the Commissariat officers got very intimate with the respective families with which they were living; little parties took place at each other's houses and there arose therefrom something more than ordinary between the young people. Fortunately however for the former, amiableness was the prevailing quality of the fair sex, beauty being altogether wanting, so that the temptation to imprudent connections was not overwhelming & all parted with only a few sighs & tears when the army moved.

My landlady got also very intimate with me, but as she was much older than me & plain, I gave her no encouragement to further familiarity, though she made decided efforts which were not to be mistaken. Her son about 18 years old was greatly annoyed at her conduct whenever he came from Paris where he was studying the law, but she heeded him not and went on as usual and to annoy him she was more communicative on some points than her national vanity should have permitted. For in his presence she told me as a matter of fact that on the day we were to have attacked Paris before the convention for its surrender had been signed, out of 42,000 men composing the national guard of that city, only 8,000 mustered or turned out to face the allies. This made him very angry, but he never spoke to me of our intimacy for had he done so I would at once have relieved his mind, for besides her want of attraction I felt I should have been more than ungrateful to have returned her hospitable kindness & liberality by any imprudent step.

A great event in the estimation of the lovers of amusement, as are the French people, took place while living at Boulogne [-Billancourt] and that was the great annual fair of St Cloud which began on the 10th of September and lasted several days. Great preparations had been in progress for some time before, it being the resort of showmen from many parts of the kingdom. Booths having been erected in the principal walks or alleys of the park & when it was at last opened to the public these alleys, which were bordered on each side by noble trees appeared like streets, with each booth surmounted by a painted sign or canvas denoting with great exaggeration what was exhibited in the interior, such as wild beasts, strange animals, men of voracious appetites, tightrope dancers, tooth drawers, sleight of hand &c including all imaginable & attractive shows & trades. And as nothing could go on without dancing there were spaces appropriated for all classes, in which bands of music attended. The crowd which daily poured in from all parts was immense for the time it lasted and it really was a most interesting sight to perceive all descriptions of people both high & low enjoying themselves in their own way; and although St Cloud & neighbourhood was swarming with Russians & English, the natives would not be denied the pleasures they had come to partake of. The cascades & fountains in the park played occasionally for the general amusement, as well as fireworks at night.

As we had only a short walk to the bridge over the Seine to be in the midst of all the gaiety, it became an afternoon's lounge for us & the French families with whom we associated & the evening usually ended in a quadrille & waltz in one of the green recesses alluded to as set apart for the purpose, a franc or two being paid to the musicians who played for us. Much to the credit of all concerned, the

7TH CAMPAIGN

affair went off without disturbance which at such a time was of some importance, for it gave the French people confidence to intermix with us. Many afterwards visited our camp in the Bois de Boulogne without hesitation or molestation, walking up and down (particularly on Sundays) the avenues on each side of which the troops were in tents or hutted.

Marshal Blucher was quartered in the palace of St Cloud, the Prussian army being partly in and about Paris & partly in echelon in the different towns on the road towards Normandy, each being occupied by them. They were not overscrupulous in the nature of their exactions from the inhabitants; nothing came wrong at hand, the contributions which they exacted having included silks, satins, laces and many objects of finery which were periodically forwarded to Prussia, convoys of this pillage were occasionally observed assembled before the main entrance of the palace undergoing an inspection from the marshal's Staff, it being currently reported that he took a tithe of them. No wonder therefore that the bad feeling of the French towards the Prussians was universal and it was mentioned to us when we went to see the palace that the aides de camp even amused themselves taking the gold bullion & fringes from the curtains & draperies of the state apartments which had evidently suffered from the hands of somebody. I must say however that the bedroom usually occupied by the Emperor had been respected when I saw it, but its contents were hardly worth carrying away for the furniture & bed had nothing striking or peculiar about them, the only thing which attracted my notice being the blankets which were made of the finest cotton, extremely light & warm. Bijoux works of art & other ornamental trifles had however been removed to avoid temptation.

While in these cantonments my brother De Vic[53] paid me a visit on his way to Spain & being gay & familiar in his manner he got on rapidly in the estimation of our French acquaintance. I became of

---

53 His brother De Vic Carey was born in 1790.

course his cicerone & shewed him all that was to be seen in Paris & neighbourhood; his stay however was short.

Although the Parisians as I have already said felt our presence as an open wound to their national vanity, yet their love of sightseeing affording amusement could not bear restraint & must be gratified at any rate & the announcement that the water works of Versailles would play for the gratification of the allied sovereigns on a particular Sunday was an object they could not resist being present at & the desire having spread to our village, my landlady borrowed a double gig & prevailed on me to drive her party there. We accordingly started on the appointed day & soon reaching the high road found it so crowded with all sorts of conveyances & people on foot &c that it was with difficulty we forced our way into the line of carriages, but once with it all went right & we reached our destination in safety, put the gig up as best we could & hurried to the gardens. I do not describe them as they are too well known by sight or hearsay to do so. The crowd was immense; all Paris & neighbourhood seemed to have congregated there and a friend having opportunely imparted to us the programme of proceedings, we jostled & crept to the spot where the sovereigns were first to make their appearance & the fete commence, for it must be understood that the water works do not all play at once but in succession. We were not long kept waiting, for a considerable bustle among the crowd announced their arrival with their respective splendid retainers who ranged themselves on spots selected for them & thus one after the other these magnificent artificial water displays took place & by good luck, having known what to do, we succeeded in seeing them advantageously, but the trouble was almost greater than the pleasure from the heat & concourse of people.

The English had not then, as they have since, appeared in great numbers & an English beauty when she appeared attracted universal admiration. On that occasion a very beautiful girl accompanied by her supposed father was conspicuous & wherever she went the young Frenchmen seemed to forget the sovereigns & water works to stare

7TH CAMPAIGN

at & admire her. She certainly was very good looking, tall & fair & as I could not help looking at her, I perceived the ladies of our party as well as most others were getting jealous of this admiration, so that I found it necessary to move on, but wherever we met her again her admirers had not apparently decreased & I may therefore say that she was one of the lions of the day. After lounging from place to place for several hours & taken refreshments at one of the numerous cafes, the evening coming on it was time to think of returning home. After some trouble we found our vehicle & got into the line of carriages which could only proceed slowly from the numbers of them. Night overtook us before we had got half way home & then commenced the most disorderly scene of the sort I ever witnessed; the carriages crowded upon each other from the desire of those inside to get to Paris as soon as possible & as the rush from the rear increased, wheels got locked into each other, the lighter conveyances were upset, the poles of others ran into the backs of those ahead; in short the greatest confusion ensued & continued until we reached home, not earlier than eleven o'clock. I thought I had succeeded in steering our carriage pretty safely but when next morning I examined it, I found many spokes of the wheels sadly damaged & not in a state to be returned to the owner, but as it was the affair of my landlady I left her (rather ungraciously I am afraid) to get out of the *scrape* as she best could.

From the extent & labour of raising the water of these water works from the River Seine to a very considerable elevation by hydraulic machinery into large reservoirs, it was stated at the time as costing each time £1,000.[54]

The Catacombs of Paris were another peculiar object of attraction, particularly to strangers in which I include the officers of the various armies. They were extensive excavations underground so intricate in their windings that it was considered dangerous to wander into their recesses without guides and it was said parties

---

54 Approximately £50,000 in today's terms.

had lost their way in them & never returned. We therefore were regularly numbered as we went in and came out to avoid further casualties, though I think the report of losses was circulated to put everyone on their guard who entered them not to separate from the guides & thereby give trouble in being sought out when found missing. Their origin was by some attributed to their being made places of refuge in disturbed times, others to being excavated for the stone required to build with, and another conjecture to places of sepulture [sic], the probability being that they served for those respective purposes when times and circumstances rendered it convenient to do so.

At this period, the service of the Commissariat was so regular that no incident occurred to disturb its everyday course excepting in occasional changes of subordinate officers and being always desirous of having under me those who appeared most active in their duties, I applied in consequence of a vacancy, for a Mr Dee,[55] from having witnessed his extreme activity. He joined me accordingly but I soon perceived that the excess of effort he made arose entirely from want of arrangement, for if he had several things to do at once his combinations were made with so little method that he gave himself double trouble in their execution. The poor fellow was therefore in constant unnecessary bustle, which I mistook for extraordinary zeal and it was of no use to attempt to correct the deficit by making his head save his heels for it was innate in him. I mention it however to shew how deceitful are appearances at times and that a well-regulated mind is far better than one under the guidance of quick impulses without method.

While thus the armies were in a state of inactivity, the diplomatists of the great powers had been busy in arranging the conditions of the Treaty of Peace, but before their labours could be brought to an end Autumn had arrived and it was no longer thought advisable from the

---

55 Presumably a clerk as not in the Army Lists.

7TH CAMPAIGN

approaching bad weather to keep the troops in huts or under canvas, and reports which had circulated of a move were in the latter end of October turned into a certainty, for I received an order from the Commissary General at Paris to accompany Deputy Commissary General Dumaresq[56] to Versailles to make arrangements with the Sous Prefect for cantoning in that town & neighbourhood part of the English army. We were selected for that service from our knowledge of the French language and as we were still in a passive state of war the expenses of the allied army were defrayed by the departments in which we sojourned. Our visit to the functionary was therefore anything but agreeable and when made aware of it his anger overcame his courtesy; it was therefore found necessary to administer a sharp rebuke by letting him know that we were not disposed to put up with any insolence, or that we had it in our power to alter arrangements already determined on. Feeling that he had committed himself, he apologised by observing that his anger was against the authorities of Paris, in burdening his already exhausted district with additional contributions to relief [sic] their own. With this we had nothing to do and having brought him to reason, we entered into the business we were required to transact & thus ended an unpleasant interview which would have ended unsatisfactorily had we not well understood the language of the country, which few of our brother officers did at the time.

The preparations for a change of quarters being thus made, our division received orders to march & reached Versailles the same day; headquarters, a brigade of artillery & brigade of infantry being stationed in that town & the [other] two brigades of infantry in St Cyr [Saint-Cyr-l'Ecole] and neighbourhood. The farewell of myself & officers with the several families with whom we had so long resided at Boulogne [-Billancourt] was really a feeling one, for we had all received from them the kindest welcome & hospitality decidedly

---

56 Deputy Commissary General Thomas Dumaresq.

more so than we had a right to expect; courteous behaviour goes a long way with French people and in this instance we felt the benefit of it. These good people particularly the young were in tears at our departure and my landlady though past that period of life was equally moved; none of us however had lost our hearts.

At Versailles I was quartered in No 2 Rue d'Anjou and though the rooms were large there was great lack of furniture, yet I had as much as I was entitled to; somehow however this good lady obtained information that I was not so comfortable as I had been under her roof and to my astonishment a waggon load of essentials in the shape of tables, chairs &c were sent by her for my use. I refused them at first but the cartman declaring that he had positive orders to leave them & seeing him obstinate, I gladly took them in & used them while we remained in that part of the country.

As we were now more isolated from the bulk of the army than before & still occupying the country in a state of war though not offensively, I received orders on the 2nd of November to provide materials for the creation of a beacon, to be ignited in case the inhabitants attempted insurrection and to serve as a mode of communication with other corps. An alarm post in case of need was also fixed on for the garrison of the town to repair to & that was the Chateau of Versailles, before the front entrance of which our guns were parked, ready loaded for immediate action, the fire of three guns being the signal for us all to assemble. Fortunately nothing of the sort became necessary, the people being apparently well disposed & tolerably quiet; yet the precaution was unavoidable for our security, but the apprehensions of a rise was I think more on account of the Prussians who were most exacting, while we ourselves demanded nothing more than our rations & kept up a strict discipline. There was therefore no cause for discontent (so far as we were concerned) on the part of the French than that of being burdened with our presence and maintenance; no doubt no slight inconvenience, but which they had brought on themselves by supporting an idol.

7TH CAMPAIGN

The 52nd Light Infantry had a bugle band, an instrument of recent discovery[57] & being harmoniously martial was flocked to by the inhabitants whenever it played as well as to the bands of other regiments. The chateau & gardens were of course open to us at all times & to the people on Sundays, we therefore made the latter our usual walk when at leisure, so that I became well acquainted with every part of both before we left. The place we were told was nearly in the same state as at the Great Revolution of 1790, Napoleon it was said never having even visited it or interested himself about it and singular enough, the letter L which figured on the ornamental parts of the building had not been displaced by his own initial as had been done to every other public building. In respect to the theatre, it would have only required the actors & an audience, with sweeping the cobwebs & a little brushing up to imagine that the Bourbons had never left.

I thought the gardens were laid out in a stiff manner, the trees being trained to imitate walls & nothing left to nature to develop its beauties, unless it was the Trianons which were laid out in imitation of [an] English landscape. As we were in winter the numerous orange trees which in summer ornament the terraces &c were comfortably housed in large conservatories with double windows to prevent the frost from reaching them; their ages were inscribed on the large wooden pots or boxes in which they were planted and many numbered several hundred years of growth, it being specified that they were sown or grafted in the reigns of such & such monarchs. They were in beautiful preservation & some had attained as far as I could judge, the height of 25 feet [7.6m] if not more.

Our presence enlivened the place in some measure, but never having been the resort of the court since the Revolution, its former prosperity had not ever since returned & it looked deserted & forsaken,

---

57 The brass bugle appeared in Hanover in 1758 and was in England by 1764, but it was only gradually accepted, Napoleonic cavalry usually being equipped with an early trumpet which lacked keys or valves.

which it must have appeared even in its best days, for when the Royal family were not there a decrease of two thirds of the population took place. It therefore principally consisted of lodging houses for the accommodation of the concourse of the nobles, ministers & other individuals in attendance & who all of course disappeared at the same time. Singular enough such had been the oversight or indifference to eradicate the vestiges of the fallen dynasty in this particular town that on the doors of the cavalry stables of the court the words *'Gardes Ecossaises'* [Scottish Guards[58]] were still legibly painted. Some persons conceived that Buonaparte felt an ominous dislike to it while others were of opinion that its great distance from Paris was objectionable to him both in regard to the ready transaction of business & the necessity of a strict surveillance over its population at all times ready for a disturbance.

In the middle of November reports were in circulation that the Treaty of Peace would soon be signed and the public announcement of its having taken place was not long delayed, for it was communicated to the French Chambers on the 25th of that month. By it the boundaries of France were the same as they [had] existed before the Revolutionary war and a heavy pecuniary contribution imposed, amounting to upwards of 28 million sterling[59] as an indemnity to the allied countries to cover in part the expenses of the war (England did not pocket her share, it being employed in fortifying the Belgian frontier), which produced a most unfavourable impression on the French people & infuriated their mercurial temperament, but not having it in their power to show any physical resistance, their anger melted away in violent language & solacing themselves with the

---

58 The Scottish Guard was formed by Charles VII in 1418 of the best 100 warriors from some 14,000 Scotsmen brought over to forge 'The Auld Alliance'. The Scottish Company (of varying size) remained a part of the Garde du Corps until they were disbanded in 1791.

59 About £1.8 trillion today.

7TH CAMPAIGN

prospect of being soon rid of the greatest part of the allied armies, which appeared then as far as their national vanity would permit.

By the terms of the treaty an army of 150,000 men of allied troops was to remain in France for 5 years & to occupy the frontier from Calais to Switzerland as a protection to the reinstated Bourbons, in case of an attempt of the people to overthrow their government & to serve if required as the vanguard of another invasion to quell such a movement. Accordingly, all the weak & second battalions of our army received orders in the beginning of December to march to the coast for embarkation to England & our quota of the Army of Occupation was at once organised & the Staff officers appointed. Everyone were [sic] of course anxious to be of the number,[60] but I made no effort to be included in the Commissariat establishment, as I thought that it would be useless to do so unless my usefulness had been perceived by my superiors and feeling conscious that I had done my duty zealously. I left the matter to take its own course and in due time learnt that I was one of the chosen ones to continue in my present post with the 2nd Division of infantry, which kept it's number & the generals & Staff with only a change in the regiments. I was therefore much gratified to find that without solicitation my services had been recognised & I may say without personal flattery, that had they been overlooked it would have shewn little discrimination in the Commissary General, for the very few of the department who were conversant with French could hardly be sent away without committing a great blunder. Although our stay at Versailles was as usual uncertain, we succeeded in remaining in it during the month of December and though the various individuals upon [whom] my officers and myself were quartered, were not on such intimate terms as those of Boulogne [-Billancourt], we still were good friends. They often enquired into our country's habits & customs and joked [with]

---

60 Being on full pay with the Army of Occupation being seen as much preferrable to being sent home to languish on half pay.

187

us about our plain cookery, our beefsteaks (as they called them) & plum pudding, the latter of which they had heard described as being a proportion of flour, raisins or currants & suet &c, put loose into a pot with water and when cooked, served up in a tureen like soup. We tried to undeceive them by a description, but as Christmas was at hand we determined to give them a practical specimen of this national dish. We therefore set our heads together & though not very artful as to its composition, each of us, five or six in number, undertook individually (from recollection) to procure in Paris or on the spot, one of the ingredients. They were obtained in what we thought regular proportions of the best quality, the raisins & currants were washed & picked, the suet chopped fine, flour dried, candied lemon peel cut in pieces with other spices, all being well stirred up in a loose paste were tied up in a cloth. Finding however the dimensions of the pudding greater than we expected, the wisest among us declared that it would never be done as it was, we therefore divided it into two. The period of boiling puzzled us also, but we ascertained that several hours were required, which having been attended to, at the end of the time & just before dinner we inspected the opening of the cloth by our cook and to our great satisfaction found that our exertions were crowned with success & the taste equal to the appearance. We therefore cut one up in slices & with proper sauce immediately distributed them among our acquaintance, keeping the other for ourselves and we quickly learned of their agreeable surprise, for one & all declared that it was most excellent & quite different to what they had been led to expect. We thus relieved the national taste from that contempt under which it had previously laid, so far at least as that particular dish was concerned, though it must be allowed that in most respects French cookery is more esteemed than that of any other nation. Towards the end of the year the weather became excessively cold, with falls of snow & hard frost, such as I had never seen before & from having been in a warm climate for years, it was doubly uncomfortable, particularly from the large size of our rooms, loose casements and not sufficient to

7TH CAMPAIGN

warm them or ourselves. The wind was particularly cutting & when accompanied by sleet & obliged to face it on horseback, which was constantly required, it was really most trying to the constitution. The frost became intense & the inhabitants being supplied with water from public pumps, the water as it fell from the spouts congealed & at last choked it, so that it was necessary to throw warm water onto the body of the pump to make the piston work; it was considered an unusual cold season but our men did not suffer from it from being in general well housed.

During the month of December all the allied troops, the Army of Occupation excepted, having gradually evacuated France and the French government appearing to improve in stability, it was thought advisable for the army alluded to, to make a demonstration of withdrawing a certain distance & thereby leave Paris & [the] country beyond it unoccupied by foreigners, so as to leave the administration to organise itself unfettered by external influence. We were therefore ordered to move back from Versailles & adjacents and occupy St Denis [Saint Denis], Luzarches, Pontoise & other places, which took place in the first days of January 1816 & there we remained nearly a month, without any incident but watching (I suppose) the march of events in the capital.

We were now maintained under the stipulations of the Treaty of Peace, at the general expense of the French nation & therefore not pressing on individual localities as before, the inconvenience [of] which the inhabitants were subject to, being that (no small one) of having to lodge us in their houses & obliged to give up a certain number of rooms with decent furniture according to the rank of the officer, the houses being chosen to meet that object according to size or capacity. My comparative rank was not above that of captain but being head of a department I was rated as Field officer;[61] even then my accommodation was not of the best, but I succeeded generally

---

61 Field officers were those of the rank of major, lieutenant colonel and colonel.

in being quartered on decent people, at times superior & at times inferior to the grade of gentility. My knowledge however of the language making me welcome almost invariably & when that did not happen I left my landlord alone, exacting only what I had a right to.

The discipline kept up in our *corps d'armée* was strict as usual & the French people could not but laud the conduct of our men, many knowing how infamously their own had behaved in foreign countries and I am sure the contrast was invidiously annoying to them, though they were deriving the benefit of it. Even the magistrates could not at times conceal their opinion in their official letters to me. I extract the following from one of the letters received by me from the sous prefect of the town of Pontoise now before me, dated the 2 January 1816:

> 'Je lui recommande de prendre toutes les mesures pour que l'armée Anglaise don't je me plais à reconnaître hautement l'admirable discipline, n'ait désormais aucun subject de plainte d'aucun genre, mes sentimens personels sont en parfaite harmonie avec les intentions formelles du roi pour le bien être des gens de Guerre de votre nation'.

> [I am recommended to take all the measures so that the English army, whose admirable discipline I am pleased to highly recognise, henceforth has no subject of complaint of any kind. My personal feelings are in perfect harmony with the formal intentions of the king for the welfare of the soldiers of your nation]

> Again, 'Les bons habitants des campagnes on vos troupes sont venus après le départ des autres armées disent que vos soldats sont des anges; ils en out logés quietement de vrais démons, et certes je ne me consolerais point success de nos Allies, qui par leur douceur et leurs parfaite discipline ont

7TH CAMPAIGN

rappelé a mes administrés l'idée du ciel n'étaient pas traites encore mieux que ceux qui n'ont montre que de la sévérité tout aux moins'.

[The good inhabitants of the countryside where your troops came, after the departure of the other armies, say that your soldiers are angels; they quietly housed real demons and certainly I would not console myself had they shown the least severity]

In a letter from the sous prefect of Bethune (north of France) of the 17 January [1816] in answer to mine announcing that we were soon to march to occupy that part of the country, he mentions without having as yet seen us, that ...

'nous ne demandons certainement pas mieux que de recevoir les troupes de sa Majesté Britannique, car nous savons l'excellente conduit et l'exacte discipline quelles observant partout'.

[we certainly ask for nothing better than to receive the troops of His Britannic Majesty, for we know the excellent conduct and the exact discipline which they observe everywhere.]

It will thus be seen that our good reputation travelled before us and I will say we fully deserved it, in contrast with our allies and for the 3 years the occupation lasted there was no relaxation of good conduct on our part to the best understanding being kept up between our soldiers & the peasantry on whom they were billeted, to the final evacuation of the country in the latter end of 1818.

During the month of January [1816] arrangements were gradually making for taking up our permanent quarters in that part of the country which we were finally to occupy while we remained in France watching its internal tranquillity & its getting gradually accustomed to a new system of government which was not exactly to their own choice, but in great degree imposed on them by force of arms.

I accordingly received through the Commissary General a memorandum dated Paris the 21 [January], containing the march Route of our division to commence on the 23rd & proceed from Luzarches, Oreil [Orry-la-Ville] &c our existing cantonments, through Clermont, Breteuil, Amiens, to St Pol [Saint-Pol-sur-Ternoise] in the Department du Pas de Calais, from whence we were to be distributed in all the adjacent towns & villages extending to a considerable distance on the road to Calais. This march occupied a week & was effected without incident to relate, the inhabitants received us with civility but could not repress their joy at being rid of foreign troops however good their conduct might be. We reached our destination on the 1 February and found St Pol [Saint-Pol-sur-Ternoise], though the head of a Sous Prefecture, a miserable town with very indifferent accommodation for either officers or men; as most of the latter however were to occupy villages & farms, their chance of being comfortably put up was greater than that of their superiors. The roads also of communication between the villages were detestable, knee deep in mud or snow & it was only on the chaussées (paved roads) that anyone could ride with any degree of comfort & these were so few as not to be of much use.

By some mistake I found on my arrival that the house intended for me had been allotted to Sir N Douglas commanding the regiment stationed in this town,[62] which led to a correspondence between our Assistant Quarter Master General Colonel Woodford[63] (whose duty it was to see me righted) & myself and as he appeared in a dilemma & yet desirous to do all he could for me, I thought it as well to give up the point & take the

---

62 Lieutenant Colonel Sir Neil Douglas commanded the 79th Foot.

63 Lieutenant Colonel John George Woodford, 1st Foot Guards, Assistant Quartermaster General.

7TH CAMPAIGN

best lodging that could be obtained, which I found quite as comfortable as I could wish, my landlord being an old man who afforded me the conveniences I stood in need of, but showed no desire to be sociable, so that I seldom saw him & our intercourse never exceeded a good morning or afternoon & thus we jogged on for four months.

Sir Henry Clinton who commanded the division had his wife (Lady Sarah [Susan][64]) with him & not finding a suitable house in St Pol [sur Ternoise] his headquarters for his family & personal Staff (viz his aides de camp) went some miles off on the road to Hesdin & occupied the Chateau d'Estruval near the small hamlet of Neulette, an excellent residence and a chateau of the *vieille noblesse*,[65] but as I was obliged to be in almost daily communication with him in respect to the supply of the troops & various other matters, I found it a great inconvenience to lose so many hours on horseback when required in the office and elsewhere. For my duties became incessant from the arrangements which should have been made by the French administration for our reception being found in a very backward state, in the immense extent of country we were spread over. For some of the troops of the division were in some instances forty miles apart & the service had to be organised to an extent little expected and embracing upwards of 140 towns, villages & hamlets.

The division consisted of the lieutenant general commanding and his personal Staff, viz an Assistant Adjutant General[66] and Assistant Quarter Master General,[67] Commissariat and Medical officers,[68]

---

64 Carey is in error here, Sir Henry Clinton had married Lady Susan (née Charteris), the daughter of Francis Wemyss Charteris, 7th Lord Elcho, on 23 December 1799. She unfortunately died on 17 August 1816.

65 The Chateau d'Estruval is now abandoned. It is in the commune of Le Parcq rather than Neulette and is 18km (11.2 miles) distant from Saint Pol sur Ternoise.

66 Major Charles Bentinck, 2nd Foot Guards, was AAG to the 2nd Division.

67 Lieutenant Colonel John Woodford was AQMG to the 2nd Division.

68 Deputy Inspector of Hospitals Summers Higgins was senior medical officer in the 2nd Division.

officers of Engineers, Commissariat Waggon Train usually called General Staff,[69] 2 brigades of artillery commanded by Major Rogers[70] & Captain Sandham,[71] with twelve guns & a brigade of artillery waggons carrying the spare ball cartridge ammunition.

The body of infantry consisted as follows:-

3rd Brigade composed of the [1/]3rd, [1/]39th & [1/]91st Regiments. Commanded by a major general[72]

4th Brigade composed of the [1/] 4th, [1/]52nd & [1/]79th Regiments. Commanded by a major general[73]

6th Brigade composed of the [1/]6th, 29th & [1/]71st Regiments. Commanded by a major general[74]

comprising a strength of upwards of 9,000 officers and soldiers, servants and followers &c and horses of all descriptions.

The British contingent of which the above formed a part & consisting of 3 divisions of infantry & three brigades of cavalry with 6 brigades of artillery & 54 field guns, included a small corps of each of the following nations viz Hanoverians, Danes & Saxons, forming

---

69 The Baggage Master for 2nd Division was named McCurry and the Assistant Provost Marshal was named Lukin.

70 Major Thomas Roger's brigade of Foot Artillery consisting of five 9-pounders and one 5½in howitzer. The Commissary attached was DACG Robert Cotes.

71 Captain Charles Sandham commanded a brigade of Foot Artillery consisting of five 9-pounders and one 5½in howitzer. The commissary attached was DACG William Lukin.

72 The 3rd Brigade was commanded by Major General Robert O'Callaghan. His Brigade Major was McPherson. The Chaplain was Edward Frith. The commissary attached was initially ACG Edward Robinson, subsequently ACG David Carruthers and Dee.

73 The 4th Brigade was commanded by Major General Dennis Pack. The Chaplain was John Metcalfe. The commissary attached was initially DACG William Miller and subsequently Nicholas Turner.

74 The 6th Brigade was commanded by Major General Thomas Bradford. His Brigade Major was Lieutenant William Elliott, 51st Foot. The Chaplain was Charles Dayman. The commissary attached was initially DACG William Cundell.

an army of 40,000 effective men besides followers. The Russian contingent of equal strength was immediately next to our right, then that of Prussia & lastly that of Austria,[75] in facing Paris we were therefore on the right of the army & the Austrians on the left.

We occupied what is usually denominated the Iron Frontier of France but not all its fortified places, each contingent possessing only those on one line of road leading clear from & into that kingdom; for example the French troops in very limited numbers held Arras, Lille, St Omer & Calais, and we the parallel fortresses of Cambrai, Valenciennes, Bouchain &c so that our communications with the Netherlands & England by Boulogne were uninterrupted in case of a renewal of active operations either offensive or defensive, each contingent having in its front or rear the same facilities of communication with Prussia & Austria. We ourselves thus held possession of the departments [of] Pas de Calais and du Nord & the other nations those in which they were cantoned forming a belt of French territory extending from Calais to Switzerland.

Since the signature of the Treaty of Peace and according to its conditions, the Army of Occupation was paid & maintained by the French government, but as we had been hitherto on the move, the arrangements connected therewith had only been of a temporary nature. However now regular contracts were entered into under the superintendence of the French Commissariat who were accordingly stationed in various parts of our cantonments with their chief at Cambrai, the headquarters of the army. The *Commissaries des Guerres* (as they are called) were generally very respectable men, but we found the contractors under them as unprincipled as they could well be, giving us constant trouble in their endeavours to impose inferior articles of provisions & forage on the troops and I am sorry to say the former gave them more support than they ought to have

---

75 The Army of Occupation comprised five armies of 30,000 men each; being Austrian, British, Russian and Prussian; the final army consisting of 10,000 Bavarians and 5,000 from each of Denmark, Saxony, Hanover and Württemberg.

done. But seeing that neither could be trusted, our vigilance became a constant duty and though we could never conquer their roguery, we succeeded in keeping them in check & at last convinced them that it would not be tolerated. They lauded our good discipline but abused our overbearing exactions in regard to the quality of the food, not perceiving as they ought to have done, that one depended on the other; their interest rendering them blind to the moral principle which governed both.

In framing the conditions of the quantity of provisions to be issued to this army, our stupid diplomatists forgot as usual the difference of the ration allowed to the British & foreign soldier and had it not been subsequently corrected would have changed the diet of the former, which he would not have put up with quietly. The principal difference was in the bread & meat, the foreign soldier receiving daily 2 lbs [0.9kg] of the former & half a pound [0.22kg] of the latter, with a small proportion of vegetables, or rice, salt & a portion of spirits, whereas our men were accustomed to 1½ pounds [0.68kg] of bread & 1 pound [0.45kg] of meat with spirits, he providing vegetables from his pay, but as the former ration was not equivalent in price to the latter, our government had to pay the difference & thus the difficulty was obviated.

In respect to the officer's rations & allowances, ours benefited by the treaty, for being framed on the continental system, which increased according to rank, while in the British army an officer whatever may be his rank only receives a soldier's ration; we consequently got more than we were entitled to or could consume in kind. A commutation in money was therefore agreed to & by it the officer as far as regarded his own interests and maintenance was not placed in contact with the contractors, so that he could use his individual efforts in favour of the soldier.

When all these points had been settled the people got accustomed to our presence & the service became progressively more regular, but in such quiet quarters the monotony became most tiresome, especially to the officers of the army, for as regarded the officers of

7TH CAMPAIGN

the Commissariat we had full employment in making up accounts, compiling returns for the Commissary General superintending the supplies and attending to many other minor details of the service.

Having had occasion for a supply of money for the public expenditure, [and] being desirous of communicating personally with my superiors at Cambrai, I proceed[ed] there one day with a few men of the 79th Highlanders (who happened to be of the grenadier company) to serve as an escort to the money I was to bring back. Our Route was by Arras, a fortified town occupied by a small French garrison and according to agreement was not to be used as a place through which detachments of the Army of Occupation could pass, or be accommodated with a night's lodging unless they deposited their arms at the gate by which they entered. It was therefore customary to be billeted in the suburbs and having gone to the Maire for the billets, the report of Scotch soldiers having arrived had reached him, he at once expressed a desire to receive them into the town unconditionally. Knowing that they would fare better under such circumstances, I at once acquiesced to his proposal and the detachment consisting of a sergeant and six men were accordingly marched in & as the report had spread among the inhabitants that soldiers without breeches & actual *sans culottes*, were coming in, the crowd collected to witness their arrival was immense, for no one would believe without ocular demonstration that such a dress existed. There they were however and being all very fine men with their high & plumed bonnets & kilts &c, continued objects of admiration until they departed early next morning. They were taken in, in some of the most respectable houses & most kindly treated; to account for this predilection would require to go back to the period when the ancient monarchy had in their service a Scotch Brigade & regularly recruited from Scotland & originating from the refugees of that nation who followed the fortunes of James the Second, the memory of whom occasionally in garrison in this town, will have lingered among the oldest inhabitants, or been handed down to the existing population. For these soldiers had the happy art of making themselves beloved wherever they happened to be, and which was imitated by their modern countrymen at Brussels before the Battle of Waterloo.

As to myself, in regard to what I have just related, having still a good deal of the day before me, I pushed on to my destination having a fresh horse at hand, a mode I usually adopted whenever I had to make the journey, by which I was enabled to perform it in the day without interruption, it being as far as I recollect from 40 to 45 miles.

In occupying the country in a military manner, it was not understood that we should interfere with the existing civil administration. The authority of the magistrates was therefore respected as if we were not on the spot, with the exception that crimes committed by our men on or in which the inhabitants were concerned, instead of being taken into custody by the native power they were tried by court martial and punished according to our code of law, much more severe than those of the country & administered under the established strict discipline kept up by us.

Whenever it was unavoidably necessary to call on the authorities for provisions or cart or waggon transport, in case of failure by the contractors, the Commissariat was the sole channel of communication between the troops & the inhabitants, the former not being allowed to help themselves on any account & to avoid wants of this nature the local magistrate or French Commissary was authorised to make an immediate but limited contract called a '*Marche d'urgence*' with any individual on the spot to meet the temporary difficulty and the operation being usually an expensive one for the government or contractors, it was seldom found necessary to have recourse to it. In this way harmony was preserved, and after a while the soldiers became so familiarised & on good terms with the farmers & their families that on Sunday evenings it was not at all unusual for the former to be seen accompanying the latter to their durafores [*sic*] or dances, held on the village green or neighbouring hamlet & mix with them, tripping on the light fantastic toe as if they had been

7TH CAMPAIGN

accustomed to it all their lives & being most of them smart handsome fellows, they became in time favourites beyond (I am afraid to say) the strict rules of morality.

In mixing thus with the country people & entering their farmhouses, it was found that one of their familiar singing airs was '*Malbrook* [*Marlborough*] *s'en va en* [*guerre*]' [Malbrough is leaving for war] and was used as a lullaby to rock their children to sleep; the origin of it was the wars of the great Duke of Marlborough & his periodical inroads in that part of the country, occasioning so much dread in the inhabitants that it became proverbial & served as a warning to their posterity; the air however is said to be by some persons of comparative modern date.[76]

In the month of April the distribution of the Waterloo Medal took place to the officers & soldiers who had been in that action, the Commissariat not being included, which was considered a great injustice on the ground that it was given to a division of the army under Sir Charles Colville stationed in observation at Halle which never knew of the action until announced to it next morning, as well as to numbers of officers & men absent & not in the ranks because they were on the strength of their regiments. The only way to account for it is that the Duke of Wellington took a dislike to the department because the supplies which were in more than adequate quantities near Waterloo were not brought up for distribution to the position, owing to the panics among the foreign troops & followers of the army (the extent & confusion of which was never made known to him) which occurred during the 17th & 18th & led to the drivers of the Commissariat wagons, consisting of peasantry forced in[to] the

---

76 The air 'Marlbrough s'en va-t-en guerre' also known as 'Mort et convoy de l'invincible Marlbrough' or 'The Death and Burial of the Invincible Marlborough' is a popular folk song in France to this day. It was written on a false rumour that the Duke of Marlborough had been killed at the Battle of Malplaquet in 1709. The song tells of Marlborough's wife awaiting his return at home, receiving the news of his death, his burial and that a nightingale sang over his grave. The melody travelled to Britain where the words 'For he's a jolly good fellow' were used.

service with their horses, to run away with their animals & abandoning their loaded waggons which no human effort could have prevented in the midst of the existing disorder. Unfortunately when once His Grace took a prejudice or dislike to anyone, nothing could remove it; it was sternly fixed in his mind & to eradicate it was impossible. Several officers of the army in the course of the Peninsular service fell into disgrace for causes over which they had no control and yet he never exonerated them; it was enough that he had so determined for him never to relent. This tenacity was a blot in his character; on the other hand however, when once he took a liking to anyone he never lost an opportunity to serve him.

Our Assistant Quarter Master General Colonel Woodford was an antiquarian & collector of curiosities and having found that the village of Azincourt usually called Agincourt in England was situated in our cantonments, resolved to make some researches if possible on the ground where the battle was fought. The priest of the village was understood to be the Cicerone[77] in pointing out the various spots most remarkable of the fight & on which the greatest slaughter had occurred & though the features of the country as far as woods & cultivated land had changed, the colonel satisfied himself that the account given was sufficiently correct to induce him to proceed in his determination. With great secrecy he first purchased from the farmers the right of excavating and immediately set to work with as many hands as could be obtained. He continued undisturbed for two or three days but a report having reached the Sous Prefect of what he was doing, that functionary ordered him to desist, but using his right of purchase he declined & continued his work. The Sous Prefect finding his remonstrances ineffectual addressed the Prefect, who wrote to the French Minister at Paris & the latter having represented the circumstance to the Duke of Wellington, orders came to the colonel to discontinue the undertaking, on the plea that the

---

77 A knowledgeable guide.

7TH CAMPAIGN

French government thought it advisable to leave the ashes of the dead to rest in peace. By the time however that the order reached him his curiosity was satisfied, in not having met with the success he expected, for though he had worked on a favourable spot & found many remains of arms, armour & bones &c they were in such a state of decay as hardly worth removing. He found however with other trifles, a ring in good preservation still adhering to the bone of a finger with a heartsease[78] & motto engraved on it with several others & a skull with a spearhead transfixed through it. When the affair was in progress the French people got annoyed, particularly when the event of the conflict awoke (as it were in their minds) and was not redounding to the national glory. It was also a singular coincidence that the site of Crecy, so celebrated as a feat of arms, was not far removed from the limit of country in our occupation.

During much part of the period that I was in the neighbourhood of Paris a good deal of my leisure time had been occupied in answering voluminous queries on my Peninsular accounts from the Audit Office in London and having at last waded through the business, rendered most disagreeable from having to trust to my memory for circumstances which were almost forgotten in that active & harassing period of life, I felt secure that I should without further trouble, be continued in my present post during the occupation of the country by the allied army. In this dream however of certainty I received unexpectedly in the month of June an order to give over my charge to a successor[79] & proceed to England without delay to answer another set of queries which it appeared I had neglected to do & I found several of my brother officers equally implicated in the same oversight. I of course lost no time in closing my public transactions and only a few hours being required to pack up, I left St Pol [Saint-Pol-sur-Ternoise] for London, proceeding by Lillers, Aire [-sur-la-Lys], St Omer [Saint-

---

78 A wild European pansy.

79 He was succeeded by Assistant Commissary General David Carruthers.

Omer], Calais & Dover & reached my destination without any incident worth relating at the end of the month.

I went at once to the office of the Commissary in Chief, reported my arrival & received orders to go to the Audit Office to transact the business for which I had been recalled to England and there I found it was a mere clerical error in adding up a column of dollars & charging one more than the real amount & carrying on the mistake to the next page, by which the public would have lost the extraordinary sum of four shillings and sixpence had it not been detected.[80] I at once acknowledged the unintentional error and refunded the amount, but I felt extremely annoyed at having been removed from active duty for so trifling a transaction and more especially as it had been already intimated to me that when no longer required to settle whatever the business might be, I was to consider myself on half pay at the expiration of one month from that date. Such was the manner of punishing officers (trifling as the cause might be) adopted by the authorities in those times, which in the end brought on considerable expenses to government which might have been avoided by simply directing me to pay back at once the sum in question, which I would have complied with without the least hesitation, for my travelling expenses from & to the army were afterwards allowed to be charged to my credit in my accounts.

Finding therefore that my case had not been fairly considered and in my opinion was an injustice not to be borne quietly, I remonstrated with the Commissary in Chief Herries[81] in as strong language as I dare do, to which I received in reply, a sharp admonition accompanied however by an intimation that a letter would be written to the Commissary General in France to ascertain if any services were required in that country & I afterwards learnt that the Duke of Wellington on being referred to, replied that he was always desirous

---

80 About £15 in today's terms.

81 Commissary in Chief John Herries.

7TH CAMPAIGN

of having officers who had previously served under him in preference to others. Waiting a reply to Mr Herries' letter which was nearly two months coming to me, I went over to Guernsey & there enjoyed myself in the bosom of my large family & while there happily occupied, I received a letter from my chief dated 9 September directing me to proceed at once to Cambray [Cambrai], the headquarters of the allied army in France & report myself to Commissary General Bisset.[82] Desirous of having another peep at Paris & go over a new road to me, I obtained leave to proceed the way I wished, on condition that no loss of time occurred or additional expense took place.

I accordingly took a passport for myself & servant for St Malo intending to go through Normandy to Paris & on to my destination. I sailed for the former place on the 19th in a small sailing cutter, the usual conveyance of those times & reached it in a few hours. I found it a large, walled, dull place & its former extensive commerce completely annihilated by the war and as it contained nothing interesting I lost no time in taking my place & that for my servant in the diligence[83] for Caen starting early the next morning of [*sic* – after] our arrival. We filled it but I was disappointed of a seat in the coupee [*sic*], which however mattered not, for some hours our progress was undisturbed & we enjoyed beautiful views of the country, among which to our left was the distant one of Mont St Michel [Mont Saint-Michel], conical in shape, surrounded by the sea, on the top or crown of which there existed a far famed monastery & now turned into a state prison. While thus on our way, the diligence was suddenly ordered to stop by a mounted gendarme who demanded to see our passports & at that time the greatest strictness prevailed in their examination. Mine was a military one & had not been exchanged by the Sous Prefect of St Malo as was the usual course with those of civilians, but merely countersigned by

---

82 Commissary General John Bisset.

83 The diligence was a large four-wheeled enclosed coach which had up to sixteen seats internally.

him which he told me was sufficient. When it came to my turn the gendarme objected to it not considering it in règle [to rule] & he ended in saying that he must detain me. I shewed him the Sous Prefect's signature & my sword, to prove my being *a militaire* on my way to join the Duke's army & moreover that I was the bearer of public papers, the responsibility of which he must take upon himself if I was not allowed to proceed. This staggered him & the other passengers getting impatient & clamorous as well as the conductor, off went the horses in the midst of his hesitation & we were relieved from a disagreeable dilemma, for he allowed us to go without further interference. No wonder however that he was puzzled how to act, my passport being in English which he was unable to read & different in shape to those he was accustomed to.

The pace we went in our lumbering machine was very slow & tedious, reaching Caen at night of which of course I saw little & being allowed only a few hours rest, we started the next day to travel until we reached Paris, stopping of course for meals &c. We reached Mantes [-la-Jolie] for supper & there the gastronomic powers of Frenchmen were fully exemplified and put to the test, for in taking our places at the table, great piles of ecrevisses (crayfish) ready for consumption, the place being famous for producing them in perfection, ample justice was therefore done to confirm their celebrity, for I may say they were devoured & how such quantities of indigestible manner could be stowed away in the human stomach has been ever since a subject of astonishment to me, for shells only remained when we were summoned to return to the diligence.

After passing through several towns among which was St Germain [Saint-Germaine-en-Laye] we reached the barrier of Paris early in the day, where our baggage was to be examined, [to ensure] that we did not introduce articles such as bread, meat, wine or other articles paying duty (octroi[84]) on introduction into the city for consumption. A process of course quite unnecessary as far as I was concerned and

---

84 A local tax on certain items.

7TH CAMPAIGN

which equally applied to my fellow passengers among whose luggage nothing of the sort was discovered; still the scrutiny was enforced though most leniently to those of whom they had no suspicion.

My stay in Paris must, I was aware be a short one & not to extend beyond two or three days, so that with the time occupied in having my passport examined & signed at different places & going from place to place as to refresh my memory & recollections, I had not a moments leisure to go either to Boulogne [-Billancourt] or Versailles to see old acquaintances.

After the exciting scenes I witnessed last year, I found the place dull & the people not over civil & meeting with no acquaintances I started for my destination on the 26th, as usual by diligence & reached Cambrai on the 28th without any material incident only that I found it was as well to say as little as possible of the allied army or my belonging to it to prevent the probability of unpleasant altercations with individuals still smarting with the recollections of grievances of which they had to complain.

On the morning of the 29th, when I knew the Commissariat Office was open, I went there and reported myself to Commissary General Bisset with whom I had a long interview. After some preliminary conversation he asked me if I knew French; I replied in the affirmative & rendered him aware of the extent of my knowledge in it. He expressed himself satisfied & said I was the person he stood in need of, to fill a situation which only a person conversant in that language was able to undertake. I was therefore obliged to give up all chance of returning to my former duty at St Pol [Saint-Pol-sur-Ternoise] with the 2nd Division, thereby exchanging a comparative easy task to one of much greater importance requiring at times great tact and constant attention.

As the French government was under the obligation of maintaining the allied army in France in pay and whatever else it required, a *Commission Mixte* (as it was called) was established at the headquarters of the four great contingents viz Austrian, English,

Prussian & Russian, composed each of four members, viz two allied and two French, which commission superintended every branch of the service, provided against existing difficulties, attended to all complaints made either by the troops or inhabitants and examined the various documents connected with items of provisions &c to prevent any overdrawing beyond what was stipulated by treaty.

When first organised the two British Commissaries appointed to our contingent were of superior rank to me, the senior Deputy Commissary General Dumaresq a native of Jersey knew French well, but the other hardly understood it which was of much inconvenience as all preliminary business was discussed in it & determined on at the meetings of the board which the latter could hardly be expected to join in effectively & enforce his opinion. The former was a testy little man & they did not long remain on good terms & just before my arrival so serious had been their misunderstandings that the Duke was appealed to & it was decided that they should be both removed, but there was no one in the Department sufficiently au fait in the required language to replace the former especially, who was the leading man. My arrival was therefore very opportune to prevent the service being put to inconvenience, and I was appointed in the first instance the junior member & to replace the senior one so soon as he had made me acquainted with the various details of the duty, which was soon effected & it is gratifying for me to mention that I remained in the execution of it upwards of two years & during the period the allied troops remained in France.

The Duke of Wellington with his immense Staff & departments were quartered in Cambrai (but he himself & his personal Staff occupied besides the Chateau of Mont St Martin some miles distant on the road to Paris) with two strong battalions of Guards, artillery & innumerable followers of the army which made billets extremely scarce and I was therefore obliged to put up with a very inferior lodging in a house in which a school was kept, the noise & racket of which, being overhead, became a great nuisance. Fortunately

7TH CAMPAIGN

however, I was seldom at home & I managed sometime after, through my intercourse with the French Commissaries of the commission, to get into a better house (*Rue de la Comédie*) in which I resided during the time I remained in Cambrai.

I had hardly been installed in my functions when preparations were to be made for the concentration of the troops in the neighbourhood of Denain on the plain of which the French had obtained a victory over the Austrians I believe, on some former occasion.[85] The Russian contingent was included in the arrangement so that we were likely to muster above 60,000 men, the Emperor of Russia & King of Prussia were to be present and it was understood that the same manoeuvres were to be repeated by those assembled troops as took place in the action alluded to.

It was of course, a Holy day & everyone of the civil administration of the army who could attend availed themselves of the opportunity and I among many others could not resist the temptation; several of us started for the field early in the morning & arrived there just before the crowned heads accompanied by the Duke had made their appearance. The British contingent including those of Saxony, Denmark and Hanover was formed in contiguous columns on the left of the chaussée or high road & the Russian contingent in the same manner on the right of the same road, the right of one being only separated from the left of the other by that road. In the midst of our troops there stood an obelisk erected by the French as a trophy to commemorate their victory & there it remains uninjured, as all we did was to read the inscription which I do not however recollect.

Every preparation being made & which was succeeded by a moment of quiescence and expectation, a bustle was perceived in the rear & immediately after the great host of distinguished persons made their appearance & at once proceeded to an eminence from which the

---

85 The Battle of Denain, fought on 24 July 1712, resulted in a victory for the French Marshal Villers over a Dutch/Austrian force under Prince Eugene of Savoy.

whole of the troops could be perceived extending to a considerable distance right & left with all the country in the front, the scene of the future operations & then a little hand map on a card containing the detail of them, was presented to the sovereigns & some of the principal persons present. After which that cavalcade proceeded to take a hasty look at the troops from left to right & on its arriving near the Russian contingent, there arose a succession of shouts from each battalion as their emperor was seen approaching. When this was over & the sovereigns had got to a conspicuous, or I should say commanding point, the manoeuvres commenced by a pack of cossacks being ordered to proceed across the river & occupy some high ground at a considerable distance. They started apparently without order like a swarm of bees, as fast as their horses could carry them, galloping over everything in their way & dashing into the water like so many ducks, reaching in a very short time their destination & there formed up. The more regular troops then commenced their movements in columns & advancing, firing and storming imaginary obstacles, crossing the river, attacking the enemy's positions & exhibiting all the operations of a fight without bloodshed, which made it the more interesting. The sovereigns were taken by the Duke to different points from which the operations could be best perceived until the day being far spent the troops returned to their respective camps.

At the commencement of the operations I perceived that the King of Prussia with a single aide de camp left the cavalcade privately & intermingled with our troops, no doubt to observe their mode of proceeding in advancing, taking up ground &c, for at that time our military capabilities stood very high in the opinion of all our allies, but I think a great deal more depended on the indomitable character of the British soldier when well led than to tactics. The great people were afterwards entertained by the Duke [of Wellington] for three days, during which a succession of parties, dinners, balls &c were given, but I was not in a position to partake of them from the preference given to the number of superior officers on the spot. I received

7TH CAMPAIGN

however an invitation to the Great Ball which was considered the crowning point of the entertainments, the decorations of which were it was said superintended by His Grace in person, assisted by several soldiers of the Guards who had before they enlisted been employed in Vauxhall Gardens. There was a garden behind his house laid out *en parterre*[86] with several small ponds and as a great crowd was expected & not sufficient room within, they were boarded over & on them the dancing parties enjoyed themselves. His Grace in his baggage had an enormous circular Indian tent which he had obtained at the taking of Seringapatam belonging to Tippoo Sa[h]ib[87] & having considerably lengthened the pole, it was suspended over the garden appearing like a dome; to all the radiating cords of which lamps were suspended, which with other decorations & the brilliancy of the company gave the whole scene a magnificence which from not being expected was the more fairy-like and striking. From the habit we had got into of frequently seeing royalty, the presence of the sovereigns was no novelty, we therefore did not run after them or their retinues, which we left to the French to do. The Ball like every other, went off with great eclat & spirit & in the course of it the supper rooms were thrown open containing all the delicacies of the season, among which I was particularly struck by observing many dishes of artificial fruits, which though very ornamental, [but] were not much esteemed by those who looked more to gratify their appetites than to admire those imitations of nature pleasing to the eye but not to the palate. As this period of festivity was attended by many & viewed in various ways, it was said that several officers amused themselves to calculate the cost & that the Duke in those three days could not have expended less than £1,000 a day.[88]

---

86 A flat area with formal arrangements of plants.

87 The Sultan Tippoo Sahib was ruler of Mysore in India. He was killed at the storming of Seringapatam in 1799.

88 At least £60,000 per day at today's values.

FEEDING WELLINGTON'S ARMY FROM BURGOS TO WATERLOO

In the autumn of this year my brother Sausmarez paid me a visit; I have mentioned before that he had entered the Commissariat in May 1815 & of course before the Battle of Waterloo & great reductions having taken place in the department at the peace, he was paid off after having been kept in Paris some time, winding [up] some accounts & when he came to me he was on his way home by Cambrai & Calais &c. I was delighted with his company & entertained him as well as I could & having two horses & the greyhounds, he found plenty of amusement in coursing, hares abounding in the country & he seldom returned home without two or three hanging to his saddle bow. One of my horses was a thoroughbred chestnut gelding which had been in the Prince Regent's stables, but being found too slight, was sent with others to France for disposal & I bought him for £50;[89] he enjoyed sport quite as much as his rider whoever he might be & when once the hare was started there was no necessity of encouraging him for all that need be done was to slack the rein, hold on & let him have his way & he was sure to be the foremost of the field & near at the death. The country was open without hedges, a little hilly & therefore affording capital runs which were however occasionally interrupted by cabbage plantations, in which the hare took shelter & was lost. By a little practise the haunts of the animal were ascertained and we found that in the neighbourhood of a particular village we were sure to obtain a course after having rode over other ground to no purpose. Although with much to do, I occasionally joined the field and afterwards partook of capital hare soup made out of what we had bagged. After keeping this horse so long as I had occasion for him, I sold him to our Commissary General Sir John Bisset who had taken a great fancy to him & intended taking him to England for his future use.

Sporting of another sort was also occasionally indulged in, but not being myself particularly fond of it, or a good shot, I accompanied a friend as a kind of retriever from possessing a good eyesight & by

---

89 About £3,000 today.

7TH CAMPAIGN

knowing the language of the country which enabled me to ascertain by enquiry where game most abounded. We usually started in a gig[90] with a dog or two, drove eight or ten miles on road & having put up our conveyance at a public house, enquired for the village functionary called *Le Garde de Chasse* [gamekeeper]; when found I informed him that we were officers of the British army desirous of a little sport & would be thankful to him to point out where it could be found. A little familiar conversation pleased him and though he told us it was not lawful to use a gun, or shoot without the leave of the landlord, his scruples were overcome on reflecting that he might make us an exception to the rule & it usually ended in his accompanying us. While my friend shot, the Frenchman & myself halted together & as we had heard that tobacco manufactured in England, though prohibited was infinitely preferred to that grown in the country, we provided ourselves with a roll of it and while walking, his pipe was replenished as often as it required & a further portion given him & in the enjoyment of it he became more disposed to point out the spots whereabouts partridges, quail &c abounded so that we never failed to bring home a good supply & to leave a favourable impression on our new acquaintance. We gave him in parting a five frank [*sic*] piece (4/2d)[91] which he no doubt found a good wage for a day's work. In returning home we showed the contents of our bag but kept to ourselves the mode adopted to fill it, as there would have been too many competitors to try it without the certainty of its failure. We had therefore recourse to it whenever leisure or inclination disposed us & it almost invariably succeeded but could not often be repeated at the same place for fear of bringing the individual into trouble for not doing his duty more strictly & warning us off according to the existing game laws, for though our position under existing circumstances was an exception not provided for, it

---

90 A gig or chaise was a light two-wheeled sprung cart.

91 About £15 in today's terms.

might be tolerated if civilly asked for. John Bull would not however do so always & therefore occasionally met with opposition.

After a residence of some months in Cambrai I had become acquainted with most of the Commissariat officers employed in the several offices there. Eight of us formed a mess which we kept at the residence of him who was the best quartered; his name was William Booth, Assistant Commissary General of Accounts,[92] a favourite of the Duke; his duty was to draw out all warrants for his Grace's signature, examine the accounts of the army & ascertain their correctness as well as all matters connected with military expenditure, which having brought them in, frequent intercourse led eventually to his being taken under the Duke's protection and being appointed to an excellent situation in Ireland, that of Ordnance Storekeeper, which he now enjoys & such was the confidence reposed in him that he was often consulted on the Duke's private affairs and I well remember seeing in his possession the accounts for examination of the Spanish estate of Soto de Roma presented by the Spanish nation to the Duke,[93] the rent roll of which amounted to 28,000 dollars, equal in sterling to £6,300 yearly[94] for the year it was made up & by this scrutiny many inaccuracies were detected, which kept his steward in check & which His Grace might not have succeeded in finding out had he himself looked into them, but for which he had no leisure. The other members of the mess were younger than our two selves but well informed and gentlemanly, so that the society thus formed proved very agreeable & lasted until we all separated to return home or to other stations.

We had our 'stranger days', for entertaining our friends & when any one of them was known to have lately come from England it was

---

92 Assistant Commissary General William Booth.

93 Sota de Roma was granted to the Duke of Wellington and his male heirs in perpetuity by the Spanish king in gratitude for his help in driving the French out. It consists of 4,000 acres of land 16km from Granada.

94 Approximately £400,000 per annum at today's values.

7TH CAMPAIGN

usual to have a dish of frogs provided & disguised under the name of stewed small birds, many ate of it without apparent disquiet after being told what it really was, but on one or two occasions it created a sensation by its bringing on sickness and obliging the individuals to leave the table for a time, although some time had elapsed before the nature of the dish was made known to them. I now & then partook of this French delicacy but did not find it sufficiently tempting to trouble it often, for I thought it insipid & less tasty than either chicken or rabbit which it resembled in whiteness of flesh.

Another relation of mine, Daniel Tupper, paid me a visit about this time on his way to England from Paris and I took him to a Ball at the municipality which was attended by all the great folks in the garrison, as well as the principal inhabitants of the town & I can with truth say he was as handsome a man as anyone present, tall, square built, manly with good features and dark complexion. This Ball was a weekly subscription one called 'Bal de Société' established by the inhabitants of the first class, to which the officers were honorary members and our subscription was one pound sterling for the season or ten pence (a franc) for each,[95] twenty-four being given in the year, which economical charge paid for the lighting, waxing the floors & music; the refreshments consumed being an extra expense & paid for by each individual & supplied from a buffet in an adjoining saloon, to those having recourse to it & we followed the example of the Frenchmen who when thirsty, ordered a bottle of wine & not consuming it at the moment, had it put aside for use in the course of the evening. These balls were frequently attended by the Duke & Duchess of Wellington (the latter a little plain woman, pock marked without any aristocratic appearance[96]) & the Duke & Duchess of

---

95 Some £65 for the season or £35 for each one in today's terms.

96 Catherine Wellesley (née Pakenham), often referred to as 'Kitty', was the unhappy wife of the 1st Duke of Wellington, by whom he had two sons.

Richmond[97] with several sons & daughters, a fine family particularly the young ladies; they had taken up their temporary residence in Cambrai to be near their sons, one of whom, the Earl of March,[98] was aide de camp to the Duke & another with some corps in the army;[99] among their acquaintance was Lord Hotham, a rich young nobleman in the Guards,[100] and as he paid some slight attention to one of the sisters, it was told me as a secret, that if I felt inclined to look on, I would soon perceive that a dead set was making at him; and being desirous of knowing how matters of this sort were carried on in high life, I amused myself watching proceedings. Hardly a person was aware of it & it therefore went on without attracting any attention or being disturbed, the family assisted evidently in the plot, for during the whole of the evening he was either dancing with one of them or in conversation with mother; their attention to him appeared overdone and he must have perceived it and seemed invulnerable to the charms for whom he was intended, the manoeuvre therefore was ultimately defeated. It was however amusing to perceive that in whatever sphere of life we are placed in, human nature is much the same, in the pursuit of what it has in view.

What with business & occasional amusements, the year 1816 was brought to a close without any incident or moment either politically or otherwise to disturb the even tenor of our life and 1817 was ushered in without the probability of any change. Christmas & New Year's Days were enjoyed in our little mess, as much as the absence from our families & friends would allow. The cold became excessive and skating the order of the day, but as I had not the opportunity of learning it in Spain & no time to make the attempt now, I left it

---

97 Charles Lennox, 4th Duke of Richmond, and his wife Charlotte (née Gordon).

98 Captain Charles Lennox, Earl of March, 52nd Foot, aide de camp to the Duke of Wellington.

99 Lieutenant Lord George Lennox, 9th Light Dragoons.

100 Lieutenant and Captain Lord Beaumont Hotham, Coldstream Guards.

to others to enjoy themselves. The people I most pitied during the frost were the market women occupied in selling vegetables & other articles in the open air, who to keep a certain warmth in their bodies had small fire pans by them, which they thrust under their petticoats when required & not being over modest or scrupulous, the operation of cooking a herring or other food under this shelter was oftentimes done & distinctly perceived though hid from sight by the hissing it produced and this is no exaggeration.

While the frost lasted the high roads were in a good state to be rode on, which to us who had horses was a temporary advantage instead of the mire & slough of wet weather and it was then time that the supplies could be conveyed with great facility to the several stations of the troops, the waggons being able to go over the then solid ground or pavement without impediment. But the moment the thaw began a chain was stretched across the road at regulated distances & no carriage permitted to go over them, for it is a curious fact that the stones of the pavement became so loose that had any sort of conveyance passed over it, the damage would have been such that re-pavement would have become necessary. After a few days the pavement became again consolidated & the chains withdrawn; it was therefore necessary to anticipate this casualty by keeping the army magazines well stored, no doubt the people adopted the same precaution. These pavements were constructed of a sandstone quarried from a strata a few feet below the surface of the ground in the neighbourhood of the roads & when first extracted are very soft, most easily worked & squared, but become extremely hard after exposure to the atmosphere for a time; this strata appeared to have been once covered by the sea, the remains of many fish being found embedded in it & preserved in museums.

Cambrai before the Revolution was an influential town in the north of France, filled with superb churches, the principal part of which were demolished during that disorderly period, open spaces with heaps of stones shewing in most instances in these sites. In one of them a magnificent tomb had been erected to the memory of one of its bishops, the celebrated Flindon,[101] which with the exception of a few [piles of] debris only, shared the fate of the building under which it stood. We had not therefore any chance of getting a sacred edifice for our protestant service, from the scarcity of those that remained & therefore had to put up with an inferior building which was arranged with seats, communion table &c for the accommodation of the Staff officers, the troops being otherwise provided for in the barracks and I can say the service was well attended & decently performed by the headquarters chaplain.[102] In a corner of the place were deposited the remains of the monument above alluded to consisting of four statues of Roman soldiers half the natural size with other fragments in marble. As there was a feeling among the inhabitants, actuated by a renewed religious tendency, to shew respect to his good bishop, a subscription was set on foot for erecting another tribute of remembrance to him, to which the officers of the garrison were invited to contribute. Many subscribed and I gave a Napoleon (16/8d[103]) and as an inducement it was mentioned in the prospectus that to perpetuate the recollection of those who thus assisted, their names would be inscribed in gold letters on the monument, so that anyone visiting the place hereafter will find on it my name with others, if it was erected & the promise carried into effect.

This place was the centre of the manufacture of Cambric muslin so esteemed all the world over for its fineness and durable quality; it was not made in large buildings exclusively applied to that purpose as is the case in other countries, but by peasantry in their respective cottages or farm houses. The hemp was grown on the spot & prepared in its simple state & natural colour & the women wove it into thread

---

101 Carey has made a mistake here. He means Bishop Fulbert who was Bishop of Cambrai from 934 to 956 AD. He is renowned for leading the defence of the city against Hungarian troops.

102 Chaplain George Stonestreet was attached to 1st Guards Brigade and headquarters.

103 About £60 in today's terms.

7TH CAMPAIGN

with a primitive distaff[104] & whenever they were expert in drawing out the thread to its greatest fineness the article was greatly improved by it & the more prized. It was then worked in the loom by the men, when the weather was wet & no out of door work could be done, in their underground cellars and when a piece was completed it was brought to market on particular market days by the farmer or his wife, who were seen in rows selling their farming produce with their roll or two of cambric. The dealers either residing on the spot or who had come for the purpose examined each piece, agreed for the price, which they chalked on it, gave their address & after the market was over it was taken to the place indicated where they exchanged it for money. To ascertain its fineness with greater certainty, the young purchasers made use of a magnifying glass about an inch square, the greatest number of threads it contained being the criterion of its superiority, older & more experienced hands had not recourse to this test. The pieces or rolls were then put out to bleach in extensive grounds near the river round the town & afterwards prepared for sale.

The merchants who had it for sale were in the habit of cutting a square from each piece, equal in size to a handkerchief, (called a coupon) which they forwarded to their customers, as specimens or samples & when returned were offered for sale and being generally of the best quality were sought after & purchased by us who were not desirous of taking so large a quantity as a whole piece, being merely required for frills to our shirts then in fashion.

In the month of March the French government appearing to assume an air of steadiness which the allied powers thought it necessary to countenance by some act of theirs, it was decided that the Army of Occupation should be reduced & accordingly the *Commission Mixte* (for that was its official import) received orders to make preparations for the supply of six regiments of infantry ordered to march to Calais & which were by degrees embarked for England as soon as transports

---

104 Spindle.

could be provided for their conveyance. This measure was the forerunner of the reduction of the occupation of five years originally, in case the country remained quiet & well-disposed to the existing dynasty and such a step was likely to produce the effect intended in gratifying the national vanity, sorely vexed at seeing part of the country occupied by foreign armies living on the fat of the land. Yet the large neighbouring towns such as Arras, Donnay [Douai] &c which had only small French garrisons became excessively jealous of those who had British troops quartered in them, so much so that it was said to be their intention of petitioning to have some also to derive a share of the pecuniary benefits which our presence afforded wherever we happened to be, and certainly the contrast was very perceptible, for in the former all was quiet, gloomy & without life while the latter presented prosperous & bustling scenes of activity indicative of an increased circulation of money. And we had hardly been a year in Cambray [Cambrai] & Valenciennes, as well as other smaller towns, when they assumed quite an altered appearance, the shops were more abundantly supplied, houses painted or whitewashed, streets kept clean with other improvements which showed that they had greatly benefited from the time we first occupied them and since the peace, no advantage could be taken by us as [a] victorious army during the military occupation of the country, as we were placed in every respect on the same footing as French troops.

The tribunals followed their usual course as well as the magistrates, who continued to be appointed by the French government as before our arrival & all municipal & other taxes were levied indiscriminately on what we or the inhabitants consumed, so that the town dues greatly increased by the great consumption we occasioned. Our presence was therefore very satisfactory to most of the inhabitants, particularly those concerned in trade & it was partly exemplified at the anniversary of the fete of the town by an unusual display of fireworks in the Grande Place which for a provincial exhibition was quite brilliant and must have cost a considerable sum which the improved state of the town funds could easily bear.

7TH CAMPAIGN

After having been stationed for some time in Cambrai, I perceived with much dismay, that my hair was falling off in hand-fulls, but I found on enquiry that it prevailed both among the young and older ones of the garrison, arising as it was said either from the nature of the water, or atmosphere of the place and it grew to such an extent that shaving the head became necessary and we obtained wigs from Paris according to the colour of our hair, samples of which were forwarded there for imitation. Being of course intimate with my brother officers of our mess, we often amused ourselves in going to parties to exchange wigs, the black with the fair and vice versa which produced so singular an effect that though recognised by our friends, they could not account for something apparently strange in our countenances and yet they did not suspect the cause of the deception which required explanation before they found it out.

General society in Cambrai was anything but enlivening or active, in consequence of the aristocratic conduct of the officers of the Guards who in wishing to save their money in France to spend when on leave among their friends in England, would not join the other officers of the garrison to give balls &c. It therefore greatly depended on ourselves to find amusements to occupy our leisure time. Several of us who could sing learnt the guitar as an accompaniment & I made so much progress that I could sing to it a dozen French songs or airs such as '*Portrait Charmant*',[105] '*Partant pour la Syrie*',[106] '*Le jeune & beau Dunois*'[107] &c but did not endeavour to attain so great a proficiency on the instrument as to play a piece of music, for I had not time for it & from the pressure of the fingers on the cords corns came on them, which were by no means agreeable to the feel.

---

105 'Charming Portrait' was a romantic song composed by Marie Antoinette.

106 'Leaving for Syria' written in 1807. The music, written by Hortense de Beauharnais, was inspired by Napoleon's time in Egypt.

107 'The young and handsome Dunois' is a song of love and gallantry, Dunois being a crusader (although in truth he was with Joan of Arc).

On market days strange characters occasionally presented themselves to gull [deceive] the peasantry bringing in their farming produce for sale & one that attracted the most notice was the itinerant tooth drawer. He was usually dressed in an old coat bedizened with tarnished gold lace & pantaloons to match, with an enormous cocked hat similarly decorated, a mustache [*sic*] on his upper lip & across his person a broad belt passing over one of his shoulders, across his breast & hanging down to his hips, as if on which to suspend a sword. The whole of which belt was fantastically ornamented with teeth extracted by him in various states of decay, a fit emblem of his calling & there he stood on a small table or pedestal two or three feet from the ground, to attract the passers-by & commenced an oration on the efficacy of the nostrums[108] he had for sale which cured toothache, itch, sores & all manner of infirmities, embellishing it by various tricks, one of which appeared curious. He stuffed his mouth with what appeared to consist of tow[109] & after he had swallowed it seemingly, volumes of smoke issued from his mouth & nostrils & he then drew out with the fingers of his two hands from between his teeth, yards & yards of narrow ribbon. This done he requested several of the bystanders to mention the coloured ribbon they might wish to appear and after having stuffed his mouth as before, turned round to the several individuals concerned drew from his mouth, to the astonishment of all present, the respective coloured ribbons which had been indicated & which he gave them without payment. Having thus drawn a considerable audience around him he discoursed on his dexterity in extracting teeth without pain of course & informed parties desirous of relief that they would find him at such an hotel at a given hour & then commenced the sale of his medicines until the time appointed, explaining their nature & giving advice to such as

---

108 Medicines prepared by an unqualified person.

109 A ball of hemp or flax fibres.

7TH CAMPAIGN

felt inclined to consult him, in attending to which he appeared fully occupied & getting money in sums suitable to the means of his dupes.

Another out of door attraction were a parcel of dancing dogs brought into the market in a cart lead by individuals whimsically dressed to draw attention to their exhibition. The dogs were in separate compartments ready dressed in a variety of ridiculous costumes & when put on the ground immediately got up on their hind legs & at once commenced capering at the sound of a fiddle. A whip kept them on the alert & there being some order in the dance, the group was as singular as could be imagined. If the manager showman however turned his head from them for a moment they at once went down on all fours & up again so soon as he again faced them, though the fiddle had not ceased playing all the time. Such were some of the modes adopted in earning a living & to all appearances it seemed to succeed from the crowd looking on and giving their mite.

The Russian army was cantoned on our right, or I should say to the east of us, its left flank consisting of cossacks being near Cambrai & extending to Maubeuge its headquarters. These children of Asia came occasionally in the former place to see & be seen, but being disciplined their appearance was uniform and not [as] peculiar as their more wild countrymen, who had been sent back home. Their horses were small but very agile & the men when on horseback appeared much taller than they really were from the saddle being very much elevated above the back of the horse & must have rendered their seat unsafe to anyone else but themselves if the horse stumbled; their bit was most powerful & with it they could rein their horses almost instantly though at full speed bringing them at once on their haunches. These men were remarkably expert with their lance and could ride up to a five frank [sic] piece laying on the ground, fix the point of their lance on it & go right round at the same rate without lifting it from the spot making it a pivot round which they moved. Their mode of salutation to us when occasionally riding through the villages they occupied, was not most agreeable, though well-meant of course, for when they perceived us approaching, themselves being on their horses in some instances without saddles, some of them would rush by us brandishing their lances, in doing which had they made a false step we might have had the point of the weapon in our bodies or those of our animals and this was considered a compliment.

The Duke from being the generalissimo of the allied armies in France occasionally visited their headquarters & it being of course known to the officer in command, he was received with military honours in the singular manner to which they were accustomed. A party of cossacks was accordingly ready at the spot where their cantonments began & when he came in a carriage they rushed at it like a swarm of bees, took the horses out, attached their own in an incredible short time & started off full tear, encircling it all round & disappearing almost instantly and this was continued all along the road by fresh *relais* [*sic*] until they reached Mauberge their destination. To regulate this and various military movements, milestones or I should say *wersts*[110] were laid down instead of those of French leagues by the Russian administration, which greatly annoyed the French authorities under the erroneous apprehension that we intended occupying the country permanently.

In the course of my duty in the *Commission Mixte* which led to great intimacy between the Chief French Commissary Monsieur Regnault and myself, I learnt some particulars relating to the mode of supplying the Russian army with provision, forage &c by the substitution of articles of inferior description for those the tariff & Treaty of Peace laid down. The soldiers it must be mentioned were serfs of the colonels of the regiments & therefore completely submissive to whatever might be arranged for them. Being of the Greek [Orthodox] church & keeping Lent, cod fish was provided for them, as well as periodically at other times & it being considerably cheaper than meat, the colonels pocketed the difference which they

---

110 *Versta* were a Russian unit of distance, equalling ⅔ of a mile or 1.06km.

7TH CAMPAIGN

received from the French government. The horses of the cavalry were also occasionally treated with banyan days[111] by a less distribution of corn & hay, in lieu of which the men were seen leading the horses along the roads or wherever they could find a bite on a common & there grazing, the difference finding its way in the same manner in the purses of the officers concerned & yet no one dared to enquire; making a singular contrast with our own men, every individual of whom had the power of complaining & exacting what he was entitled to & they did so whenever there was cause for it.

We had heard a great deal of the excellence of the Russian church music & being desirous of having a peep at the Russian cantonments, three of us started one morning early to pay a visit to Mauberge, which I before mentioned as being the headquarters. A short distance from Cambrai brought us among the troops of that nation & all along the road we perceived the werst [*verst*] stones before alluded to as annoying to the French authorities & as we passed through the villages the soldiers were either drinking or occupied otherwise as our own men might have been. The only thing observable that struck us was that the peasantry did not look so contented or cheerful as they did in our cantonments. After a long ride we reached our destination, a fortified town full of Russian officers & soldiers without any matter of interest to attract our attention. It had been besieged several times & the walls were studded with the marks of cannon balls, the effects of the bombardments. We soon went to the Greek church or chapel, the principal object of our visit; its exterior was quite unpretending having been temporarily fitted up for the Russian garrison & the priests had commenced mass & were assisted by a numerous choir of splendid voices which harmonised most delightfully & rendered the service a most impressive one & no wonder it was perfect, for to compose it, it was said the finest voices of the whole army had

---

111 Banyan Days was a Royal Navy term for a day when no meat was served, so for horses a day without their normal corn or hay.

been selected & brought together for the purpose. Finding nothing to amuse us, our visit was soon over and we returned to our homes quite satisfied that there was no reason to complain of the place allotted for our residence when contrasted with what we had seen. We were two days in this excursion.

As the month of June [1817] drew near a rumour got in circulation that the anniversary of Waterloo was to be commemorated by a grand dinner to which all officers who had been on the field were to be present. The idea soon matured into a tangible shape by the appointment of a committee of management, which decided that it should be by a subscription & there being plenty of time to obtain from Paris & elsewhere what would make it worthy of the event in a gastronomic point of view, the day was pleasurably anticipated by those who were to participate in it. A room suitable for the occasion was fixed on, as capable of accommodating from 150 to 200 guests & was ornamented with flags & military trophies & the attendance of military heroes was perhaps more numerous than ever took place afterwards, for it included every officer from Lord Hill down to the lowest subaltern including Staff officers & those of the Commissariat & Medical departments. The repast was as splendid as expense could make it including all the luxuries of the season; military bands attended & when the cloth was removed, or I should say the dining part was over toasts & speeches succeeded rapidly & continued to a very late hour, each one being drank to by a bumper & the glass required to be emptied at one draught which ultimately led sooner or later to scenes of intoxication, as strong or weak heads could bear it. Some made their retreat in time but others remained until unable to move & dropt [*sic*] under the table & there they lay until removed to their quarters. Among the doors of exit or entrance in the room there happened to be two on the same side near to each other to correspond, one that opened & the other not, being a sham one. I was seated near the latter & perceiving a move of two or three officers leaving the room in a tottering state, I saw one of them, Lord March, eldest son of the Duke

7TH CAMPAIGN

of Richmond, make a bolt at the sham door & whilst endeavouring to open it fell on the floor unable to rise, being overcome with the enjoyment of the night. Several of us nearest to him in a decent state yet, rose up & assisted in taking him out and returned no more, feeling that they had had quite enough, thus by degrees the greater part of the assembly dispersed leaving the joyous & determined few, reckless of consequences to continue as long as it was in their power & go home by daylight as well as they could. The Duke did not attend, from a wish it was supposed, not to be a check on the unbounded hilarity which was expected & did take place on the occasion, certainly more boisterously than if he had been present.

In remuneration for the capture of Paris one million sterling[112] out of the contributions exacted from France was appropriated to each of the armies that fought at Waterloo, and the arrangements for its distribution being at last completed, I received a letter from the Agents, Messieurs Herne & Furmidge[113] dated 5 July 1817 informing me that my share net of their expenses was £33 15[s] 3[d][114] being the allowance to a lieutenant, though my comparative rank was that of captain, that classification however having been settled by the authorities in England for all grades of non-combatants, it was admitted without remonstrance. Out of it I bought a silver bread basket to commemorate my having been present at a series of events so glorious to our country.

My situation as member of the *Commission Mixte* brought me as I have said before & as time went on more & more in contact with the French Intendant Monsieur Regnault, Monsieur Robert the Sous Intendant his colleague next to him in rank and many of their subordinates including the contractors who all seemed to be on a greater footing of intimacy than our own ideas of difference

---

112 About £60 million today.

113 The Army Agents Herme & Furmidge of 35 Great George Street, London.

114 Equivalent to £2,500 today.

of position would permit. For as representatives of government, the British Commissariat had to see that justice was done to the soldier in the quality & quantity of the supplies furnished by the contractor who oftentimes endeavoured to provide articles of inferior description if not refused; no intimacy could therefore exist between such parties without impropriety. While with the French administration, all parties seemed united to make the soldier & horse consume what was fairly objectionable and had we not constantly resisted these fraudulent attempts we would have been subject to perpetual imposition. Every complaint of this nature from every part of our contingent were referred to the *Commission Mixte* and being the one of the two British Commissaries of the board who could translate the English reports & freely discuss them, my hands were constantly full of work & trouble & it was a difficult undertaking for me from being naturally of a quiet temper to correct existing evils, but experience taught me by degrees that it was a valuable ingredient in this part of my duty, for I found that gentleness and courtesy, produced more effect in correcting attempts at abuse than a boisterous or bullying conduct could have done and the Intendant often told me that he would do more for my conciliatory manner of conducting business than what the service required.

Another unprincipled mode adopted by the French contractors was to corrupt by bribes the English quartermasters & sergeants, to induce them to wink at the inferiority of the supplies received by them, but I am glad to have it in my power to state that at the conclusion of the service when our army had embarked, the Intendant declared to me in confidence that though every endeavour had been made to effect that purpose during the three years of the occupation it was only successful in one instance. A fact he meant as illustration of the moral principal existing in the British army little understood or practised among his countrymen & therefore as something extraordinary or new to him, to which he could not avoid doing justice, though not a friend to the English, and the only apology he had to offer was that it was customary

7TH CAMPAIGN

in that service & that it was therefore a justifiable attempt on the part of those whose interests were concerned. Himself and all his people were rank Bonapartists having been brought up in that demoralising school. They had little or no religion & evidently disliked the existing government, which was endeavouring to instil religious ideas in the minds of the people by the renewal of processions on Saints days &c. He was of course invited to attend these ceremonies & being in his private office on several occasions when getting ready to go, he made no concealment in throwing ridicule on such endeavours & being made to play a part in pageants in which he had no feeling or interest. He was otherwise a good man living respectably with his wife and family & I found in paying them occasional evening visits at their house that the society consisted of the best of the town's people.

The hay harvest of this year [1817][115] having been indifferent in the north of France from prevailing heavy rains, gave rise to serious inconvenience to the service and trouble to myself in having to attend to innumerable complaints from all quarters against the contractors, who availing themselves of the deficiency & inferior quality of the article, had recourse to every expedient in imposing on the troops such as could not be consumed and it becoming at last too serious to bear it any longer I received orders to proceed to the town of La Fère (from the neighbourhood of which our contractors drew their principal supplies of forage) to ascertain by a personal investigation the real state of the harvest.

I took a passport as an officer of the army, but travelled privately passing through S[ain]t Quentin to my destination; I visited various places & farms, collected information from dealers & every other source within my reach and being in plain clothes and speaking the language perfectly, I succeeded most completely in my object, and ascertained that the crop of hay, though deficient was not so bad as

---

115 Carey may have mixed up his years, as 1816 rather than 1817 has been dubbed 'the year without a summer' when harvests were incredibly poor.

had been represented. Armed with this information I suspect the contractors considered me a great bore on my return, in being able to rebut many of their exaggerations & keep them under salutary check. La Fère is a great artillery station & college where I believe Napoleon received some of the rudiments of his education, but being desirous of not making known publicly the object of my visit, I kept very quiet and aloof from everyone with whom I had no concern, or who might wish to pry on what I was doing & therefore saw little of the place or its military establishments to enable me to give any description of it.

On my return home I visited the grand tunnel[116] which opened by canal a water communication between the Netherlands and the interior of France for the conveyance of merchandise & especially coals. It was designed by Buonaparte[117] and excavated by the numerous prisoners of all nations detained by him during the war, many of whom it was said lost their lives in the progress of the work by the occasional fall of loose stones & rubbish overhead under which they were crushed. Being then a novelty in the art of civil engineering it was much admired, but would not in the present times be considered anything extraordinary excepting from its great utility when both countries were united under one government.

My duty frequently took me to the Mairie or municipality and being there one day I was told of a dreadful murder which had been committed within our cantonments and that suspicions fell on our soldiers owing to a button found on the spot & supposed to have been torn off in the scuffle that took place. It was an English military waistcoat button evidently, with the number of the regiment on it, but that corps was not in the Army of Occupation & though it weakened to a certain degree the suspicion first entertained, the French authorities could not easily be persuaded to fasten the guilt on

---

116 The Grans Soutterain is on the Canal de Saint-Quentin near Riqueval and is the longest canal tunnel in France, running for 5.67km (3.5 miles).

117 The project had actually begun in 1769, but work was interrupted in 1773. It was revived by Napoleon and opened by him in 1810.

7TH CAMPAIGN

their own countrymen. After however the most diligent & searching investigations, the murderer was at last fortunately discovered and relieved our men of the culpability of such an act; he proved to be an old French soldier who had served in the campaigns in Spain & Portugal & had stripped a dead English soldier of his waistcoat with other clothes on a field of battle, which waistcoat he had brought home & happened to wear at the time of the murder, for when arrested it was found in his possession with the button missing & the corresponding ones still on it; on that & other corroborative proofs he was found guilty and sentenced to the guillotine & was afterwards executed in the great square at Cambrai while we were still in garrison. The event, an unusual one, created much excitement in the place for several hours, most of the shops were closed, the large bell of the principal church tolled most solemnly, gloomy stillness prevailed & [the] only persons seen in the streets were those hurrying to the scene of execution, the generality of whom were women. The guillotine was in the centre of the square and at the appointed hour the culprits, for there were two of them, made their appearance surrounded by gendarmes & ascended the scaffold accompanied by a priest. One of them made a short harangue to the people & immediately after they were seized in turn by executioners, laid on [a] board & strapped down to it & died under the fatal knife which at once descended & their heads were seen falling into a basket & the blood spouting out of the neck. The bodies with the heads, were then put in coffins & at once carried away for burial; in an hour after not a vestige of the ceremony was perceptible, the guillotine being removed & quantities of sawdust having been laid under it to absorb the blood, all was swept clean and people were passing over the spot on their business as if nothing had happened.

While at Cambrai I occasionally felt indisposed, from effects as was supposed, of the Peninsular campaigns & was recommended to use a shower bath. There was no other place to place it but a corner of the main entrance of the house in which I had my lodging &

229

which led into a small square or courtyard into which several other lodgers looked from their windows. I chose an early hour to avoid observation & strapping my nakedness in a blanket, stole quietly from my door into the bath; it was an operation quite new to me and having pulled the string to let the [cold] water fall, the shock was so great that without one moment's consideration, I rushed completely stripped, into the yard back to my room & while in the act saw the faces of several persons looking on, both men & women; I felt of course annoyed at the occurrence and took care to avoid it afterwards but the blame was on their side in indulging their curiosity at the expense of their modesty. The landlord recommended my taking a little more care in future, though he found fault with them for prying into things with which they had no business.

An agreeable trait in the good understanding which existed between our soldiers & the peasants with whom they were living was the assistance offered by the former in getting in the harvest, which in consequence was sooner accomplished, immediately after which the troops were brought together & encamped for the purpose of drilling, manoeuvring in corps & masses; accordingly the glacis around Cambrai were studded with innumerable tents which gave additional liveliness to the place by the concourse of officers & men who since the last review had been rusticating in the various villages in which they were cantoned. During these bursts of excitement we were visited by sundry individuals from Paris, such as ventriloquists, actors & singers &c among whom was the celebrated ventriloquist Alexandre[118] who certainly was wonderful in sleights of hand & deceptions and inimitable in holding apparently conversations with several individuals, for he threw his voice down a cellar, then at the farther end of the room in which he was, as well as in the garrets upstairs, making it appear that several persons were speaking together about some business in which they were concerned. His

---

118 Alexandre Vattemare (1796–1864).

7TH CAMPAIGN

sleights of hand were also extraordinary, among which was that of sowing [a] seed in a flower pot, which progressively rose out of the ground, grew, flowered and produced seeds which he distributed to the persons present. He was also noted for his practical jokes in his journeys, one of which might have proved serious, being in the diligence & passing through a town, the vehicle got intermingled with a funeral procession in a narrow street and at the moment the coffin came near the window of it, out of which he was looking, he threw his voice into it making the corpse cry out for air as he was not dead. An alarm arose among the bystanders, the bearers put the coffin on the ground & the procession, horror-struck, began to disperse during which, room having been made, the diligence proceeded on its journey the passengers & conductor wondering at the occurrence & totally ignorant of the originating cause of it. On another occasion being also in a diligence travelling by night, he thought to frighten the passengers by making them believe in the possibility of a robbery from one moment to the other and finding a favourable opportunity he threw his voice outside, as that of several men calling out to the conductor to stop at the peril of his life; the carriage stopped & the supposed men came up in the dark, Alexandre hurriedly collected from the various persons with him something to give the robbers, while holding a conversation with them & having given them what he had obtained & with which they appeared satisfied, they desired the conductor to proceed. On his arrival at the first stage he informed his fellow passengers who he was & the deception he had practised on them, returning to them at the same time their property which he of course had cunningly concealed, though they were all impressed with the conviction as far as the darkness permitted, that they had seen it put out of the window & carried off.

The garrison of Valenciennes, being composed of regiments of the line, there was much more sociability among them than at Cambrai; they got up private theatricals & other amusements during the season

& having heard that the famous tragedian Talma[119] was to exhibit there for a few days, I went over to hear him. It was not however for the first time, as I had before seen him in Paris; he gave us several chosen extracts of his best parts which of course delighted all that heard him, but being short of stature, it took away I thought much from the dignity of the characters he represented and though his gesticulation was graceful it appeared to us overdone, accustomed as we were to much less action in our theatres. One interesting feature in his dress was his classical imitation of that supposed to have been worn by the ancient potentates & heroes he personified & it was said that when Napoleon assumed the Imperial title he took lessons in gesticulation from him which enabled him to act with that dignity which became a crowned head.

From the various avocations which the Duke of Wellington had to attend to independent of the command of the allied army, not the least of them was that of being consulted on every point connected with the diplomatic policy of Europe over which he exercised a great deal of influence & which caused his being frequently absent from our headquarters. The French King Louis the 18th & the French princes looked up to him also as a man in whom they could confide for advice in every circumstance and were therefore always desirous of paying him every attention & respect. The latter hunted the wild boar occasionally in the forest of Compiegne, once celebrated for its palace & stables to which he was frequently invited and his mode of doing so when up with the army was quite characteristic & shewed his wonderful physical powers. He rode down there from his Chateau of Mont St Martin a distance of 45 miles, hunted during the day with the princes & returned on horseback before dark & it was said hardly one of his personal staff could keep up with him though of course much younger in age, besides which if public papers awaited him &

---

119 François-Joseph Talma (1763–1826).

7TH CAMPAIGN

required to be despatched he attended to them either before dinner, or before retiring to rest.

In a former part of my narrative of the Peninsular campaign, I alluded to his patience in carefully reading over at Badajoz the claims of various people for supplies furnished by them to the army during the years 1808 & 1809, engrossed in several quires of paper; since which, owing I suppose to an immense increase in business his manner of despatching it had quite altered, for he wrote afterwards in a hurried manner on the turned up corner of each despatch or letter his decisions or instructions in pencil but oftentimes so illegibly that they could not be made out by his Military Secretary, Lord Fitzroy Somerset and yet no one would ask him their purport. The writing therefore of such words as could be read were finely passed over with a pen and the dispatch handed over to the other officers in his confidence and well acquainted with his handwriting to make out what they could and thus the remainder of the words were deciphered, for when once His Grace had discharged his mind of any subject he was not again disposed to revert to its details.

During the years 1816 & 1817 many officers of the French army had been reduced, several of whom returned home to Cambrai. They were generally young men, rank Bonapartists and inclined to be insolent and quarrelsome. Seeing that we took little notice of their conduct, their arrogance led them into quarrels with our officers and at last it was found necessary to bring a certain number to trial before their own courts and being convicted, were sentenced to be banished from the cantonments of the allied army, while others less guilty were permitted to remain on good behaviour and superintendence of the police. No duels were permitted with these townspeople, but the officers of the garrison were obliged to carry their swords to resent any attempted insult by which peace was preserved and the existing good harmony between us and the generality of the inhabitants suffered no diminution.

In the meantime however, an unfortunate event occurred which produced considerable sensation for a while. The evening walk for the inhabitants and garrison was on a walk just below the glacis of the citadel and between it and the town; several officers of the Guards being one day seated on one of the seats with a French female acquaintance, she made some disagreeable remarks on a Frenchman passing by and in his hearing, which he resented warmly and the officers having interfered a quarrel ensued. His appearance being respectable, an exchange of address took place, a challenge followed but was not accepted at once, for the individual being a stranger and not known it was necessary to ascertain previously if he was in a sphere of life which would entitle him to have the satisfaction of a gentleman. It was found on enquiry from the French authorities that he was a captain in the French army & therefore a meeting was arranged for next morning and it took place in one of the outworks just outside the town; at the first fire the Guardsman was mortally wounded and while expiring, his second who was within hearing of the sentry on the ramparts called out for assistance to convey the body into the town.[120] The Frenchman fancying that it was with the intention of laying hold on him remonstrated as being a breach of the forms of duelling, but he was told at once that such was not the intention & that he and his second were at liberty to retire and would not be interfered with, or measures taken against them for some hours at least, as that would depend on the authorities. On further enquiry it was ascertained that the fellow was a great duellist, a good swordsman & a sure shot and that he had come up to revenge his country's wrongs by picking a quarrel with the first of our officers who would give him an opportunity and thus fell a promising young officer who after all was not most to blame in the affair, but was singled out by his antagonist to give him justification. A military funeral took place at which most of the two regiments of the Guards assisted and the angry feelings of the soldiers could hardly be restrained from insulting

---

120 Again Carey has the wrong year. Ensign Alexander Gordon of the Coldstream Guards was killed in a duel with a French officer at Cambrai on 1 April 1818.

7TH CAMPAIGN

the French spectators and had it not been for the high character of the corps, and its great discipline serious quarrels between them & the inhabitants must have occurred, as the irritation continued for a considerable time.

The autumn of the year 1817 was fast passing away & the troops had returned from their encampments to their usual winter quarters without any political event occurring to disturb the routine of the service. France appeared quiet and we accordingly sunk into the dull reality of another winter on its frontier. After the autumnal rains, the by roads became as usual almost impracticable from their muddy state & therefore unfit for equestrian exercise and there was little inducement to ride on the chaussée pavements[121] which would in a short time injure the hoofs of our horses; we therefore were confined most of the time to the precincts of the town which being fortified, afforded round its ramparts a nice clean walk of nearly three miles & in dry weather we could extend our lounge round the outside of the fortifications and when the weather permitted coursing the hare was not forgotten. The Duke kept a pack of hounds which went out two or three times a week but none of the Department joined the field that I recollect except his own company, attributable to our not having sufficient leisure time at our disposal, as many would have enjoyed it. On one occasion in turning out the hounds some French General officers who were on a visit to His Grace were mounted by him on his hunters, but after riding some distance & making some leaps, which their horses took without being consulted, they abandoned the sport as too rough & dangerous for people like themselves, unaccustomed to ride over hedge & ditch without the thought of consequences.

The usual '*Bals de Société*' [Society Balls] were a great resource and there we acquired a proficiency in dancing quadrilles & waltzes which

---

121 French and Belgian chaussées at this time had a central section laid with stones and known as a pavement, wide enough for two carts to pass each other. Either side of this was a strip of mud which was softer for horses, but at times of excessive rain these became very boggy.

rendered us acceptable on returning home; at the same time that we were improving our knowledge of conversational French. The French ladies generally were not however prepossessing in their appearance and Cupid was in consequence anything but active in his usual efforts, for I have no recollection of a marriage having taken place in Cambrai during the occupation between us & the inhabitants & only one instance of an intimate flirtation between an officer of the Guards and the daughter of his landlord, a respectable bookseller. She was rather good looking but it ended in nothing, although he was much found fault with by most of the garrison for having continued his attentions so long without a declaration; the fact was the generality of the higher classes in the town and neighbourhood consisted of a few landowners, members of the law, medical men & shopkeepers &c, possessing little fortune or rank in life to render a matrimonial connection desirable, added to which the difference of religion was another serious obstacle; so that not one of us returned to England leaving affectionate remembrances behind him, but it was not so with our soldiery in their cantonments, the particulars of which will be related in their proper place.

Among the multifarious duties I had to attend to & which kept me fully employed; the task devolved on me of ascertaining the expense which a regiment of cavalry, infantry & a troop of artillery occasioned while serving with the Army of Occupation in France, for though it fell almost entirely on the French government it was supposed the Duke of Wellington was desirous of the information to enable him, with other materials which the Commissary General could furnish, to form an aggregate of the expense of our whole contingent; the details of my calculations will be found among my papers.[122]

My correspondence at this time may be said to have been confined to professional matters with the officers of the Commissariat stationed in various places affording neither interest or amusement; among them however was one (Mr Robert Cotes) who had been in our mess, a fine

---

122 Not extant.

7TH CAMPAIGN

young & intelligent man, extremely prepossessing in his manners & well informed, who occasionally wrote to me. He was quartered in the village of Marquise[123] with a regiment of cavalry in the neighbourhood of Calais & having much leisure time he amused himself in investigating on the spot the probable place from which Julius Caesar embarked for the conquest of Britain & I transcribe the result of his enquiries as very entertaining & probably correct; his career poor young man was a short one for he did not long survive our withdrawal from France, having died of consumption a year or two afterwards in Belgium.

He writes: 'Among other occupations, I have been exploring the remains of the Romans in the neighbourhood with the view of ascertaining a point (insignificant enough to a general observer but which acquires some interest in the eyes of one who is so near the spot), that is where Julius Caesar embarked when he invaded Britain. Different places have been fixed on & among them Boulogne & Calais occupy a higher place in the scale of probabilities, but Wissant (situated between them in a bay now blocked up by sands which continually increase on this coast though it was formerly a place of consequence & the principal point of embarkation & disembarkation for travellers to & from England) appears from the testimony of ancient authors as well as from local circumstances to have a greater claim to the honour in question. One of the strongest arguments however in favour of that theory is drawn from the existence in the immediate vicinity of Wissant, of several Roman camps which are nowhere else to be found on the coast & are supposed to have been constructed by Caesar's lieutenant whom he left at this side of the water with a large force to keep the country in awe & above all to secure the harbour when he embarked. The principal work goes by the name of Camp de César; it is in a surprisingly good state of preservation considering the number of years which have passed since the supposed date of its erection; it is of a circular or rather oval shape, much smaller than the

---

123 Approximately 10km north-east of Boulogne-sur-Mer.

one we saw near Bomhain [Bohain-en-Vermandois?], but the ditch & rampart much more strongly delineated than in that one. The rampart is excessively steep and nearly sixty feet high from the bottom of the ditch. It is probable that some of the artillerymen will be employed in the summer in cutting into one of the mounds or barrows & perhaps something remarkable may be discovered.' Letter dated 21 April 1818.

In attending occasionally the soirees of the French Intendant Militaire Monsieur Regnault I perceived an increasing intimacy between his wife's sister, Mademoiselle Fengnagell & the Sous Intendant Monsieur Gaston Robert, next to him in rank in the *Commission Mixte* which ended in their marriage. Being well acquainted to them both I received a formal intimation of it which I transcribe to shew the forms then used to acquaint the friends of the parties of the ceremony having taken place; the bride was Dutch, her sister having married Monsieur Regnault in Holland when the French occupied that country & which accounts for all the names alluded to not being French. It is as follows:-

'M[onsieur].
Madame La Baronne de Fengnagell née de Dopff, Madame Regnault, Mr Regnault, Intendant Militaire, Chevalier du L'Ordre Royal de la Légion d'Honneur, ont l'honneur de vous faire part du marriage de Mademoiselle Angelique de Fengnagell leur fille, soeur, et belle soeur, avec Monsieur Gaston Robert, Sous Intendant Militaire, Officier de L'Ordre Royal de la Légion d'Honneur. Cambrai le Juin 1818. Addressed to Monsieur Cairrey, Député Commissaire General, Cambrai'.

[Madame La Baronne de Fengnagell nee de Dopff, Madame Regnault, Mr Regnault, Military Intendant, Knight of the Royal Order of the Legion of Honour, have the honour to inform you of the marriage of Mademoiselle Angelique de

7TH CAMPAIGN

> Fengnagell, their daughter, sister and sister-in-law, with
> Mr Gaston Robert, Deputy Military Intendant, Officer
> of the Royal Order of the Legion of Honour. Cambrai
> June 1818. Addressed to Monsieur Cairrey [*sic*], Deputy
> Commissioner General, Cambrai].

The bride, though young, was neither good looking nor interesting, having strong carroty hair, but she was amiable. The bridegroom with nothing remarkable in his person was some fifteen years older than her & for a Frenchman was sullen and evidently disliked the English; he however spoke that language tolerably, for which reason he had been selected to be a member of our *Commission Mixte* and finding there was no cordiality in his manner we never became intimate but I kept on good terms with him for the good of the service.

When the army first took its quarters in Cambrai we found that a '*Société d'Émulation*'[124] existed there consisting of the literary & scientific men of the place which held their periodical meetings in the *Hôtel de Ville* to which any of our officers who felt inclined might become members; I was invited to become one, but was too much occupied to think of the sciences. I must moreover confess that I did not possess attainments which would have rendered me capable of contributing my mote [speck] on any subject which might have amused or instructed the society. There was however one of the Commissariat who joined it, the ci-devant Colonel Hill, then an Assistant Commissary General[125] whose wife was with him and was said to be a blue stocking[126] and had the credit of having assisted him in composing an essay which was translated by a Monsieur Felix of our Commission & read by him at the meeting held on the 17 August

---

124 A name commonly given in the eighteenth and nineteenth century to learned societies in France, Wallonia and Flanders, to study the arts, literature and science.

125 Assistant Commissary General Hugh Hill.

126 A derogatory name for a literary woman.

239

to which I received an invitation to be present. I knew beforehand of the composition from having seen it in course of translation in M[onsieur] F[elix] hands who evidently would have preferred composing it himself than have waded through its translation. The subject was the influence which works of imagination exercise on public morals. Assistant Commissary General Hill had been colonel of the Battleaxe Guard in Dublin,[127] a situation connected with the court of the Lord Lieutenant, which he had been obliged to throw up in consequence of pecuniary embarrassments. He was a quiet little man and well informed and his wife was talented, short & ugly.

The British contingent consisted of the following numbers on the 1 October of this year as ascertained by official returns exclusive of the Danes, Hanoverians and Saxons - viz:

Officers	1,223
Soldiers	21,801
Servants	975
Women	1,636
Children	2,799
Horses	8,287

The spring & part of the summer of 1818 passed on with great sameness in the routine of our life, but towards the month of September when the subject of the usual autumnal concentrations of the troops for exercise was in agitation, rumours of a speedy evacuation of the country got into circulation and soon ripened into fact by the great powers having decided that the occupation should be reduced from five to three years, in consequence of the tranquil state of France rendering our presence unnecessary & perhaps inimical to the consolidation of the existing government. Few among us were

---

127 The Battleaxe Guard was established at Dublin Castle in 1662 and was analogous to the Yeoman Warders at the Tower of London.

7TH CAMPAIGN

sorry to hear of this determination for most were desirous of a change even at the prospect of half pay, so that when all doubts of its taking place were removed no one can be said to have regretted it.

The *Commission Mixte* received accordingly in the beginning of October, an intimation that arrangements would have to be made for the concentration of the British contingent including the Danes, Saxons & Hanoverians between Cambrai & Valenciennes for a grand review preparatory to its dismemberment & return home and everything being ready the troops commenced their march from their respective cantonments to the points indicated, the details of which will be found in a document prepared in the office of the *Commission Mixte*, which enumerates in a very neat & comprehensive manner the strength of the different corps of cavalry and infantry &c & the various villages in & about which they were to encamp or occupy; this paper which will be found among my papers is endorsed as follows:

'Detail of the concentration of the British contingent of the Army of Occupation in France preparatory to a grand review & subsequent withdrawal from that country in the autumn of 1818.'[128]

The troops being soon assembled the review took place on the 23 October in the presence of the Dukes of Kent & Cambridge[129] who came from England for the purpose. The army was in the highest state of discipline & order and a finer display of military array could hardly be witnessed anywhere, for though not so numerous as many concentrations on the continent, the men individually could not be equalled except by the foreign Guards, consisting of picked men who were better adapted for grand parades than rough service, as

---

128 Not extant.

129 Prince Edward, Duke of Kent, and Prince Adolphus, Duke of Cambridge, were the 4th and 7th sons of King George III.

casualties in their ranks could not easily be filled up. The Danes, Hanoverians & Saxons were also fine-looking men, the two former dressed as ourselves in red or scarlet and the latter in green.

The troops having received the Royal dukes by a salute as usual & with whom the Duke of Wellington made his appearance of course with a numerous & splendid Staff, broke into columns & commenced a series of manoeuvres which were carried on during a great part of the day, in advancing & attacking points supposed to be occupied by an enemy, which it is unnecessary to detail. After which & before sundown the troops being ranged for the purpose marched past the Royal dukes, in columns of regiments which occupied so much time that night was coming on before it could be ended; the cavalry bringing up the rear were therefore obliged to trot past & the British regiments leading those of Hanover, Denmark & Saxony were obliged to gallop to keep close up, their horses being much smaller; it shewed the superiority of the pace of our animals which since the battle of Waterloo & occupation of Paris had not escaped the observation of the allied sovereigns, for they immediately set about improving their race by large purchases in England & I perceived many years after in travelling in Germany that their horses had much improved both in bone & blood.

I had lent for the event my old cossack horse to Mr R[obert] Cotes before mentioned which I had purchased on entering France in 1815 & while returning from the field he broke down completely, which obliged me to get rid of him for he fell & tumbled Mr C[otes] over his head while galloping in the midst of our party, but fortunately in such a way that he alighted on his legs & found himself running along by the impetus he had acquired. The poor brute being behind him rolling on the ground & endeavouring to rise with his knees very badly lacerated & all bloody.

After the review the troops according to their march routes proceeded towards Calais & Boulogne and were disposed so as to follow each other on the road and embarked in succession as transports were provided during the first fortnight of November; the

7TH CAMPAIGN

Guards in Cambrai & 52nd Regiment in Valenciennes being the last to take their departure & bring up the rear.

Some days after when in conversation with Mr Regnault on the evacuation, he remarked to me that the opinion entertained by the French of the English soldier was that as long as he had spirits or wine at command he thought of nothing else, but said he; 'your people have come out in a new character for I grieve to say & am quite ashamed to acknowledge, that my countrywomen have behaved most shamefully, numbers of them having abandoned husbands & parents to follow the English army, to such an extent that it was found necessary by the authorities to place gendarmes on the roads to prevent this female exodus & oblige them by force to return to their homes'. It showed in one respect the good feelings which had existed between the soldiers & peasantry & could not after all be a subject of wonder after an intimacy which had existed for upwards of three years with fine young men living in idleness & hardly anything to do but to be attentive to the female part of the family with which they lodged & possessing personal attractions. Notwithstanding the precautions taken many succeeded in making their escape disguised as drummers & in male attire intermixed with the soldiery & followers of the army. The scandal must have been great & annoying to French vanity to be unable to avoid its publicity.

As the accounts of the *Commission Mixte* relating to the supplies issued to the army could not be closed without some delay, I received orders to remain behind & assist at their completion as long as it was necessary.

When the day of the departure of the Guards came & which completed the evacuation, I dressed myself in plain clothes & went to see them march out & for the purpose [I] intermingled with the French crowd to observe the feeling expressed on the occasion. Some were passive, merely looking on, others exulted at their country being rid of foreigners; a few were most violently vociferous in expressions of enmity and some spoke in favour of our people as 'bon enfants'. I was therefore surrounded by persons of different ways of thinking but perceived that a trifle might have from one moment to the other occasioned a row; this was however kept in check by the stern attitude of our men & I may add by many of the women present, who in their remarks expressed much kindly feeling & an old woman in particular spoke very plainly on the subject in my hearing to the most violent of her countrymen, in observing that they would soon find out to their cost the difference between a large wealthy English garrison & a small French one, which appeared to have a good effect, for the troops continued their march without disturbance. The crowd consisted principally of poor people, among which there was a number of discontented old Imperial soldiers and the refuse of the population, for the respectable inhabitants could not [but] be satisfied with the uniform good conduct of our men.

Our people were soon replaced by the arrival of a French detachment and wishing to see them also, I went in the market place where they were already formed up, but their reception did not appear at all enthusiastic; they looked anything but prepossessing being undersized men & recruits so that the contrast between them & our men was such that I thought the townspeople were almost ashamed of them.

After some days the town looked as if deserted, for the few French troops which had arrived did not enliven it and I felt quite strange at being left alone with a clerk & hardly any other Englishmen (not of the army) but such as had still some private affairs to settle & with whom I had no acquaintance. The people were however civil and took no notice of us, so that we were likely to get on quietly & meet with no molestation, besides which we were under the protection of the police but found no occasion for their assistance. To be however thus situated for a period of two or three months was anything but agreeable and it was therefore with infinite pleasure that I received an official letter from the Commissary General at Calais intimating to me that arrangements had been agreed upon between the Duke of Wellington & the French Minister at War for the immediate dissolution of the *Commission Mixte* at the several headquarters &

7TH CAMPAIGN

withdrawal of its members and that consequently I was to leave the business in an unfinished state & proceed to England, in complying with which I lost no time. The fact was the French government had become impatient of any individual connected with the allied army remaining any longer in the country, from a desire to show to the people as soon as possible that there was no longer a vestige of any foreign control over the sacred soil of France.

Tired of the isolation I had been in for three weeks, my arrangements were soon made for an early departure and having wished adieu to my French friends of the Commission, with whom I had kept on good terms, I started on the 1 December for Calais by Lille, Cassel &c passing hurriedly through the former place, situated in a flat country, I perceived the immensity of its fortifications which, though low in their appearance were very strong from being surrounded with wet ditches which rendered them most difficult of approach by a besieging army. It is considered the key into France on that frontier & the French authorities were jealous of anyone even looking into the works, so that I only remained in the place for an hour to refresh myself in which short time I only saw that it was a nice town in a general point of view.

Having heard a great deal of the beautiful view from the heights of Cassel, I could not resist the temptation of remaining there an hour or two to see it. I put up at one of the inns of the town & was told that I must ascend the neighbouring hill for the purpose, which having done & got up to the mill which crowned the top and being fortunate in the weather, my curiosity was fully recompensed; looking northward a great part of the Netherlands it may be said, was perceptible for being a flat country; I could distinctly see the steeples of churches (dotted here and there) of the principal cities, such as Dunkerque [Dunkirk], Bruges, Gand [Ghent] & even Brussels, with those of the intervening small towns & villages as far as a spy glass could carry, a distance of nearly thirty leagues, embracing as the miller reported, upwards of 200 towns and villages. To the left of this panorama the British Channel was distinctly seen with the coast of England bounding the horizon and on the extreme right of the picture the view extended to another part of the Netherlands and yet the height of the hill on which I stood did not exceed 800 feet above the level of the sea. Looking backwards towards France the view was limited by ranges of low hills; it was certainly the most extensive prospect I have beheld not excepting that from Mount Vesuvius or those from the Estrella Mountain in Portugal, the Alps or Pyrenees, each however having their respective beauties quite different from each other.

On the road from Cassel to Calais the spot was pointed out to me near Guines famous for [the] interview between our Henry the 8th & Francis the 1st called the Field of the Cloth of Gold;[130] its present appearance was not interesting being a bare space or field without any pleasing feature to recommend it; the weather was cold & disagreeable and nothing about the locality tended to remind one of this vain pageant, which could only be brought back to the imagination by the descriptions contained in the chronicles of those times.

I reached Calais in due time without incident to write upon & went over the town to see such remains as existed of the period during which it was in possession of the English but with the exception of an old gate, the principal church & a dilapidated building said to have been a palace in olden time, there was little to interest a traveller.

On the 3rd of December I took my passage with several officers who had lingered behind the army in one of the packets, though the weather was very unfavourable, being crowded in a small sailing cutter many of us had to lay down from sea sickness on the floor of the cabin for want of better accommodation. I happened to be near an officer of cavalry dressed in his uniform, who had a basin by his side and as the steward had plenty to do he neglected emptying the contents. In the meantime a heavy lurch of the vessel occasioned by an increase of wind took place & the officer feeling himself sliding to leeward made a grab at the basin & in a moment I perceived that he was deluged

---

130 The meeting at the Field of the Cloth of Gold lasted from 7 to 24 June 1520.

7TH CAMPAIGN

with the contents all over his person, which put him indeed in a sad plight & to add to our misery on reaching the vicinity of Dover late in the evening, the tide was too low to get into the harbour; the sea was rolling heavily and we were apparently doomed to lay out all night in the midst of it. A large boat however ventured out to us and for a round sum offered to take us on shore, but it was a matter of some danger in being transferred from one vessel to the other which a few only would attempt. I was one who risked it and we were accordingly directed one by one to jump into the boat every time it came alongside the vessel, the boatmen being obliged to fend off as soon as one was taken in, for fear of being swamped by remaining too long near the packet & thus we got in by degrees & were afterwards safely landed on the shelving pebbly shore of Dover, delighted as may be well supposed at again returning to England in safety & enjoying the comfort of a good dinner & night's rest in a comfortable bed instead of remaining out at sea beating about, as the other folks did almost all night until the tide rose again to enable the vessel to get in.

Next morning I started by coach for London & having reported myself to the Commissary in Chief at the Treasury, I received the intimation that I should be put on half pay at the expiration of two months from the day of my landing in England.

In consideration of the services rendered in the *Commission Mixte* the French government were pleased to honour me with the decoration of a Chevalier of the Legion of Honour, and though I never received permission from our government to wear the cross, the distinction was not the less gratifying to my feelings; the diploma is among my papers,[131] and the reason given for not allowing it to be worn was that no orders founded by the Emperor Napoleon were then recognised by the government of England.

In thus bringing my narrative of upwards of ten years of my life employed on a foreign service & connected with the most celebrated

---

131 Not extant.

epoch in the history of the world, I must say I feel a pride in having personally participated in it. It is a proud record of England's exertions in a righteous cause & it is almost wonderful that comparatively with a mere handful of soldiers, victories should have been achieved over the conqueror of Europe which gave such a stimulus to the vanquished nations as led at last to their emancipation & it is gratifying to have it in my power to declare that as an eye witness to many of the events, the account of them as recorded in the press of England bear a noble contrast by their fairness & truth to the attempts made by French historians to disguise their defeats by increasing the numbers of their enemies & decreasing their own forces so as to make it appear that they were in most cases the few against the many instead of honestly admitting that they had the worst of it in fair fields. For although numbers might have been equal in some instances, the French armies being a national unity were opposed to ours composed of different nations not understanding each other's language which in a battlefield proved a great disadvantage. On our side however we had a great helping hand, to whom we must ascribe all our advantages, for had not the great disposer of events come to our aid, it would have been an impossibility for us to have contended against such gigantic & experienced armies & I have no hesitation in declaring that the hand of God was perceptible in many instances. An example of which was in our chief the Duke of Wellington, who though he exposed himself in every action, was signally preserved, for had he been killed or even disabled for a time, there was no general in the army who could have replaced him with equal talents. To the Almighty therefore must be ascribed the glory of having preserved England from the sad casualties of internal war which all other nations endured so much to their misery and cost.

THE END

7TH CAMPAIGN

Extract from the Memoirs of General Sir Thomas Brisbane GCB &c who commanded a brigade in the Peninsular war &c and was on familiar terms with the Duke of Wellington, which I annexe to shew how effective the Commissariat was during those great events.

'On my arrival in Paris in 1815 from America, I had the honour of dining with the Duke of Wellington on the following day. He spoke in the most feeling manner of his old army namely, the cavalry, the artillery, the infantry & the Commissariat & he summed it up with these remarkable expressions: that when he broke up on the Garonne, after the Battle of Toulouse he had commanded the most perfect army that ever was in existence.'

In confirmation of which Sir Thomas mentions that his brigade (infantry) in the march through Portugal & Spain to the south of France was without rations but one day.

I contemplated writing something on my voyage to the Mauritius, sojourn there & return home, embracing a period from the beginning of March 1820 to January 1824, as also my going to Malta and serving there in my official capacity of head of the Commissariat Department from April 1837 to the month of July 1845, during which time we visited Italy twice, Switzerland, Tyrol, Bavaria & down the Rhine, into the Netherlands, Brussels to Ostend & home.

Appendix A

Commissary Tupper Carey's Correspondence

The following have been copied from Tupper Carey's papers contained in a Note Book labelled 'Family Records'.

Commissary General Carey never applied nor sought for testimonials, but he annexes copies of four which were sent to him without solicitation and it appears another was received by Sir J[ohn] Bissett from General Sir Lowry Cole commanding the 4th Division of infantry under whom he served in the most active campaigns in the Peninsula.

Copies of Testimonials.

16 Fludyer Street, 23 December 1818

Sir,
It might be satisfactory to you to be in possession of the enclosed copy of a letter which I addressed to the Secretary Harrison on the 14th instant, respecting your claims for promotion. I now enclose it. I have the honour to be Sir, your obedient servant J[ohn] Bissett Commissary General

APPENDIX A

16 Fludyer Street, 12 December 1818

Sir,

I do myself the honour to enclose to you, to be laid before the Lords Commissioners of his Majesty's Treasury the copy of the letter received by me from Lieutenant General Sir Lowry Cole in favour of Assistant Commissary General Carey who began his services under Sir John Moore and continued them throughout the whole of the Peninsular war and the late service in France, where for nearly two years, he was the senior member of the *Commission Mixte* appointed for deciding on all cases of complaint between the British and allied contingents and the French administration, a situation in which I placed him, from his commissariat experience, his knowledge of the French language and conciliating manners, the last of which was not the least of the requisites necessary for a due execution of the often delicate duties, he was then called on to perform and which having executed highly to my satisfaction, I take leave strongly to recommend him to their lordships' protection as a most deserving officer. I have the honour to be Sir &c &c J[ohn] Bisset

Mon Plaisir, Mauritius, 10 June 1823

Dear Sir,

I should not do justice to the opinion I entertain of your services were I to permit you to retire from this command, without serving testimony to your zeal for the interest of the public and your indefatigable exertions to forward the service on all occasions. I can only add that, I should consider myself fortunate in having the benefit of your assistance wherever I might be hereafter employed and I beg you will accept my best wishes for your success. your very faithful humble servant R[alph] Darling Major General

FEEDING WELLINGTON'S ARMY FROM BURGOS TO WATERLOO

Commissariat Accounts Office 11 July 1823

Sir,

I do myself the honour of herewith returning you the triplicate sets of your cash and provision accounts from the 25 April to 6 June and of your accounts of oxen, carts, harness, magazine implements and office furniture from the 25 March to the date of your giving over charge on the 6 June last and beg to acquaint you, that the original sets of all these accounts have this day been forwarded to the post office for transmission to H M Treasury by the ship *'Exmouth'* expected to sail on the 13th instant.

In returning you the closing accounts of your administrations of the Commissariat Department on this station, though it may appear unusual on the part of one, so much your inferior, yet at the risk of being deemed presumptuous and conceiving that the close abbreviation thereof, which my situation imposed upon me as a duty, may perhaps give it some value in your estimation, I cannot resist the impulse of the respect and esteem which your public conduct has produced too often my humble testimony to the conscientious and honourable integrity, the unabating zeal, regularity and ability which have marked your proceedings, during your three year's service in this colony, in the whole course of which period you have undeviatingly pursued a line of conduct so exemplary and meritorious, that while it has secured to you the good opinion of everyone who has had an opportunity of observing it, cannot have failed to have called forth the unqualified approbation of your superiors and what is more to be valued must have been for your own mind, a retrospect to which you can at all times recur, with unerring and never failing satisfaction.

I shall ever consider it one of the more fortunate events of my life to have been placed in relations of such business, with an officer whose openness of conduct on all occasions, bespoke the disinterested of the motives by which it was activated and whose habits of official regularity

APPENDIX A

and probity and readiness to attend to every suggestion, which had the public interest in view, lightened to me the duties of a situation which I can say from experience is not always exempt from a degree of painful anxiety and solitude. For the advantage and gratification which the discharge of your official duties has thus conferred on myself, I beg leave to make you my best acknowledgements and at the same time to express my confident and earnest hopes that your public merits may be duly appreciated and regarded by the high authorities in England, whose notice they must have attracted. Wishing you most sincerely a good and prosperous voyage to your native land that you may soon be happily reunited to your domestic aide and every happiness. Believe me to remain with much truth, respect and esteem your most faithful and humble servant, Deputy Commissary General Lithgow[1]

Note by Tupper Carey,
Mr Lithgow had to examine my accounts as Commissary of Accounts and being on the spot would judge of their accuracy in a twofold point of view and as he had many difficulties to contend with, with my predecessors by their loose adherence to instructions, his painful position was greatly alleviated by my conscientious discharge of duty, which led it is presumed, to his expressing himself in the above terms.

Treasury, 11 September 1845

My dear Sir,

I had attentively read the paper relative to the mode of conducting business at Malta, which you wrote for the information of your successor, and a copy of which you have been so kind as to send me, with your note of the 9th instant.

---

1   Deputy Commissary General William Lithgow.

I have often remarked the regularity and exactness with which the duties of the Commissariat department at Malta are conducted notwithstanding the magnitude of many of the operations and your paper was regarded by me with much interest as it shone a strong light on the causes of this successful management. After these will be no doubt be of much use to Mr [?] and I beg that you will accept my thanks for this additional proof of your zeal for the public service.

I am happy to say that we have at last nearly completed the revision of the Commissariat regulations and I shall have much pleasure in sending you a copy of them, which I am sure you will be glad to have, although your connection with the active duties of the department has for the present ceased. I remain, yours sincerely CE Trevelyan

Note by Tupper Carey,
Sir Charles Trevelyan, as under Secretary to the Board of Treasury, conducted the business of the Commissariat Department both at home and abroad, and as such addressed the above letter.

I add the following copy of a letter lately found among my papers from the senior officer of the department with Lord Hill's corps of which the 2nd Division formed a part in the Netherlands before the Battle of Waterloo and which was written some days before my joining from England.

Grammont, headquarters of Lord Hill's Corps, 28 April 1815

Sir,

I beg you will send me a Return of the Commissariat of the 2nd Division to which you are attached and that you will report to me the state of the supplies and every other circumstance which you may consider necessary to advert to.

APPENDIX A

I beg you will be so good as to come to Grammont some early day next week as I wish to speak to you on Commissariat matters. I am glad that I have the good fortune to have an officer of such very good and correct conduct as yours has always been, attached to a division of this corps of the army. I am, Sir your obedient humble servant T Ogilvie Deputy Commissary General

The following is an extract from a letter lately found among my papers conveying the approval of the Lords Commissioners of Her Majesty's Treasury of my public services while at the head of the Commissariat Department at Malta during a period of eight years.

N° 452.
Treasury Chambers, 15 April 1845

'At thus releasing you from your present duties, my Lords desire to express to you their sense of the satisfactory manner in which you have invariably conducted the business of the department committed to your charge' C E Trevelyan

Appendix B

The Court Martials of Deputy Commissary General Charles Pratt and William Moore

Charles Pratt Esq, Lewisham Hill, Kent

6 March 1819

Sir,

The Lords &c having had under their consideration varied reports from the Auditor General at Lisbon, relative to your improper conduct whilst employed in the peninsula in the years 1814 and 1815, in the settlement of claims for mule hire, together with the whole of the examinations taken before that officer upon oath in support of the following specific charge alleged against you (viz)

1st That you interposed unnecessary delays and difficulties in the settlement with the claimants.

2nd That you demanded and accepted gratuities from the claimants in consideration of the payments made to them.

3rd That you purchased depreciated claims and drew their amount for your own purpose from the Military Chest and their Lordships having likewise had before them a report from the Comptrollers of Army Accounts thereon, accompanied by your defence, with your explanations and remarks upon the evidence taken by the Auditor General, I am commanded to acquaint you, that My Lords after fully

APPENDIX B

and maturely weighing all the circumstances of the case, are of opinion that the explanations offered are by no means such as can satisfy their lordships that the charges preferred against you are unfounded & as they cannot in justice to the public, permit any officer of the Commissariat to retain his Commission, when by his own misconduct he has forfeited every claim to confidence. My Lords have felt it to be their duty to submit to H[is] R[oyal] H[ighness] the Prince Regent that you should be dismissed the service. George Harrison

Mr W B Moore, 12 Old Burlington Street

6 March 1819

Sir,

The Lords &c having under their consideration various reports from the Auditor General at Lisbon, relative to your improper conduct whilst employed under the orders of Deputy Commissary General Pratt in the Peninsula, in the years 1814 & 1815; in making applications to the claimants for mule hire to induce them to pay to Mr Pratt a gratuity upon the settlement of their claims and My Lords having likewise had before them a report from the Comptrollers of Army Accounts thereon, accompanied by your defence, with your explanations and remarks upon the evidence brought forward in support of the charge against you & this Board having fully and maturely weighed all the circumstances of the case, they are of opinion that the explanations afforded by you are by no means such as can satisfy their Lordships that the charges preferred against you are unfounded; and as they cannot in justice to the public, permit any officer of the Commissariat to retain his commission, when by his own misconduct, he has forfeited every claim to confidence. I am directed to acquaint you, that their Lordships have felt it to be their duty to submit to H[is]

257

R[oyal] H[ighness] the Prince Regent that you should be dismissed the service. George Harrison

D[eputy] C[ommissary] G[eneral] Pratt, Lewisham Hill, Kent

23 June 1819

Sir,
The Lords &c having had before them your letter the 18th of March last, praying for the issue of your Half Pay as a DCG to the date of your dismissal from His Majesty's Service, I am directed to acquaint you, that My Lords have been pleased to authorise Mr Hill to issue to you the said Half Pay, after deducting therefrom the balance of £28 5[shillings] 1¾[pence] due from you upon your account from 4 October 1808 to the 24th of February 1809 as stated by the Commissioners of Audit. SR Lushington

Index

1st Division 57 fn
1st Line Battalion KGL 119
2nd Division viii, 31 fn, 57 fn, 117, 118, 119 fn, 120 fn, 156, 187, 193 fn, 194 fn, 205, 254
2nd Duke of York Battalion 119
2nd Line Battalion KGL 119
3rd Division 4, 13, 71 fn
3rd Dragoons 114
3rd Duke of York Battalion 119
3rd Line Battalion KGL 119
4th Division 3 fn, 4, 11, 29, 64, 85, 86 fn, 114, 123, 250
4th Line Battalion KGL 119
6th Division 27, 29, 50, 77
6th Inniskilling Dragoons 130
7th Division 68
7th Fusiliers 79 fn, 89, 168
10th Hussars 62 fn
18th Hussars 14 fn
20th Foot 17, 26, 47, 66
23rd Foot 29, 66
24th Foot 50, 98
27th Foot 89 fn
40th Foot 28, 89
52nd Foot 44, 48, 67, 120, 137, 185, 194, 214 fn, 243
71st Foot 120, 194
79th Foot 194

Abrantes 96
Adam, Major General Sir Frederick 118, 120 fn
Adour River 61, 63, 68
Aire 67, 201
Algeciras 103
Almeida 29, 95
Amiens 192
Antwerp 134
Arcangues 57
Arras 195, 197, 218
Arrauntz 59, 60
Ascain 50, 52, 59
Ath 118, 119, 121, 139, 145
Auch 85
Auchmuty, Major Samuel, 7th Foot 79
Audit Office, the 201, 202
Austria, Emperor of 168, 175
Avon, HMS 109 fn

Badajoz 92 fn, 99, 114, 233
Baden 171
Barca de Alva 1
Basques 22 fn, 23 fn, 24, 60
Bath 113
Battleaxe Guard, the 240
Bavaria 171, 195 fn, 249
Bavay 144

FEEDING WELLINGTON'S ARMY FROM BURGOS TO WATERLOO

Bayonne 13, 21, 53, 59, 60, 61, 63, 64, 91, 98
Bazas 69, 72, 90, 91
Beauvois-en-Vermandois 148
Belgian troops 129, 131, 133, 140, 171
Bell, Major John, 4th Foot, Assistant Quartermaster General 37, 87
Bentinck Major Charles, 2nd Foot Guards 193 fn
Beresford, Lt General William Carr 61, 64, 68, 71
Berrioplano 9
Bidache 62
Bidassoa River 33, 36, 43
Bilbao 33, 34
Biskarreta-Gerendiain 22
Bissett, Commissary General Sir John viii, 203 fn, 205, 210, 250, 251
Blucher, Field Marshal Prince 122, 138 fn, 148, 154, 160, 179
Bois de Boulogne, 159, 163, 179
Bolton, Captain RA 120
Bonaparte, Napoleon 55, 58, 60, 80, 113, 115, 140, 144, 186, 228
Booth, Assistant Commissary General of Accounts William 178, 212
Bordeaux vii, 68, 69, 71, 75, 86, 90, 94
Bouchain 195
Boulogne-Billancourt 159, 177, 178, 183, 205
Boulogne-sur-Mer 195, 237, 242
Bowles, Deputy Commissary General x

Bowman, Deputy Assistant Commissary General David 120 fn
Bradford, Major General Thomas 194 fn
Braganca 94, 95
Brazil 100
Bremervorde Battalion, the 119
Brock, Captain Saumarez, 43rd Foot 98
Bruges 117, 245
Brussels 117, 118, 123, 125, 126, 127, 129, 131, 134, 137 fn, 142, 146, 198, 245, 249
Burgos 8, 94
Byng, Major General John 31

Cadiz 15, 102
Caen 61, 203, 204
Calais 90, 187, 192, 195, 202, 210, 217, 237, 242, 244, 245, 246
Cambrai viii, 148, 195, 197, 203, 205, 206, 207, 210, 212, 214, 215, 216 fn, 218, 219, 221, 223, 229, 230, 231, 233, 234 fn, 236, 238, 239, 241, 243
Campbell, Colonel Sir Neil, 54th Foot 155
Canada ix, 89 fn
Candie Cemetery x
Canterbury 116
Captieux 69, 172
Carbajales de Alba 2
Carey, Augusta ix
Carey, Charles ix, xi
Carey, De Vic 79
Carey, Francis ix
Carey, Isaac x

INDEX

Carey, Marguerite x
Carey, Lt Colonel Octavius,
 Calabrian Free Corps 98
Carey, Sausmarez, Commissariat
 Clerk 116, 143, 210
Carey, Tupper (son) ix, xi
Carruthers, Assistant Commissary
 General David 192 fn, 201 fn
Cassel 245, 246
Castelnaudry 82
Castelo Branco 96, 101
Champ de Mars, the 160
Chantilly 148, 152
Charleroi 125, 135
Charters, Commissariat
 Clerk 7
Ciudad Rodrigo 91, 95, 99 fn, 114
Clauzel, General Bertrand 19 fn
Clermont 148, 150. 192
Clinton, Lt General Sir Henry viii,
 118, 119, 120, 123 fn, 129 fn,
 148, 156, 158, 193
Clinton, Lady Susan 193
Cugnac, Jules Emilien, Marquis de
 86 fn
Colborne, Colonel Sir John 137
Cole, Lt General Sir Lowry vii, xii,
 5, 25, 26, 27, 29, 30, 37, 57, 58,
 76, 123, 250, 251
Commission Mixte 122, 205, 217,
 222, 225, 226, 238, 239, 241,
 243, 244, 247, 251
Compiegne 148, 232
Conde 121
Condom 85, 86, 88
Cordeaux, Deputy Assistant
 Commissary General William 7
Cossacks 147, 166, 167, 169, 174,
 208, 221, 222, 242

Cumberland Hussars, the 140
Cundell, Deputy Assistant
 Commissary General William
 194 fn

Dalby, Commissariat Clerk 120fn
d'Angouleme, Louis Duke 60,
 69, 71
Darling, Major General Ralph ix,
 251
Dawbiney, Commissary Clerk
 120 fn
Dax 67
Dayman, Chaplain Charles
 194 fn
Dee, Commissariat Clerk 182,
 194 fn
Denain 207
d'Espagnac, General Charles
 21 fn
d'Estruval, Chateau 193
Dobree, Deputy Assistant
 Commissary General John
 Saumarez 98
Dobree, Commander Nicholas RN
 101, 108, 110
Donahoe, Lt Colonel Daniel, 11th
 Portuguese Line 65 fn
Douai 218
Douglas, Lt Colonel Sir Neil, 79th
 Foot 192
Dover 202, 247
Downie, Major General
 John 41
du Plat, Colonel George 119
Dumaresq, Deputy Commissary
 General Thomas viii, 3 fn, 183,
 206
Dunkirk 245

Dunmore, Commissary General Thomas 117

Dutch troops 128, 133, 140, 171

Egypt 29, 219 fn
Elizondo 25
Elliott, Lieutenant William, 51st Foot 194 fn
Enghien 121
Errentaria 33
Etxalar 32
Exeter 113
Exmouth, HMS 252

Falmouth 111
Flanner, Deputy Assistant Commissary General John 51
Frith, Chaplain Edward 194 fn

Gazan, Marie Reiss, Madame 14
Genappe 128 fn, 138
Ghent 144, 245
Gibraltar viii, 102, 104, 110
Gordon, Ensign Alexander, Coldstream Guards 234 fn
Graham, Lt General Sir Thomas, Lord Lynedoch 2, 12, 13
Grammont 119
Gramont, Captain Antoine de, 10th Hussars 62
Granicus, HMS 104 fn
Greig, Commissariat Clerk 120
Grenade 74
Grenade-sur-l'Adour 68
Guards, the 54, 59, 98, 176, 192 fn, 193 fn, 206, 209, 214, 216 fn, 219, 234, 236, 243

Guernsey x, 65, 101, 107, 113, 116, 118, 203
guillotine, the 229

Haines, Deputy Commissary General Gregory 118 fn
Hake, Colonel 140 fn
Halkett, Colonel Hugh 119, 120 fn
Hanoverian troops viii, 119, 120 fn, 140, 171, 194, 195 fn, 207, 240, 241, 242
Hardy, Commissariat Clerk 98
Herme & Furmidge, Army Agents 225 fn
Herries, Commissary in Chief John 202, 203
Higgins, Deputy Inspector of Hospitals Summers 193 fn
Hill, Assistant Commissary General Hugh 239, 240
Hill, Lt General Sir Rowland 12, 25, 57, 61, 66, 119, 224, 254
Hondarribia 33
Hope, Lt General Sir John 57
Hotham, Lieutenant and Captain Lord Beaumont, Coldstream Guards 214
Hougoumont Farm 123, 129
House, Commissariat Clerk 7

Invalides, Hotel des 153, 170
Ireland, Ensign De Courcey, 87th Foot 68 fn
Ireland, Lieutenant Stanley, 87th Foot, Acting Deputy Assistant Commissary General 68
Ireland, Ensign William, 87th Foot 68 fn
Irun 33

INDEX

Jenkins, Chaplain George 86 fn
Jersey 206

Keller, Major von 138 fn
Kennedy, Commissary General
  Sir Robert 9, 25

La Fere 227
La Haye Sainte 136, 137 fn
La Rhune, mountain 43
La Serre, Ensign Nicholas 87th
  Foot 98
Labastide-Beauvoir 82
Lady Arabella, Packet 111
Langon 71, 72
Languedoc Canal (Canal de Midi)
  84
Le Cateau-Cambresis 145
le Fevre, Pierre, Commissariat
  Storekeeper 51
Le Marchant, Captain Carey, 1st
  Foot Guards 54, 98
Le Mesurier, Anne ix
Le Mesurier, Lt Colonel Havilland,
  12th Portuguese Line 29, 98
Le Mesurier, Ensign Henry, 48th
  Foot 98
Le Mesurier, Captain Peter, 68th
  Foot 98
Le Mesurier, Lieutenant Peter, 9th
  Foot 98
Le Mesurier, Captain William, 24th
  Foot 50, 98
Legion d'Honneur viii, x, 238,
  239, 247
Lennox, Charles, 4th Duke of
  Richmond 214 fn
Lennox, Captain Charles, Earl of
  March, 52nd Foot, 67 fn, 214

Lennox, Lieutenant Lord George,
  9th Light Dragoons 67 fn, 214 fn
Lesaka 25, 32, 33, 38, 40
Life Guards, the 166
Lille 195, 245
Lisbon viii, 9, 90, 95, 96, 99, 100,
  101, 108, 110, 256, 257
L'Isle-Jourdain 85
Lithgow, Commissary of Accounts
  253
Louis XVIII, King viii, 60 fn, 89,
  117, 144, 152, 232
Lukin, Assistant Provost Marshal
  194 fn
Luxembourg Palace 159, 170
Luzarches 189
Lynch, Count Jean-Baptiste, Mayor
  of Bordeaux 71

Maclaurin, Deputy Assistant
  Commissary General David 120 fn
Madrid xiii, 8, 68 fn
Maling, Staff Surgeon John 120 fn
Malplaquet 144, 199 fn
Malta vii, ix, 29 fn, 249, 253,
  254, 255
Marlborough 113
Maubeurge 221
Mauritius ix, 249, 251
May, Lt Colonel John, RA,
  Assistant Adjutant General 38
Maya 25
McCrea, Captain Rawdon 87th
  Foot 98
McCulloch, 2nd Captain William,
  RE 98
McCurry, Baggage Master 194 fn
McPherson, Brigade Major 194 fn
Metcalfe, Chaplain John 194 fn

Miller, Deputy Assistant Commissary General William 194 fn
Mons 143
Mont Marsan 67
Mont St Jean 132, 134. 135, 141
Mont St Martin Chateau 206, 232
Montdidier 148
Moore, Commissary Clerk William 256, 257
Morillo, General Pablo, Count of Cartagena 56
Muffling, Baron, Commandant of Paris 164
Muhammad, Sulayman bin, Emperor of Morocco fn 104
Murray, Maj General Sir George Quartermaster General xii, 37

Napier, Lt Colonel Charles, 102nd Foot 155
Napoleon, King Joseph 11, 14, 16
Nassau troops 58, 171
Neuilly 158, 163
New South Wales ix
Ney, Marshal Michel 122
Nisa 96
Nive, Battle of vii, 54
Nivelle, Battle of vii, x, 114
Nivelles 121, 123, 135, 137, 138, 143, 145

O'Callaghan, Major General Robert 194 fn
Occupation, Army of vii, viii, ix, 122, 187, 189, 195, 197, 217, 228, 236
O'Donnell, General Henry, Conde de La Bispal 21 fn

Ogilvie, Deputy Commissary General James 71, 119 fn, 255
Orry-la-Ville 192
Orthes, Battle of vii, x, 61, 64, 65, 69, 114
Osma 10
Ostend 117, 134, 146, 249

Paget, Lt General Henry, Earl of Uxbridge 118 fn
Pamplona vii, 17, 18, 19, 20, 21 fn, 23, 26, 27, 29, 30, 40, 45, 98, 114
Paris viii, 71, 80, 116, 118, 148, 153–89, 192, 195, 200, 201, 203, 204–06, 210, 213, 219, 224, 225, 230, 232, 242, 249
Passages (Pasaia) 33, 45, 52
Peronne 148
Picton, Lt General Sir Thomas 4, 26, 27, 30, 76
Pipon, Deputy Commissary General James 101, 111
Platov, General Count Matvei 169
Pontoise 189, 190
pontoon train, 2, 61, 63, 64, 73, 74, 76, 163
Portuguese Contingent, the vii, 3, 6, 29, 49, 53, 65, 66, 75, 88, 90–4
Pratt, Deputy Commissary General Charles 95, 256–8
Pratt, Deputy Purveyor George 96 fn
Provost Marshal 53
Prussia, King of 168, 169, 207, 208
Prussian troops xii, 122, 133, 137, 138, 141, 148, 150–4, 155, 159, 160, 161, 165, 167, 170, 171, 173, 179, 206
Puente-Arenas 8

INDEX

Quatre Bras 121, 125, 138

Radford, Commissariat Clerk 194 fn
Ramsgate 117
Recquin, French sloop 71 fn
Regnault, Commissary General
    122, 222, 225, 238, 243
Reindeer, HMS 109 fn
Richmond, Duke of 67, 113, 132,
    214, 225
Robert, Sous Intendant Gaston
    238–9
Robinson, Assistant Commissary
    General Edward 194 fn
Rogers, Major Thomas, RA 194
Roncesvalles 19, 20, 21, 23 fn, 25,
    26, 32, 56
Roquefort 69
Ross, Major General Robert 66
Roverea, Major Alexandre de,
    Sicilian Regiment 29
Royal Staff Corps, the 74, 172
Roye 148, 150
Russia, Emperor of 160, 168, 169,
    176, 207

Saint Boes 65, 66
Saint Denis 153, 154, 156, 167, 189
Saint Quentin 227
Saint-Cyr-l'Ecole 183
Saint-Felix-Lauragais 82
Saint-Germaine-en-Laye 204
Saint-Just-en-Chaussee 150
Saint-Macaire 72
Saint-Paul-sur-Ternoise 192, 193,
    201, 205
Saint-Sever 68
Salamanca x, xiii, 2, 54, 91, 95, 98,
    114, 168

Salzgitter Battalion, the 119
San Marcial 36
San Martin de Elines 8
San Sebastian 37, 38 fn, 114
Sandeman, Helen ix, 11
Sandham, Captain Charles RA 194
Sanguesa 19
Santa Barbara 43
Santarem 96
Sare 46, 47
Saxon troops viii, 194, 195 fn, 207,
    240, 241, 242
Scots Greys, the 130
Smith, Captain Harry, 95th Foot 92
Smith, Assistant Surgeon
    John Gordon, 12th Light
    Dragoons 142
Smith, Juana 92
Socoa 52, 61
Soignes Forest 125, 126, 131, 135
Somerset, Lt Colonel Lord Fitzroy,
    Military Secretary 38, 233
Sontag, Major General John 7
Soto de Roma Estate 212
Soult, Marshal Jean-de-Dieu, Duke
    of Dalmatia 21, 25, 28, 36, 39,
    52, 56, 61, 62, 63, 64, 68, 72,
    73, 79, 82, 85
Spanish forces xii, 1, 3, 21, 27, 33,
    36, 41, 47, 49, 53, 56, 68, 78,
    90, 140
St Cloud 159, 178, 179
St Jean de Pied de Port 22, 26
St Malo 203
St Quentin 148
Stonestreet, Chaplain George
    216 fn
Strachan, Assistant Commissary
    General Alexander 175

FEEDING WELLINGTON'S ARMY FROM BURGOS TO WATERLOO

Suchet, Marshal 72
Sympher, Lt Colonel Augustus, KGL Artillery 65
Sympher, Captain Frederick, KGL Artillery 65 fn, 120

Tafalla 19
Talavera, Battle of x, 98, 114
Talma, Francois Joseph, actor 232
Tangiers 104, 106, 110
Todd, Captain Alexander, Royal Staff Corps 172
Tolosa 13, 91
Toro 94, 95
Toulouse, Battle of vii, x, 77, 114
Treaty of Peace 182, 186, 189, 195, 222
Trevelyan, Sir Charles, Under Secretary to the Board of Treasury 254, 255
Tudela 19
Tuileries, the 159, 170, 172
Tunney, Reverend Robert 120 fn
Tupper, Amelia ix
Tupper, Daniel 213
Turner, Deputy Assistant Commissary General Nicholas 194 fn

Ustaritz 60

Valenciennes 195, 218, 231, 241, 243
Valladolid 13, 94
Vane, Charles, 3rd Marquess of Londonderry 140 fn

Vattemare, Alexander, ventriloquist 230 fn
Vera (Bera) 45, 46
Versailles 154, 162, 180, 183, 184, 187, 189, 205
Villarcayo 94
Villasandino 8
Villava 19, 21
Villecourt 150
Vitoria, Battle of vii, x, 9, 11, 12, 13, 16, 18, 19, 91, 92, 114

Wasp, USS 109
Waterloo 118, 125, 143, 146
Waterloo, Battle of vii, 113, 139, 155, 198, 210, 242, 254
Watteville's Regiment, 29 fn
Wellington, Duchess of 213
Wellington, Duke of vii, 8, 10, 41 fn, 67 fn, 70, 113, 117, 122, 123, 126 fn, 139, 140, 141, 142, 143, 148, 151, 158, 160, 168, 199, 200, 202, 204, 206, 207, 208, 209, 212, 213, 214, 222, 224, 225, 232, 235, 236, 242, 244, 248, 249
Weymouth 113
Wise, Captain William Furlong, RN 104 fn
Woodford, Lt Colonel John, 1st Foot Guards, Assistant Quartermaster General 192, 193 fn, 200
Wurtemberg 171

Zamora xiii, 94, 95
Zenobia, HMS 101

266